FOR ALL PEOPLE

Viggo Mortensen

FOR ALL PEOPLE

Global Theologies in Contexts

ESSAYS IN HONOR OF VIGGO MORTENSEN

Edited by

Else Marie Wiberg Pedersen,
Holger Lam,
and
Peter Lodberg

William B. Eerdmans Publishing Company
Grand Rapids, Michigan / Cambridge, U.K.

Wm. B. Eerdmans Publishing Co.
255 Jefferson Ave. S.E., Grand Rapids, Michigan 49503 /
P.O. Box 163, Cambridge CB3 9PU U.K.

Printed in the United States of America

07 06 05 04 03 02 7 6 5 4 3 2 1

Library of Congress Cataloging-in-Publication Data

For all people: global theologies in contexts /
edited by Else Marie Wiberg Pedersen, Holger Lam, and Peter Lodberg.
p. cm.
Includes bibliographical references and index.
ISBN 0-8028-6086-9 (pbk.: alk. paper)
1. Church. 2. Globalization —Religious aspects — Christianity.
I. Pedersen, Else Marie. II. Lam, Holger. III. Lodberg, Peter.

BV600.3.F67 2002
270.8′3 — dc21

2002026483

www.eerdmans.com

Contents

Acknowledgments

We express our gratitude to Aarhus University Research Foundation, to the Church of Denmark Council on Inter-Church Relations, the Ecumenical Council of Denmark, and the Danish Mission Council whose financial support made the publication of this book possible.

For meticulous assistance with editing the manuscripts we wish to express our deep gratitude to Anna Marie Baden Olsen and Bente Stær at the Department of Systematic Theology, University of Aarhus.

To all the authors who despite often extremely full schedules undertook the task of writing a contribution to this book and thus paying Viggo Mortensen a tribute, we express the deepest appreciation.

Last but not least we owe thanks to Bill Eerdmans for taking the risk of publishing a book edited by a bunch of Danes of whom he knew nothing.

Else Marie Wiberg Pedersen,
Holger Lam, *and* Peter Lodberg

Introduction

ELSE MARIE WIBERG PEDERSEN

This book is about the challenges facing religion, especially Christian theology and the Christian churches today. One such major challenge is the interconnectedness of the world, now much debated under the general term "globalization," and how that affects the way Christians and churches act or ought to act. But also, the new world situation has made it very clear that God might be challenging the world. The title of the book is *For All People: Global Theologies in Contexts* first and foremost because it is written for all people in a postmodern "globalized world," to take two of the most employed concepts in our present time, and likewise important because Christianity from its very inception claimed to be universal, stressed by the resurrected Christ's call: "Go into all the world, and preach the gospel to every creature" (Mark 16:15) or, in another version, to "teach all nations" (Matt. 28:19). Second, the title reflects the character and career of Viggo Mortensen who — having made the move from a chair in Ethics and Religion of Philosophy, to a chair as director of the Department of Theology and Studies in the Lutheran World Federation, to now holding the chair as professor in Global Christianity and Ecumenism — always tried to be a theologian for all people, open to particularity and to the challenges of his time. Allow me to illustrate that by citing him from his inaugural lecture as a professor in 1999, "Globalization as a Challenge to Missiology and Ecumenical Theology":

> It is a matter of building a bridge between the living pluriform religious world and the rationality of the globalized world. The different religions'

> capacity to do so will be crucial for their survival capacity. In this respect Christianity has the advantage of being a missionary and global religion. When meeting the challenges of globalization there is nothing wrong about becoming "local," about reflecting upon one's context and roots. Yes, it is not only natural, it is necessary. It must, however, be complemented by an openness to the global realities, acknowledging the responsibility, in a wider perspective, also for the victims of globalization.
>
> Globalization actualizes the old idea of a united humanity, originating in enlightenment and explicated in modernity. Does this idea today need a religious or at least a transcendent foundation in order to survive? The ecumenical movement also has its dreams about a united humanity. But due to globalization the historic part played by Christianity in the shaping of the religious values on which societies and institutions were built is being questioned. The challenge now is to bring together people, nations and races who can foster a more just society — acknowledging and respecting these people, nations, and races in their particularity.[1]

Building bridges between different worlds, being open to the realities of the world and responsible in relation to the victims of the day's order, and not least keeping alive the idea of and working for a united humanity, this is the challenge for the globalized world. Shaping a world for all people.

The colleagues from different contexts and continents such as Africa, Europe, North America, and South America who have contributed to this book represent Mortensen's outreach within both Lutheran and ecumenical theology.

Globalization as Challenge to Mission and Ecumenism

Robert Schreiter brings the question of globalization a step further by viewing it from the juncture of postmodernity. By virtue of a new understanding of catholicity, or what Schreiter calls "a new catholicity," he explicates the challenges for the church which, now covering 34 percent of the

1. Viggo Mortensen in his inaugural lecture, "Det Globale og Multireligiøse. Teologiske Udfordringer" (The Global and the Multireligious: Theological Challenges), Center for Multireligious Studies, University of Aarhus, 2001, pp. 17-18. (my trans.)

world's population, has become for the first time "a world church." The main question is how a genuine catholicity understood as the fullness of faith ought to be. To answer this question Schreiter urges us to critically evaluate globalization as a modern phenomenon that can actually be a vehicle in the search for more humane forms of interconnectedness and the rethinking of difference. Here postmodernity provides us with a platform to analyze and critique. Thus the new catholicity has as its goal to have sensibility to culture and the question of difference without falling into the hegemony of a single system.

Johannes Nissen continues along this line in his article on mission and globalization in a New Testament perspective. Christian mission done in the world of plurality, if it is to follow the understanding of mission "in Christ's way" emphasizing the unconditional love of God and the infinite dignity of every human being, has to take place as an open invitation with due respect for different cultures. Nissen contends that if mission is taking place in open dialogue, leaving the former imperialist methodologies of "conquest" or market-oriented methodologies of expansion, then globalization can really be seen as an opportunity that challenges false opposites to becoming true dialectical relations.

Peter Lodberg also takes up the theme of globalization, but following James H. Mittelman he views globalization as a syndrome of different processes and activities, and following Anthony Giddens as a new network in which space and place are disconnected while different and distant places are being tightly connected. Thus globalization contains the paradox of being a connecting factor yet simultaneously with its dynamic and flexibility exposing the particularities of culture and religion. Lodberg poses the question whether people and the church can learn to live with this given dilemma of globalization, and if the World Council of Churches will really be able to make the paradigm shift in its ecumenical approach to and analysis of present-day challenges such as it already called for with the new world order in 1989.

Friedrich Wilhelm Graf pronounces the old *homo oeconomicus* dead, and demonstrates on the basis of different economic theories how religion and economy are interwoven, both being expressions of the cultural mentalities in which they are molded. As religion seems to shape the economic *habitus* of diverse cultures by providing the needed certainty for capitalism of whatever kind, the progressive globalization and pluralization will not subjugate religion. Rather, religion will continue to exist as the powerful cultural framework and identity that will deliver the symbolic languages necessary for the creative agents of global capitalism in order to interpret the many new risks of a highly flexible and mobile world. Therefore, what we will witness in the future is not the "clash of civilizations" but a plurality of value conflicts, namely between those who let religion adapt to capitalism and those who cling to old religious traditions, all going straight through societies.

Challenges to Ecumenism and Christian Identity

Vítor Westhelle poses the bantering question whether Europe is really Christian but immediately reverts it to the question whether one needs to be European in order to be truly Christian. Taking his point of departure in European inventions and discoveries since the Renaissance and in the whole symbolism of the Copernican turn, Westhelle skewers Europe's self-understanding as the absolute center of the world and as, in a famous Hegelian phrase, the end of world history, thus entangled in the myth of being the "new" Jerusalem. This sense of having reached the end, according to Westhelle, is founded on the specific European sense of being sinful, a *Schuldigsein* directed only toward the supreme Good, the total Other, that blinds the Europeans and makes them incapable of seeing the relative otherness in the others outside of Europe. The rational and enlightened Europeans, who colonized and taught others, have not yet learned to see the evangelical possibilities of the world's others. It remains for these others to teach or bring back to Europe the good news *(eu-angelion)* that there is more.

John W. de Gruchy focuses on the connection between ecclesiology and ethics. With the various controversies between the two during the twentieth century, expressed in different organizations and in conflicts such as the German *Kirchenkampf* and the South African apartheid, as an illustrative background, de Gruchy explicates Dietrich Bonhoeffer's interconnection of ecclesiology and ethics. Through a thorough exposition of Bonhoeffer's works, particularly his *Communio Sanctorum,* he demonstrates how to Bonhoeffer ecclesiology, Christology, and ethics were always interacting factors. Furthermore, de Gruchy shows how Bonhoeffer developed the ecclesiological ethics of "being-church-for-the-people" on an "ethics of free responsibility" inspired by stays in Anglo-Saxon contexts, thus correcting false dichotomies such as the German misappropriation of Luther's teaching of the two kingdoms.

The relation between ecclesiology and ethics is also of paramount significance in Jens Holger Schjørring's description of the Nordic Lutheran churches' identity as it developed in an international perspective during the twentieth century. By virtue of central case studies, Schjørring critically analyzes the Nordic churches' influence on the international scene, from their leading role, forming more or less one Nordic block as representatives of evangelical freedom and equality and as ecumenical mediators after the two world wars, to their weakened and differentiated theological position from the 1960s. Regretting how the church in Denmark thereafter developed an even anti-ecumenical strain, Schjørring holds that exactly such majority churches in affluent countries as the Nordic ought to take up their heritage of playing a leading role in the interfaith dialogue so necessary in the globalized world.

Else Marie Wiberg Pedersen in her article "Lutheran Ecclesiologies Today — Custodians of the Past or Guides to the Future?" discusses the Lutheran practice of the ordination of women as one point that has taken the Protestant principle *ecclesia reformata semper reformanda* seriously. Wiberg Pedersen finds the inclusion of women in the ordained ministry to be the most significant move in twentieth-century Lutheran ecclesiology and one where it has moved considerably forward towards, though not having reached the goal of, full communion. This is discussed in relation to the Lutheran World Federation's studies on a communio-ecclesiology. The chapter concludes with a reference to the wider ecumenical discussion on the ministry in the case of the Porvoo Common Statement between Anglican and Lutheran churches in the Northern part of Europe.

Musimbi Kanyoro observes that ecumenical or international church studies have a major impact on the development in local churches, challenging them to follow the gospel they proclaim. Focusing on the ordination of women, Kanyoro urges the church as such to enact its proclamation by showing solidarity with all of God's creatures as well as accountability to humanity as a whole, in which respect international studies have an important role to play. Coming from the Evangelical Lutheran Church in Kenya that does not allow for women's ordination, she concludes by expressing her hope that the church as a community may eventually live out its calling to be a sign of the kingdom of God, thus acting as a liberative, transformative, and inclusive force.

Anna Marie Aagaard sketches the ecumenical debate on ecclesiology and ethics, highlighting the unknown or ignored approaches to ethics and policy decisions on moral issues. Aagaard describes the different strands within this debate, which has to a large extent been characterized by an inculturation of ethics as political ethics rather than as social ethics. According to Aagaard, however, an ecclesial ethics inspired and promoted by the Orthodox churches developed in the World Council of Churches during the 1990s. By virtue of such an ecclesial ethics articulated as "a liturgy after liturgy," a body language — various configurations of community as the body of Christ — is provided, Aagaard contends, that might make it possible to simultaneously contrast the church and the world and make social ethics a common cause of church and the secular world.

God Challenging the World

Philip Hefner defines the mission of Christianity and of the church as transformation on the presumption that the world is created and inscribed to be transformative by God. That this is so is underscored by our belief in the Triune God, witnessed in both Scripture and tradition. Hefner contends that this transformation today is carried out in newness and change, ecclesially for example in the *semper reformanda* principle and especially expressed in the Christian hope for a new world lived out in a community engaged in the possibilities and transformative work of God. If the church claims to have reached the end, it does not engage in mission in consonance with the gospel or in consonance with creation, whose character it is to transform certainty to riskiness and comfort into challenge. Thus transformation as integral to creation is our mission, the very epitome of Christian belief.

Walter Altmann illustrates the Latin American, liberation theology view on suffering as a perspective of hope. In contrast with traditional images of Christ as the dead Jesus, the risen Christ, entailing the cry and hope for a new life, is more often depicted in recent Latin American art and base community material. It is Altmann's clear message that history has not come to an end, but rather, despite the fall of crude regimes, there is still a long way to a just social order. While the traditional pictures convey the prevailing circumstance of being not only exploited people but now, under the conditions of a globalized economy, also an excluded people, depictions of the indigenous crucified Christ and of the cross are so symbolically enriched that they portray a suffering endowed with hope, meaning, and future.

Niels Henrik Gregersen brings the view of the cross of Christ further by inscribing it in the trinitarian theology of risk-taking and thus in creation itself. In discussion with various sociological risk theories and acknowledging the givenness of risk, Gregersen proposes a perception of God as a risk-taker who not only risks the giving of creative freedom to creation, acted in autopoietic processes, but who also risks the self-giving to risk. Thus understood, Gregersen contends, Christian theology has always known life as risk conditioned in a positive and creative way, and therefore the cross should never be seen in isolation from the resurrection of Christ.

Viggo Mortensen: A Tribute to a Theological Character

PETER LODBERG

Professor Viggo Mortensen holds the Chair of "Global Christianity and Ecumenism" at the Theological Faculty at the University of Aarhus, Denmark. He is at the same time Director of the Center for Multireligious Studies, which documents and analyzes religious developments as part of the larger process of globalization. From 1991 to 1999 Viggo Mortensen served as Director of the Department of Theology and Studies in the Lutheran World Federation, Geneva.

Colleagues and friends want to pay tribute to Viggo Mortensen on the occasion of his sixtieth birthday on May 15, 2002. We want to thank him for his friendship and loyalty, and for his encouragement to deal with Christian theology in all its aspects in order to teach and preach with honesty and clarity. Viggo Mortensen is a creative and innovative theological researcher and teacher. He acts as a fine intermediary of theological and pastoral issues related to mission, church, and globalization.

In the words of Viggo Mortensen's own mentor, the Danish theologian and philosopher K. E. Løgstrup, theology is a matter of existence. As Dean of the Theological Faculty Viggo Mortensen has often welcomed new students and challenged them to become "theological characters." Thus, to Viggo Mortensen theology is both an academic enterprise and a way of life that involves one's whole personality. This has led Viggo Mortensen to take part in the discussion about the future of Christianity in a multicultural and multireligious global world.

Viggo Mortensen was one of the first Danish theologians to take part in the post–World War II discussion on the relationship between theology and natural science as documented in his doctoral dissertation from 1989, *Theology and Natural Science — Beyond Restriction and Expansion.* The dissertation tries to bridge the historical and philosophical contrasts between a metaphysical concept of theology and a natural science that tends to make a worldview out of its methods. The inspiration of Viggo Mortensen's bridge-building is the phenomenology of K. E. Løgstrup rendered as a "cosmo-phenomenological philosophy of religion" that paves the way for a friendly interplay between theology and natural science.

Already during his time as Director of the Department of Theology and Studies in the Lutheran World Federation, Viggo Mortensen began to study the process of globalization as a challenge to the theology and mission of the Lutheran churches today. A series of studies around the world concerning the relationship between religion, ethics, and economy was undertaken in order to show the complexity of the matter and to challenge the Lutheran churches to engage in socio-ethical discussions and actions.

Viggo Mortensen started his academic career in the field of ethics and philosophy of religion. During his time in the Lutheran World Federation he worked out several important contributions to Lutheran ethics in an ecumenical context. Today he is able to relate all his previous work and international experience to the study of religion and globalization, which is of the utmost importance to a well-informed theological character of today. The contributors who in different ways have followed Viggo Mortensen on his way offer this book as a tribute to a highly respected friend and theologian.

PART I

Globalization as Challenge to Mission and Ecumenism

Globalization, Postmodernity, and the New Catholicity

ROBERT J. SCHREITER

Introduction

Viggo Mortensen's career as an academic and as a churchman has taken him far beyond the confines of Denmark. Especially his years with the Lutheran World Federation brought him to all parts of the world. This broad experience is reflected in the programmatic paper he wrote for the new Center for Multireligious Studies at the University of Aarhus.[1] There he sets out the global, multireligious, and multiethnic dimensions of the world today. He rightly identifies these areas as the ones that must be addressed in order to understand religion in contemporary Danish society, as well as within the larger world picture.

The programmatic paper ends with the theological challenges, both within the church and in a multireligious society. One of the theological issues for the church is how to frame the dialogue that will need to take place, within the church, in the larger world, and especially between religious traditions. I would like to look at one dimension of that broad agenda by examining the theological concept of "catholicity" as a way of engaging globalization. This by no means can carry the full weight of the agenda as Mortensen has sketched it out. But it does, I

1. Viggo Mortensen, *Det Globale og Multireligøse Teologiske Udfordringer,* Center for Multireligiøse Studier, Occasional Papers/Aktuelle Skrifter, 1 (Aarhus: Aarhus Universitet, 2001).

hope, provide one way of getting a theological grasp of the phenomenon of globalization.

After giving a brief reminder of some of the ways in which catholicity has functioned in Christian theology, I want to take the traditional concept a bit further and speak of a "new catholicity." A new catholicity takes the phenomenon of globalization into account, and is concerned especially with communication in a multireligious, multiethnic, globalized world.

"Catholicity" is understood here as a theological way of imagining the Christian church in its wholeness, but also as a whole at this point in time. Referring to the church as "catholic" is of course an ancient concept. The term is traced back to Ignatius of Antioch.[2] It is enshrined in a special way in the Nicene-Constantinopolitan Creed, where we profess the church as "one, holy, catholic, and apostolic." Catholicity is seen there as one of the traditional "marks" or characteristics of the true church. To be sure, there have been different perspectives throughout church history as to which characteristics or marks — and how many of them — described the church of Christ. The number has varied from as low as two (as, for example, with Luther) to as high as one hundred (with the Roman School in the eighteenth century). The four noted in the Creed, however, have been the most widely accepted.

Catholicity traditionally understood referred both to the church as it sojourns in this world, and its eschatological fulfillment with the Trinity in heaven. With its theology becoming increasingly entwined with canon law, the Western church in the Middle Ages emphasized the catholicity of the church in its earthly form, to be found in its physical extension of the church throughout the known world, and in the fullness of faith *(regula fidei)* it confessed in Jesus Christ. Orthodoxy and the Reformation emphasized the spiritual and eschatological dimensions of the church's catholicity, although work by the World Council of Churches and the Faith and Order Commission has tried to include both dimensions.[3] In this account here I will be emphasizing the this-worldly dimensions of catholicity, since these most closely pertain to a discussion of globalization.

At certain moments in the history of the church, one or other of the

2. "Where Jesus Christ is, there is the catholic church." *Smyrn.* 8, 2.

3. For a recent summary of thinking on this matter, see Wolfgang Beinert, "Katholizität der Kirche," *Lexikon für Theologie und Kirche,* 5:1370-74.

four marks — one, holy, catholic, and apostolic — came to the fore as particularly defining the church as a whole. At the time of the christological controversies, and again during the Great Schism, the unity of the church held pride of place. The holiness of the church was particularly at stake during the Donatist controversy, when the holiness of the ministers of the church, and the state of those who had lapsed in their faith under persecution, was under question. The sixteenth-century Reformation can be seen as a concern for the apostolicity of the church, i.e., whether the Latin church of that time had lost its claim to have carried on the tradition of the apostles.

In our own time, at the beginning of the third millennium, it seems to me that catholicity now takes a central place in defining what it means to be the church of Christ. For the first time, Christianity does indeed come close to being found everywhere. About 34 percent of the world's population is Christian today. What is most striking about the extension of Christianity around the world today is its great diversity, as it has been incarnated in so many different cultures of the world. We are indeed, for the first time, part of a world church. The question, of course, is whether this world church has moved beyond the hegemony of Europe and the West. It is precisely this looking toward the catholicity of the church that calls us to examine just how fully participative Christian communities around the globe have become in the totality of the church, and to what extent a colonial mentality still remains. At the same time, questions have been raised about whether the fullness of the church is present in local communities. This question was raised especially at the time of the rise of the African Instituted Churches. Some of these churches have now become members of the World Council of Churches, which has to be construed as a positive answer to that question.

To ensure that genuine participation *(koinonia)* takes place, which is a way of speaking of the fullness of the church in the local community, and the participation of local churches in the whole, I propose that a third element must be added to the traditional definition of catholicity, namely, that of communication and exchange.

The worldwide nature of the church today, and the challenges raised by the inculturation of faith, were the reasons that I spoke of a "new catholicity" in the book by that same name.[4] In this presentation, I want to go

4. Robert Schreiter, *The New Catholicity: Theology between the Global and the Local* (Maryknoll, N.Y.: Orbis Books, 1997).

into the nature of the "new" in more detail, since it is this new situation that directs both how we understand the church in its extension, as "throughout the whole," and what we see as the theological challenges to confessing the faith handed down to us in all its fullness.

The newness as we are experiencing it today grows out of the conjunction of two phenomena: namely, globalization and the postmodern condition. I have already spoken extensively of globalization in the aforementioned book, but we have had considerable experience of globalization since that book was first drafted (in 1995), and an immense literature has developed.[5] Globalization was then still a relatively new concept, at least in theology. Today it is part of everyone's awareness. We are now into the second decade of globalization, which gives us both some view back on its development, and some prospective ideas about its future.

Postmodernity is a broad concept, but one increasingly important if we are to understand our current world. I will be using it in a somewhat specific sense as coming to terms with the limits of the modern, in ways to be explained below. The reason why postmodernity is important here is the peculiar way it interacts with globalization. Globalization is a phenomenon of modernity, and our experience of the limits (and limitations) of globalization is partly tied up with our understanding of the limits of modernity. It is precisely at those edges of modernity, if you will, that Christians find themselves asking fundamental questions and seeking to understand what is going on from the perspective of faith.

This presentation falls into two parts. The first looks at the context in which Christians now find themselves: at the intersection of the second decade of globalization with postmodernity. Thus, globalization and postmodernity will each be looked at in turn. The second part then turns to the new catholicity, and examines the challenge of a genuine catholicity in terms of extension, fullness of faith, and communication. A brief, concluding word will be said regarding the possible theological frames that can help develop both the theology of a new catholicity, and the spirituality to live within such a view of the world.

5. Perhaps the best single work is David Held et al., *Global Transformations: Politics, Economics, Culture* (Oxford: Polity, 1999).

Globalization in the Second Decade

Just what is globalization? The concept has technological, economic, political, and sociocultural dimensions. I will try to summarize briefly these dimensions, and then speak to the "second decade" phenomenon. I would like to do this in five points.

1. Advances in communications technologies make globalization possible. "Communication" is understood here both in terms of the conveying of information and the transport of people and goods. Thus, the development of the telegraph and the telephone in the nineteenth century, but also the introduction of the steamship, launched the most recent earlier period of globalization, from roughly 1850 to 1914. The development of the computer and the Internet since the 1980s has been the driving force behind the current wave of globalization.
2. Those who benefit from globalization note especially its capacity, via communications technologies, at once to compress and to expand time and space. The compression is experienced in the collapse of time in the process of communication, and the capacity to store huge amounts of information on a computer chip. The expansion is experienced as profound interconnectedness, because of the great access those who have the technology are able to achieve. A considerable literature has developed, especially in India and Latin America, about the underside of globalization where, instead of interconnectedness, people experience exclusion. What these two views — of interconnectedness and exclusion — give us when taken together is the deep paradoxes, even contradictions, that mark globalization.
3. These contradictions are nowhere clearer than in the economic dimension of globalization. There is interconnection in that a single form of economy is increasingly the case: a market-driven capitalism based on neoliberal principles. While there are variations of form in this capitalism, it is all interconnected. At the same time, while holding out promises of improving the lot of the entirety of humanity, large numbers of people are at this time excluded from its benefits. Not only are they excluded, but in many instances their own local economies have been severely disrupted and their economic lot has indeed worsened. Economists debate whether this is a

temporary dislocation (as was experienced in Europe in the eighteenth and nineteenth centuries with the Industrial Revolution), or whether it is indicative of an ever deepening divide between the few rich and the many poor. From the side of those suffering from globalization's effects, those debates are academic in the worst sense of that word. When people's livelihood and very lives are threatened, debate on how to measure the pace and impact of economic change seems like so much quibbling. It is the economic dimension of globalization that has drawn the most attention — and protest — in recent years.

4. Globalization is closely tied up with processes of modernization. Democratic government, concern for individual choice and liberty, and the separation of spheres of action create the conditions in which globalization flourishes. The communications capacity of globalization seems to speed up the processes of modernization. It channels, through the media, the message of individual choice and liberty on the one hand, and a kind of conformity to icons and mores that flow from modernity on the other. The speed and the force of these messages about the individual and about fitting in to this brave new world are profoundly disconcerting for many in the world whose lives have been gauged by (religious) traditions, and not by the market or the latest fashion communicated through the social media. The head-on clash between the modern and the traditional is one of the features, as we shall see, of the second decade of globalization.
5. All of this points to important realignments of power. Many people experience it as a loss of local autonomy, as nameless and faceless agents decide their fate and socialize their children in ways against their will. Patterns of domination, reminiscent of nineteenth-century colonialism but yet distinctively different, reshape human relations. The experience of being deliberately excluded, yet at the same time taunted with images of wealth and visions of the human as producer and consumer, feed a smoldering and increasingly consuming anger among the poor and disenfranchised. While domination by the wealthy and the few is much in evidence, one cannot discount the agency of those who are oppressed. One way of reading the events of September 11, 2001, is from the gaining of agency in the midst of rage.

Globalization, then, bristles with energy and with contradiction. Its sheer scope gives it an aura of inevitability, yet historians are pointing out that a previous period of globalization came to an end with the collapse of the great European powers in the 1914 war. As we enter into the second decade of the current globalization, what are some of the characteristics evident after ten years of experience with it? Three things stand out.

First of all, patience is running out with the promises of globalization. The protests in Seattle, Prague, and Genoa point to a broadly based antipathy toward globalization, an antipathy that can turn into rage. In the Muslim world, much of the modernity flaunted by globalization (at least the cultural dimension of modernity, if not its structural, scientific side)[6] has led to a fundamental rejection of globalization in its cultural and social dimensions. Even those most avid proponents of globalization know that this situation cannot continue.

Second, and building upon the first point, there are more and more calls to develop a more humane form of globalization that restores local autonomy, and does not live by the cut-throat laws of an unbridled market. What social and political forms will need to be conceived to make a more humane form of interconnectedness possible? Utopian thinking has not fared well since the rise of globalization. Now alternatives need to be thought through, with social action accordingly. While there is doubt on many fronts that such more humane forms of globalization can be achieved, it nonetheless behooves those concerned with the deleterious effects of globalization to work toward something different.

Third, a further step needs to be taken to come to understand and deal with difference in the world. Affirmations of solidarity work best in situations of resistance. What does dealing with difference mean in the reconstruction of societies, or what does it mean when one can no longer presume a peaceable society? Thinking is just getting under way to begin to conceive what living with real difference can mean.[7]

The beginning of the second decade of globalization finds us at something of a turning point, then. A lot of effort in the first decade was put by scholars and religious leaders into understanding and describing

6. The distinction is from Bassam Tibi, *The Challenge of Fundamentalism: Islam and Politics in the New World Disorder* (Berkeley: University of California Press, 1998).

7. See for example Giles Gunn, *Beyond Solidarity: Pragmatism and Difference in a Globalized World* (Chicago: University of Chicago Press, 2001).

globalization. Now the time has come for more critical evaluation and the imagining of humane alternatives. Part of that rethinking will have to deal with how globalization, as a largely modern phenomenon, comes up against its limits precisely as a product of, and vehicle for, modernity.

Postmodernity as the Context of the New Catholicity

The term "postmodernity" first appeared in art criticism in the 1920s. In the humanities and in religious studies, it has often taken its meaning from Jean-François Lyotard's report for the Quebec government, published in 1979.[8] Notable characteristics of the postmodern as Lyotard describes it are the fragmentation of lifeworlds and the disappearance of overarching master narratives. I am using the polyvalent term "postmodern" here in the sense of a range of responses to the limits of the modern. This understanding does not reject the modern, since postmodern responses are not intelligible without reference to the modern. While building on the modern, they recognize the limitations and try to move to the next step. I wish to elaborate this idea, as it will be developed further in this presentation, by focusing on two things. The first is regarding the postmodern as it creates what is called in Latin America *tiempos mixtos,* and the second has to do with providing a kind of rough mapping of the postmodern as it pertains to this discussion of the new catholicity.

As a result of the modernization brought by globalization, and the postmodern response this in turn has engendered, many people of the world — especially the urban dwellers, and the poor especially among them — live in "mixed times." That is to say, the premodern, the modern, and the postmodern are experienced together. Poor urban dwellers, coming in from rural areas, carry with them a strong sense of tradition and a premodern way of living. To survive in a large city, one must adopt some attitudes and practices of modernity, such as the separation of the spheres of home and work. Especially for women, this can mean leaving their own homes, where premodern patterns are followed, to work as domestic servants in middle-class homes or in hotels where the modern and the postmodern are routinely mixed. They find themselves constantly negotiating these different concepts of time and the worldview each entails. The

8. ET *The Postmodern Condition* (Minneapolis: University of Minnesota Press, 1984).

point I am trying to make here is that living in a postmodern world does not mean the disappearance of premodern and modern forms. This is especially important to remember when considering religious attitudes and practices. Indeed, the prefixes "pre" and "post" are misleading, since they imply an evolutionary or linear development, driven by the modern. The experience of mixed times questions that sequencing, both as a concept and as a strategy to reconcile traditional and modern ways of thinking.

The terrain of the postmodern is by definition varied and hard to trace. Yet I would like to suggest a simple mapping that highlights three of the major responses to the postmodern condition as they relate to religion and theology.

The first response focuses upon the limits of the modern, and opts for some reappropriation of the premodern. The modern has failed, on this view, because it is built on premises that ultimately show its bankruptcy. Extreme examples of this reappropriation of the premodern can be found in the various forms of fundamentalism. Fundamentalism cannot be understood without reference to the modern. It is a peculiar, antimodern selection of beliefs and practices of faith that become identity markers for the faithful. This selection rarely encompasses what in calmer times would be seen as the genuine fundamentals of belief (Christian fundamentalists rarely emphasize the Trinity; Muslim fundamentalists do not begin with the five pillars of Islam).[9] A more moderate form of reappropriation of the premodern can be found in the "radical Orthodoxy" of John Milbank and his associates, or even more moderate in the postliberal theology of the New Yale School.[10] Among the radical Orthodox, the genuine Christian response to the world today comes through a postmodern critique of modernity, and postmodern reading of premodern Christianity. For postliberal theology, following a cue from Ludwig Wittgenstein, Christian faith must be anchored in cultural-linguistic communities, which read the world through the lens of their own language games, and live by the rules of those language games.

A second type of postmodern response sees the limits of modernity

9. An excellent study of fundamentalism as a modern reaction to modernity is Bruce Lawrence, *Defenders of God* (Durham, N.C.: University of North Carolina Press, 1989).

10. Signature text for radical Orthodoxy is Milbank's *Theology and Social Theory* (Oxford: Basil Blackwell, 1991); for postliberal theology, a basic work has been George Lindbeck, *The Nature of Doctrine: Religion and Theology in a Postliberal Age* (Philadelphia: Westminster Press, 1984).

not in any inherent shortcomings of the modern project, but rather due to the fact that it has not been completed. The emancipatory dimension of modernity is emphasized here, both in terms of emancipation from premodern oppression, and emancipation toward full participation in the discourse of modernity. Among philosophers, Jürgen Habermas has been the clearest proponent of this approach.[11] Such theologians as Helmut Peukert and Edmund Arens have worked out the theological implications of this.[12] While this approach could be seen as an extension of modernity, it is a view of the modern seen from a distinctively postmodern perspective.

A third type of postmodern response would embrace the postmodern condition described by Lyotard more directly. There is no master narrative; the deconstruction of the subject is part of getting at the experience of the postmodern. This embrace of the postmodern again permits a range of responses, from the radical a/theology of Mark C. Taylor and the work of Thomas Altizer to much more measured probings of the postmodern condition.[13] This type of response recognizes how much North Atlantic people are immersed in the uncertainties of the postmodern, and tries to delineate what a faith response would be to this condition.

The Conjuncture of Globalization and the Postmodern

At the beginning of this presentation, I posited that the new catholicity finds itself today at the juncture between globalization, now in its second decade, and postmodernity. Globalization is, in the main, a phenomenon of modernity. Part of its agenda is precisely the extension of modernity to all parts of the world. It seeks autonomous subjects who are willing to sub-

11. See for example his *Die Moderne. Ein unvollendetes Projekt* (Frankfurt: Suhrkamp, 1981).

12. See for example Edmund Arens, ed., *Kommunikatives Glauben und christlicher Glaube. Ein theologischer Diskurs mit Jürgen Habermas* (Paderborn: Schöningh, 1997); *Christopraxis. Grundzüge theologischer Handlungstheorie* (Freiburg: Herder, 1992).

13. See Mark C. Taylor, *Erring: A Postmodern A/Theology* (Chicago: University of Chicago Press, 1984); *Altarity* (Chicago: University of Chicago Press, 1987). A more measured approach would be found in the work of David Tracy, *The Analogical Imagination* (New York: Continuum, 1981).

mit themselves to the rules of the market economy, not only in the economic sphere itself, but also in political and sociocultural spheres. It holds out as values progress (i.e., greater autonomy and economic prosperity), inclusion in the benefits of globalization, and equality as a producing and consuming subject (equality at least in the sense of equality of access or of opportunity).

Globalization has failed to deliver on these promises in a manner adequate to the expectations of those who have either entered its processes voluntarily, or been drawn into them against their will. One can argue from statistics, as do economists, that those countries who have entered this process have indeed seen their lots improve: China would be the best case. Yet the period of transition from premodern or non-capitalist economies to neoliberal capitalism is a rough one, and it damages many along the way. It is the anger against this transition that is being heard so clearly today.

Other things besides globalization as such have contributed to this questioning of the modern project. Most notable has been the experience of war in the twentieth century, in which genocide has played an all too prominent part. Is this carnage the result of emancipation and greater enlightenment? Our immediate reaction would be to say "no," but the death toll remains undeniably evident. Postmodern responses, in all their variety, are attempts to seek out less optimistic and more measured understandings of the human, to plead for other rationalities, to make room for differences that cannot be subsumed in the modern paradigm of globalization.

The critiques of globalization have underscored the contradictions of globalization as a system. It is highly conflictual, based as it is on competition. Its allocations of power create even more conflict and violence. It has spawned many attempts to understand it as a potential political order, from fears that nation-states will disappear altogether to Samuel Huntington's now famous "clash of civilizations." It is itself a totalizing system, and one wonders whether it may not ultimately go the way of other totalizing systems from the twentieth century, such as Leninist and Stalinist varieties of Marxism. The postmodern becomes, therefore, a platform on which to stand in order to analyze and critique globalization. That critique may come from any of the three directions indicated in the general mapping of globalization — reversion to the premodern, recommitment to the modern, and immersion in the postmodern.

The New Catholicity

How does a new catholicity situate itself within the conjuncture of the second decade of globalization and postmodernity? How does one imagine the whole? Let us examine what this new catholicity must address under the three headings of extension through space, the fullness of faith, and the imperative of communication and exchange.

The New Catholicity as Extension

Four points stand out when thinking about the new catholicity as the extension of Christian faith throughout this globalized and increasingly postmodern world.

First of all, the theological basis for responding to this extension. The new catholicity brings with it a special sensibility to culture and the question of difference. Theologically, this has found its basis traditionally in a theology of creation or in a theology of incarnation. In the former instance, creation itself is a celebration of the plenitude of God's creative power. Difference, in this perspective, is therefore constitutive of the created order, not a deviation or defective form of it. To try to eliminate difference as such is therefore wrong-minded. To be sure, such a point of departure does not answer the question about legitimate and illegitimate difference, i.e., difference that is destructive of itself or of others. But God creating, and God seeing that "it was good," becomes the basis for a theology of culture.

The incarnation has also served as a basis for understanding the relation between Christianity extended throughout the whole world and in the encounter with cultures. That the "Word became flesh and dwelt among us" (John 1:14) serves as a warrant for honoring culture. Christ's taking on humanity in a specific culture sanctifies the idea that the gospel is capable of being heard in each culture. Indeed, one could say that we will not be able to grasp the full implications of the incarnation until Christ's message has been able to be heard in each culture and takes on flesh, as it were, in those cultures.

To these more commonly known understandings of a theology of culture based upon creation and the incarnation, one might add an eschatological understanding of God's design. In this reading, the conflict and contradiction we experience now in difference will have a divine outworking in the final reconciliation of Christ in all things. Read in the context of creation and the incarnation, such a reconciliation will not erase difference, but will allow every tribe and tongue, people and nation, to come together without violence. Following the Book of Revelation, such a coming together will be preceded by passing through a great tribulation, that is, through a transformative process that we cannot yet understand. What is important is that the story is not intended to end in violence and death. There is a way to come through all this, led by the grace of God.

Second, central to the new catholicity as extension is the negotiation of the global and the local. This is an area that still needs much exploration. This is partly due to the fact that the global has changed for us, and the local is on the agenda in a way it may not have been before. In the global-local relationship, each has both a positive and a negative dimension. For the global, the positive dimension, in its religious form, is offered in the translocal nature of Christianity. The experience of the translocal itself is a form of transcendence: transcending the immediate and the local, but also possibly transcending the human, the intercultural itself. A mild form of this is a kind of theological cosmopolitanism; a more profound form is the experience of communion that comes from knowing that one is part of something greater than oneself.

But the positive dimension of the global extends beyond this immediate experience of the translocal or even the transcendent. It has to do with the message of Christianity itself, that God has acted in a definitive way in the life, death, and resurrection of Jesus Christ. Sensitivity to the local and the different may make us hesitate before all too quick generalizations about the universal, and historical memory of the equating of universality with earthly empire in nineteenth-century missionary efforts. But even with all of this, one cannot deny what is for Christians the significance of the Jesus story for the entire world. Again, understanding the global in terms of the new catholicity requires a renewed sense of the meaning of universality for our world today.

The global can also be negative. This is most evident in the erasure of the local and of difference. Centralizing tendencies, such as are currently experienced in the Roman Catholic Church, ignore or suppress the local, resulting in often strong, localizing reactions. The global as oppressive and dominating is unfortunately all too common in the world today. It is this negative dimension of the global that receives the most attention. And at this point in time, one must say: deservedly so. The oppressive dimensions of the global — manifested either in the forms of economic or sociocultural globalization, or in its ecclesiastical incarnations — must be analyzed, deconstructed, and dismantled.

The local has positive and negative dimensions as well. The local, both in itself and in its intersection with the global, is the site of individual and communal identity formation. Most people live, move, and have their being in their immediate locale, even though they may be influenced by global factors. What it means to be and to live as a Christian is enacted in the local. Here the concrete finds its manifestation. Just as Jesus of Nazareth lived a specific life in a particular cultural setting, so too most human beings do not live in some supracultural reality. The best of the local, then, is about the humanization process, our ways of becoming human. The complexities of identity formation reach beyond what can be done here, but suffice it to say that attending to the local provides the best window into anthropology. As has already been noted, the global can interact with the local in a positive fashion by affirming the insights into the human of the local, and expanding them in such a way as to give access to the translocal and the transcendent.

The local has its negative aspect as well, especially when it becomes confining and restrictive of the human spirit. Anyone living in a small-scale or rural society has had the opportunity to experience this. What is of special interest today in negotiating the interaction between the global and the local is the negative impact of the global on identity formation, where the resistance that the local is forced to undertake distorts the process of identity and community formation. Certain kinds of ethnification lead down this path, where ethnic identity becomes reified and ideologized. In such instances, local identity becomes a legitimation of violence against neighbors. Distortions of identity that emerge no longer liberate or allow the human to flourish, but constrict it and turn it to violence. In the recent past, the need to create space for difference has sometimes permitted a too uncritical view of the local, even a romanticizing of it. At this point in time, particularly as ethnic identities seek religious legitimation, becoming more critical is important.

The third dimension of extension for the new catholicity takes up the interaction of the global and the local in another way, and refocuses the question from a more general perspective: How does a new catholicity negotiate sameness, difference, and pluralism? All three of these must be addressed together. In emphasizing especially the unity in belief, Christians have been prone to stress the sameness dimension (one thinks of Vincent of Lérins's famous definition of tradition — *quod ubique, quod semper, quod ab omnibus creditum est)*. Much of the focus of the last four decades has been on exploring difference. As time has gone on, difference has become, so to speak, more differentiated. A good example has been feminist theologies, which have seen a continuing differentiation from initial statements about the experience of all women, to the experiences of women of different class and ethnicity. Perhaps now is the time to bring questions of sameness and difference into closer relation so as to avoid ideological distortions of either of them. These together form the basis for articulating an understanding of pluralism that is more than a luxuriation in difference, which takes the plural nature of human experience seriously, yet avoids the totalization of such a point of view. This becomes especially important in multicultural societies when one tries to move to a possibility of genuine living together (cf. the Latin American idea of *convivencia*), which is more than avoiding conflict.

Fourth and finally, the challenge of a new catholicity in its dimension of extension brings us back to some specifically theological issues, namely, that of inculturation or contextualization, and our concepts of communion. The second decade of globalization calls perhaps for a second generation of concepts of inculturation as well. If first-generation concepts of inculturation focused on making room for culture, second-generation concepts build in concern for ideologization or totalization of a given ethnicity, which stokes the fires of nationalism or intolerance. Here perhaps two strands of inculturation — those focused upon identity, and those committed to liberation — might find a place to come together.

Communion is a theological term used widely in Christianity today to express how Christians live in difference. Based on the Greek *koinonia*, communion evokes living together in peace, and a sense of full participation. As with any term of this scope, it is broad in its range of meanings. It is being suggested strongly in a recent document of the Lutheran World Federation on globalization, and has become the favored term of an understanding of the church in Vatican circles. Here is not the place to debate its various meanings or the sources of those meanings — be they the communion of persons within the Trinity or the relation between God and a chosen people. Certainly part of the theological agenda of a new catholicity would be to widen and deepen this important concept, so as to include the riches of biblical and theological tradition, but also to encompass the discussion of sameness, difference, and pluralism that an understanding of the new catholicity as extension presses upon us.

The New Catholicity as Fullness of Faith

The catholicity of the church has also been measured by the *regula fidei*, the fullness of faith. The root of the word "heresy" is to select, that is, to accept only parts of the belief that has been handed down from the apostles. What does the fullness of faith entail for the new catholicity? Three things come to mind in a special way here.

First of all, Christian faith must take into account the many faces of faith that the world presents today. Even for the more intellectually or theologically inclined Christian, the fact that 20 to 25 percent of all Christians today are Pentecostal or charismatic in their faith is something that cannot be neglected.[14] Nor should one neglect those uncounted numbers of "culture Christians" in the People's Republic of China who show a positive appreciation for Christianity as a spiritual tradition, but for a variety of reasons choose not to accept baptism.[15] There has been a growing appreciation in Roman Catholic circles in the last three decades for the varieties of popular faith *(religiosidad popular)*, which heretofore had been seen as deficient forms of Christianity in need of better evangelization. One of the tasks of the new catholicity is a deeper understanding and appreciation of the different faces of faith in the world today. One cannot restrict oneself to Western Christianity as practiced by theological elites. Here, it seems to me, we find ourselves still in a "first-generation" stage of learning to appreciate and understand why people would choose these forms of Christianity. A good deal needs to be done here before moving into more thoroughgoing critique. To this point we have been all too ready to critique what we barely understand.

Second, connected with the faces of faith is the phenomenon of secularization. Thinking about secularization has made quite a turn in the last

14. See Murray Dempster, Byron Klaus, and Douglas Peterson, eds., *The Globalization of Pentecostalism* (Oxford: Regnum, 1999).

15. See Edmond Tang, "The Second Chinese Enlightenment: Intellectuals and Christianity Today," in Werner Ustorf and Toshiko Murayama, eds., *Identity and Marginality: Rethinking Christianity in North East Asia* (Frankfurt: Peter Lang, 2000), pp. 55-70.

decade. From earlier predictions that it was an inexorable outcome of modernization, part of the disenchantment of the world, secularization is seen to be a possible consequence of modernization, but not an inevitable one. Secularization is clearly present in Europe, also (albeit in different form) in Canada, Australia, and New Zealand, and to a lesser extent in the United States. The move of secularization has most recently evoked a resurgence of religion in many parts of the world. Some of that resurgence has been linked especially to violence, and therefore should not be welcomed. But researchers have noted that, even in secular Europe, one can detect an unevenness in secularization, that religious sentiment continues to brood beneath the surface.[16] A new catholicity does not simply exult in a return of religion, but tries to understand the different approaches within secularity, and what these mean for interpreting Christian faith in a postmodern world.

Third and finally, the concept of tradition makes a return in the postmodern world. Tradition as an overarching concept was much criticized in the European Enlightenment. In the postmodern situation, one can speak of a certain "retraditionalization." This is an understanding of tradition that does not return to the premodern, but emerges under postmodern circumstances. In the case of those whose postmodern stance is to privilege the premodern, a selective return to the tradition is undertaken. In those who thoroughly embrace the postmodern, even while proclaiming the death of all master narratives, tradition is reappropriated, perhaps along the lines of Robert Redford's "little traditions," or as the heritage of cultural-linguistic communities, in George Lindbeck's sense. What the latter cases show is that narratives of some sort cannot wholly be jettisoned from the processes of identity and community formation. Narratives may not be shared on a wider scale, but they continue to be there nonetheless.

The New Catholicity as Communication and Exchange

I have already noted that the new catholicity requires a special attention to communication and participation if it is to ensure genuine extension and

16. See, for example, Grace Davie, *Religion in Modern Europe: A Memory Mutates* (Oxford: Oxford University Press, 2000).

fullness of faith. It must somehow embrace and connect the whole. I do not want to go into the whole area of intercultural communication and hermeneutics here, nor explore the understanding of the concept of communication for fundamental theology,[17] but rather wish to focus on two points.

First of all, a world church cannot take its form uncritically from the economic and sociocultural globalization now taking place. This may seem to be a simple truism at first glance. But it must take into consideration how often the church has sought its form uncritically from sociocultural and political forms around it. One need only remember the Constantinian church, monarchical and absolutist forms of the papacy, and instances of identification with empire in the modern missionary period. When seeking how to embody the whole, the church must find non-dominative, inclusive, and liberating ways to embrace the entirety of Christian faith.

Second, communication in the new catholicity involves not only dealing with difference, but discovering within difference ways to be able to speak universally. The local may have a certain existential priority, but there are reasons also for seeking the ontological, which will give the global a certain priority. This is the case not the least because, in seeking a critical base from which to work, some kind of criteriology will have to be worked out. The cultural and the local lead us to think about the intercultural and the translocal, again something that will call for more than existential reflection. And there are compelling crises that we face — of war and peace, but especially of the environment — which require us to think on more than a local scale. How will this be done?

In *The New Catholicity,* I suggested that the indeterminacies of narrative may create the space for a certain kind of universality. Narratives that are especially compelling exhibit a polyvalent nature that not only include many possible meanings, but also the capacity to hold together many of those meanings at the same time. A similar feature may be found in the articulation of certain Christian dogmas, such as the Chalcedonian formula on the two natures of Christ, where a line is drawn regarding what *cannot* be said, although what is sayable is never entirely and exhaustively

17. See Bernhard Fresacher, "Kommunikation. Leitbegriff theologischer Theoriebildung. Fundamentaltheologische Anstösse," *Zeitschrift für katholische Theologie* 123 (2001): 269-83.

articulated. Under certain conditions, these present workable approaches, at least until meanings are identified and possible utterances are indeed spoken. One wonders whether one can move beyond generalities here, given the diversity of human life.

This is most obviously present in the various attempts to articulate a global ethic. Most people would agree that such an ethic is desirable, if for no other reason that there be peace on earth. But to what extent it can actually be articulated remains a point of much debate.[18] Even on apparently fundamental issues, such as "Thou shalt not kill," divergence remains.

Heretofore, the paths to universality through difference have largely been negative ones — resistance to evil, the struggle for justice, working toward a not yet articulated vision of humanity. As societies move toward moral reconstruction after violence, and creating institutions that will prevent violence in the future, can we begin to make a turn to the positive, without falling into a hegemony of a single system? Or does that universality remain for the Christian essentially something eschatological? Is it to be found in the reconciliation of all things in Christ that the opening hymns in the Letters to the Ephesians and the Colossians promise?

The postmodern warns us of all that can go wrong with communication, of how to attend to silences that may be sites of suppressed speech, of how to detect hidden patterns of hegemony that need to be exposed. Language of the universal comes under special scrutiny. Yet it is precisely to such language that we must turn, to honor the full aspirations of the local, and to create institutions that will protect human life and community as a whole. The concept of a new catholicity can, I believe, contribute to that project and bring Christian faith into interaction with the most powerful conjunction in its environment today, globalization in its second decade and the postmodern.

18. I have tried to formulate some of this in "Weltethos — Eine Illusion?" *Theologisch-Praktische Quartalschrift* 149 (2001): 1-12.

Mission and Globalization in a New Testament Perspective

JOHANNES NISSEN

Defining Terms

The title of this paper brings together three terms, "mission," "globalization," and "New Testament Perspective." Since these terms can be understood in various ways I shall begin with a brief explanation of how they are used in this contribution.

The first term, "mission," is used in a comprehensive sense. Mission is more than evangelism. It includes proclamation as well as social action. The comprehensive understanding of mission can also be described by means of a tripod: *leitourgia*, *martyria*, and *diakonia* — worship, witness, and welfare work.[1]

Mission is an affirmation of the love of God in Jesus Christ. It is a proclamation of how God loved the whole of humanity in Jesus Christ. Mission is an *invitation* to come and see how God's fullness, the abundance of his kingdom, is realized. And it is a challenge to *go out* to tell other people about this abundance — in words and actions.

The second term, "globalization," points to the fact that the cultures

1. See also Johannes Nissen, *New Testament and Mission: Historical and Hermeneutical Perspectives* (Frankfurt: Peter Lang Verlag, 1999), pp. 18-19, with reference to various aspects of mission in the New Testament: (1) mission as *sending* (especially the Fourth Gospel); (2) mission as *disciple-making* (cf. the Gospel of Matthew); (3) mission as *deliverance and emancipatory action* (cf. the Gospel of Luke); (4) mission as *witness* (especially the Book of Acts and the Fourth Gospel).

of the world become increasingly open to each other, knitting the globe into one.[2] Heads of multinational corporations talk about themselves as the engineers of a world culture, a secular *oikoumene.* MTV, Macintosh, and McDonald's are just a few agents of the global forces of market, media, and modernity, tying the world together by communications, information, entertainment, and commerce.

The process of globalization means that European Christians have met people of faith from other traditions and have found a deep spirituality, wisdom, and holiness in other religious traditions. Globalization also means that the global nature of the problems of economy, ecology, and war have become evident and that religions are called upon to help to solve these problems. However, as a counterforce to globalization, we also find a return to ethnic, cultural, and religious identities, which are perceived as being threatened by the hegemony of Western capitalism and other global forces.

What, then, about the understanding of the phrase "in New Testament perspective"? I use this term to indicate that the main aim of this essay is the *interaction* between biblical texts and present experiences.[3] My purpose is not to offer a historical analysis of mission in the New Testament. Rather it is to enter into a dialogue between "the text" of life (our experiences) and the text of Scripture, and this dialectic is the kernel of my interpretative enterprise.

The interaction means a mutual challenge between text and interpreter. On the one hand: "When we read the Bible, we are not so much interpreting the Bible as much as *interpreting our own lives and life of our community* in the light of the Bible." On the other hand, the biblical texts have a *transformative role.* "The authority and interpretation of scripture has to be considered from a perspective that asks the question of the capacity of scripture to bring about transformation."[4]

2. Cf. C. Duraisingh, "Gospel and Cultures: Some Key Issues," in *Break the Chains of Injustice,* ed. P. Reámonn (Geneva: WARC, 1996), pp. 30-55 (32); K. Ahlstrand, "Moving with God's Mission," *Swedish Missiological Themes* 88, no. 1 (2000): 37-43 (39).

3. See J. Nissen, "Scripture and Experience as the Double Source of Mission: Hermeneutical Reflections," in *To Cast Fire Upon the Earth: Bible and Mission Collaborating in Today's Multicultural Context,* ed. T. Okure (Pietermaritzburg: Cluster Publications, 2000), pp. 178-93 (182-84).

4. The two quotations are taken from P. Holtrop et al., "Witnessing Together in Context," in *Breaking the Chains of Injustice,* ed. P. Réamonn, pp. 56-71 (60 and 62).

Text and experience are two points of departure that must be kept together.[5] If, on the one hand, we begin theological reflection from the traditional perspective of revelation, Scripture, and tradition, we are in danger of a theological imperialism that overlooks the crucial importance of every local human situation. If, on the other hand, we begin with local experience and culture, we are in danger of reducing Christian faith to a human creation designed to solve problems humanly defined.

Globalization as Opportunity and Challenge for Modern Mission

In this essay it is impossible to deal with all aspects of the encounter between the biblical traditions and present challenges. Where, then, do I see the "link" between mission, globalization, and the New Testament? Globalization is both an opportunity and a challenge for modern mission.

First, globalization is an *opportunity.* Even though globalization is a modern phenomenon, it is not totally unprecedented in human history.[6] In a sense, globalization had already occurred at the time of Christ in the Greco-Roman world. Thanks to the favorable conditions and impressive facilities and infrastructure created by the *Pax Romana* and metropolitanism, the first Christian mission was able to reach out to most parts of the Roman empire in just a couple of generations.

Migration, both voluntary and forced, is a significant phenomenon today. People have migrated from one place to another throughout history. But the accelerated movement of peoples across the world in the last decades is qualitatively new. Migration is also an important aspect of Christian mission.

Mission is traveling.[7] It is being on a journey. It is a restless moving towards the time when God will be all in all in creation and salvation (1 Cor. 15:28). Christians are in transit.

5. Cf. E. W. Poitras, "St. Augustine and the *Missio Dei:* A Reflection on Mission at the Close of the Twentieth Century," *Mission Studies* 16-2, no. 32 (1999): 28-46 (44).

6. Cf. Choong Chee Pang, "Globalization: Challenge and Opportunity for Mission," in *Into the Third Millennium: Together in God's Mission* (Geneva: LWF, 1998), pp. 93-100 (95).

7. Cf. J. Andrew Kirk, *What Is Mission? Theological Explorations* (London: Darton, Longman & Todd, 1999), p. 232; J. Nissen, "Firmness and Flexibility: Paul's Mission to the Greeks," in *Dialogue in Action* (FS J. Aagaard), ed. L. Thunberg, M. L. Pandit, C. V. Fogh-Hansen (New Delhi: Prajna Publications, 1988), pp. 58-84 (56-58).

Because mission is global, the missionaries will also be global in their outlook. "Missionaries are at home everywhere, but not quite at home anywhere. They are persons who can move easily from one place to another, from one culture to another, and not become confused, or lost, or incapable of action."[8]

Second, globalization is also a *challenge* to modern mission. There are at least four areas where this challenge becomes evident:[9] (1) The exclusion and marginalization of people; (2) the "oikoumene" of dominion versus the "oikoumene" of solidarity; (3) the relation between universality and particularity; (4) the encounter between religions.

Mission at the Margins

One World — Many Divisions

The process of globalization has a double effect on people.[10] Those who have great access to the communication technologies experience a profound interconnectedness. They belong to the rich part of the world, and they profit from the global capitalism. Other people, however, have the experience of being deliberately excluded. The majority of these people are living in the South.

About two decades ago J. de Santa Ana wrote that "one of the most compelling paradoxes of our time is the fact that, more than ever before in human history, we live in *one world,* where communications are fast and where what happens in one point of the planet is related to events in other parts of the earth; however, in this one world, barriers between human beings, separating and dividing societies, are still very strong."[11]

8. A. Bellagamba, *Mission and Ministry in the Global Church* (Maryknoll, N.Y.: Orbis Books, 1992), p. 10.

9. Two other areas are partnership in mission and reconciliation. On the first issue see J. Nissen, "Unity and Diversity: Biblical Models for Partnership," *Mission Studies* 14:1-2, no. 27-28 (1997): 121-46. On the second issue see my final remarks in this contribution.

10. Three processes in particular have shaped the globalization phenomenon. The first is political, the second is economic, and the third is technological. On these processes see R. J. Schreiter, *The New Catholicity: Theology between the Global and the Local* (Maryknoll, N.Y.: Orbis Books, 1997), pp. 5-8.

11. J. de Santa Ana, "The Mission of the Church in a World Torn Between Poor and Rich," *International Review of Mission* 72 (1983): 20-29 (20).

The sad thing is that nothing has changed. Life is still full of distorted relationships. Today millions of people are living at the margins of society. These include the poor, the refugees, the migrants, and many others. Therefore, one of the most pressing issues to confront Christians in all parts of the globe is the presence of these marginalized people.

Jesus and the Marginalized

The Bible underscores that the marginalized are given a special place in history. In both the Old and New Testaments God shows a bias towards those on the margins of human society. In the Old Testament God is understood as the God of the poor, the orphans, and the widows. In the New Testament the "good news to the poor" is of special importance. This point is stressed by Jesus' proclamation in the synagogue of Nazareth (Luke 4:16-30), which in recent years has become one of the major motivations for mission.[12]

An important feature of the primitive gospel is that the disadvantaged — the women, the poor person, the stranger, etc. — suddenly take center stage. The poor are seen as "agents of the dawning Kingdom."[13] The non-privileged came into this world not as mere recipients of gifts from the wealthy, but as those upon whom the future of the world is dependent. A "sinful woman" (Luke 7:36-50), a tax collector (Luke 19:1-10), and a Samaritan, an outsider (Luke 10:30-37) represent the signs of the "economy of the Kingdom."

It seems that we have become so familiar with the text of the gospels that the power of the scandal of Jesus' associations is almost always lost on us: His highly risky association with women of ill repute. His touch for the leper and his face-to-face encounter with the Gerasene demoniac. His meals with tax collectors and friendship with zealots. And to cap it all, his first resurrection appearance to Mary Magdalene of all people. "There can be no doubting the fact that Jesus spent a disproportionate amount of time with those whom others sought to marginalize and

12. Cf. J. Nissen, *New Testament and Mission,* pp. 50-52, 57-60.

13. Cf. J. Nissen, *Poverty and Mission: New Testament Perspectives on a Contemporary Theme* (Leiden: Interuniversity Institute for Missiological and Ecumenical Research, 1984), pp. 171-73.

that he would wish us to do the same until humanity achieves that state of wholeness in which all belong and there are no more centres and no more margins."[14]

The special concern of Jesus for those marginalized represents a decentering of perspective and a reversal of the world as it is presently known and legitimized. Universality passes through the particularity of the weakest and the smallest ones in humankind. As pointed out by M. Arias: "Globalization is inseparable from contextualization. The 'little ones' in the strange strategy of Jesus became not only the objects but also the subjects of mission!"[15]

Mission from the Periphery

What does it mean for today's mission that the starting point of Jesus' ministry is located in the Galilean periphery? According to the American-Hispanic scholar O. Costas the accent on Galilee in Mark's Gospel has three implications for contextual evangelization.[16]

First, Mark's Galilean model implies that contextual evangelization should have a sociohistorical foundation based on the periphery. When the gospel makes "somebody" out of the "nobodies" of society, when it restores the self-worth of the marginalized, then it is truly good news of a new order of life.

Second, evangelization not only has a public message, but also takes place amid the multitudes. The Galilean multitudes can be found everywhere. There is not a neighborhood, town, city, state, nation, or continent that does not have a Galilee. One must always look for the powerless, the marginalized, and the voiceless to discover the concrete reality of Galilee.

Third, there is the global scope of evangelization: that is, communicating the gospel from the periphery of the nations. Some make the mistake of starting in Jerusalem rather than in Galilee and end up frustrated

14. *A Whole New World Together: Four Spotlights on Mission.* The CMS Bicentenary 1799-1999 (London: Church Mission Society, 1999), p. 6.

15. M. Arias, *The Great Commission: Biblical Models for Evangelism* (Nashville: Abingdon Press, 1992), p. 32.

16. O. Costas, *Liberating News: A Theology of Contextual Evangelism* (Grand Rapids: Eerdmans, 1989), pp. 61-90. It should be noticed that Costas uses the term "evangelism" almost in the same way as I am using the term "mission."

or co-opted by the powers. They gear the message to a select few rather than the harassed multitudes and find themselves left with a historically harmless church, a private gospel, and a plastic Jesus. Instead a prophetic, liberating, and holistic mission must ask: *Where* is our base, *who* is our target audience, and *what* is the scope of our evangelistic task?

Mission to "Foreign" Structures

The Church and the Powers

Our globe is not just a world of living beings; it is also a "jungle" of multiple and complex structures and systems. Paradoxically, we human beings and other creatures are both served and enslaved by these structures and systems. Such structures are relevant in a missionary setting. This is particularly true of the economic structures created by the debt crisis.

This aspect has often been neglected by Christian mission, as was made clear by the WCC Assembly in Canberra 1991: "There is an urgent need today for a new type of mission, not into foreign lands, but into 'foreign' structures. By this term we mean economic, social and political structures which do not at all conform to Christian moral standards."[17]

Here we find a redefinition of mission. Mission is not just about sending a person from a so-called Christian country to a non-Christian country. Mission is more than this. Today we live in a global village in which we all are caught in economic, social, and political structures that are worldwide in character — structures that are competitive and divisive, creating hostilities, exploitation, injustice, and death. The mission to which we are called takes place in a world whose economic structures are contrary to our understanding of reconciliation and justice and peace.

Several passages in the New Testament letters (particularly Colossians and Ephesians) speak of the "principalities and powers." Some of the concrete modern structures might be structurally analogous to these powers. This might include religious structures (e.g., -ologies and -isms), moral structures (codes and customs), and political structures (the tyrant, the market, the schools, the courts, race and nation). The totality is over-

17. *Signs of the Spirit. Official Report. Seventh Assembly,* ed. M. Kinnamon (Geneva: WCC, 1991), p. 66.

whelmingly broad.[18] A survey of the New Testament material points to three aspects. First, as created by God these powers are essentially good. Second, they have rebelled and fallen. And third, they are redeemed "in Christ."

According to the WCC Assembly in Canberra, the Spirit of truth re-establishes and restores the integrity of the human person and human communities: "As Christians and as churches we constantly experience the danger of becoming captives to the systems and structures of the world. They are principalities and authorities, 'the cosmic forces of darkness, the spiritual forces of evil' (Eph. 6:10) which induce all human beings to be tempted to do injustice to others."[19] Today the basic question is: Do the churches bless the existing powers instead of depriving them of their authority and power?

The "Oikoumene" of Domination and the "Oikoumene" of Solidarity

Globalization has resulted in a new awareness of the inhabited earth as an interrelated whole. When the one world, however, is experienced as a closed system of domination and dependency, this awareness can be oppressive and paralyzing in its effects. This experience is not new. In the New Testament, particularly in the Book of Revelation, there is a critical perception of the imperial oikoumene of the *Pax Romana* as a threatening reality.

Two forms of the oikoumene are opposed to each other: the oikoumene of domination and the oikoumene of solidarity.[20] While the first form obeys a logic of power aiming at total control and threatens to make the earth uninhabitable, the second form proves to be a liberating impulse: it is an expression of living interactions instead of death-dealing autonomous laws. It lives in the certainty that the earth is habitable, because God has established his covenant for the whole of creation, and it is

18. Cf. J. H. Yoder, *The Politics of Jesus* (Grand Rapids: Eerdmans, 1972), p. 145. On mission to the "principalities and powers" in Colossians and Ephesians see my book, *New Testament and Mission*, pp. 129-44.

19. *Signs of the Spirit*, p. 73.

20. Cf. K. Raiser, *Ecumenism in Transition: A Paradigm Shift in the Ecumenical Movement* (Geneva: WCC, 1991), pp. 63-65, 86-87.

guided by the hope that God will dwell with humankind, with God's people (cf. Rev. 21:3).

The biblical vision of the oikoumene is characterized by *sharing in solidarity* expressed in various ways. One of the most impressive is the idea of *Jubilee.* The importance of the Jubilee year in the New Testament should not be overlooked. The Lucan paradigm for mission is proclaiming the Jubilee. In his inaugural speech in the synagogue of Nazareth, Jesus directly refers to the Jubilee by speaking about the "favourable year of the Lord" (Luke 4:18). In this way it is indicated that the ministry of Jesus will be one of liberation, healing, and justice. It will be a ministry where words and actions are woven into one. The aim of Jesus is to mend the whole of creation.

The Jubilee was a proclamation of renewal: the restoration of people, of social relationships, of nature itself. It has a critical and prophetic potential that can help to uncover the self-destructive tendencies of the present global system of finance.[21] The global market economy is said to create "the best of all worlds." But if we look at it from the perspective from below, the perspective of those who are excluded from enjoying its benefits, it has become an ideology that serves the interests of defending power and domination.

The Global and the Local

A Re-reading of the Missionary Mandate

In its essence, Christianity is a global religion. This is especially clear in Matthew 28:16-20. In the past this text was sometimes understood as a mandate to an aggressive militant mission, as a "crusade." It was imaged as a "conquest" — the winning of "souls" for Christ.[22] It is now widely recognized that the geographical understanding of Matthew 28 is a mistake. The emphasis tended to be on the "going" rather than on the "making of disci-

21. Cf. K. Raiser, *Ecumenism in Transition,* p. 18. On the biblical resources for an economy of life see also U. Duchrow, *Alternatives to Global Capitalism: Drawn from Biblical History, Designed for Political Action* (Utrecht: International Books/Heidelberg: Kairos, 1995), pp. 142-202.

22. Cf. G. M. Soares-Prabhu, "Following Jesus in Mission: Reflections on Mission in the Gospel of Matthew," in *Bible and Mission in India Today,* ed. J. Kavunkal and F. Hrangkuma (Bombay: St. Paul's, 1993), pp. 64-92 (85-86).

ples." The locality, not the task, determined whether one was a missionary or not.

There is no doubt that the concluding words in Matthew 28:16-20 was a text that spoke to the European Christian consciousness and culture in a powerful way. It was referred to as the "Great Commission." The fundamental social context that gave rise to the kairos for this text was the European "discovery" of "new" worlds which Europeans entered, conquered, colonized, and exploited. Matthew 28 spoke to the hearts and souls of sincere, zealous Christians. There *were* ends of the earth; there *were* new nations to be evangelized; there *were* new disciples to be won. And most of all, the modern age finally provided the technology to achieve the relatively rapid movement of comparatively large groups of people around the surface of the earth.[23]

Today we find ourselves in a very different Christian community living in a vastly different social context. Modern culture with its "scientific" certainty is being transformed into the global culture of multicommunal networking and high-speed information technology. The question arises, then, whether the church's missionary activity is in need of a different biblical paradigm to inspire the same missionary zeal and commitment as Matthew 28 did previously.

The missionary mandate in Matthew 10:5-16 might be seen as the basis of a new paradigm for mission in this culture and civilization. At least three aspects should be noticed.

First, the text underlines the *contextual aspect* of mission.[24] In Matthew 10 the mission is to the lost sheep of the house of Israel. This means that it is to the community, culture, and society of which Jesus and the disciples are part. Here then is another difference to Matthew 28, where the mission is to other cultures, communities, and societies. This commission then is not to those outside but to those within.

Second, the text points to the *holistic character* of mission. Jesus announces the good news of the kingdom by teaching and healing (cf. Matt. 5–7 and Matt. 8–9). The disciples who share in the mission of their master must engage in a similar holistic mission in which verbal proclamation is joined to liberative action. Healing is concerned with restoration of the

23. Cf. S. C. Bate, "Matthew 10: A Mission Mandate for the Global Context," in *To Cast Fire Upon the Earth,* ed. T. Okure, pp. 42-56 (44-45).

24. Cf. S. C. Bate, "Matthew 10," p. 48.

fullness of human life in those who have lost it. A more holistic understanding of sickness and health is one of the signs of the postmodern age.

Third, *mission as directed to the "lost"* means that "the locus of mission . . . is not determined by the predilections or ambitions of the missioner, but by the need of the people to whom he or she is sent." Moreover, the demands raised to the disciples are radical: "Poverty and powerlessness are for Matthew an absolutely indispensable part of Christian mission."[25]

One Gospel — Many Cultures

Today we are facing a complex problem: How can the unity of humanity be related to cultural diversity? Somehow the globalization process seems to support the dream of a modern Babel.[26] Babel offers a promise of unity for all through one language, one culture (cf. Gen. 11:1). It allows no room for the identity of each language, each culture. Pentecost in Acts 2:1-13 is the reversal of Babel, holding together both "all" and "each." Local identities are confirmed within a larger community. By emphasizing that each heard the gospel in his or her own language, Luke indicates that the identities of the hearers were affirmed. In the presence of the Spirit, differences need not mean division. No longer can any group or place or time be more "sacred" than another.[27]

The Book of Acts as a whole is the story of the gospel being unfolded, opened up, its beauty increasingly revealed as it is appropriated and reappropriated by culture after culture.[28] It is through the encounter of the Jewish Christians with the cultures of people like Cornelius that the horizon of theology is expanded (ch. 10–11). Thus, it is in facing the religio-cultural milieu of Athens that Paul's grasp of the gospel is enriched (17:17-34).

In its broadest sense the biblical story moves from the uniform to the

25. The two quotations are from G. M. Soares-Prabhu, "Following Jesus in Mission," pp. 78 and 81.

26. Cf. V. Mortensen, *Det globale og multireligiøse Teologiske Udfordringer* Center for Multireligiøse Studier, Occasional Papers 1 (Aarhus: Aarhus Universitet, 2001), p. 11.

27. Cf. *Spirit, Gospel, Cultures.* Bible Studies on the Acts of the Apostles (Geneva: WCC, 1995), p. 11.

28. Cf. C. Duraisingh, "The Day of Pentecost: Acts 2:1-13," in *Gospel and Cultures: Reformed Perspectives,* ed. H. S. Wilson (Geneva: WARC, 1996), pp. 37-43 (37).

pluriform. At its deepest level, Christianity is not an ethnocentric religion and its vision is not one of uniformity. Gentiles need not become Jews; Chinese need not become Italian or Polish. The universalism of the gospel means that in faith one can find solidarity in and through the plurality of nations. Multiplicity, not conformity, is what characterizes Christianity. The vision is one gospel, diverse cultures, one community. People in different parts of the world speak different languages, see the world through different eyes, and live their lives in different ways. But when people accept Jesus Christ, they become members of a new community, with a new identity and a new way of living. The question is: How can the various cultures encounter the gospel — and be transformed by it without losing their distinctiveness and vitality? On the other hand, how can the distinctiveness and integrity of the Christian faith be lived in each culture?

In relation to the intersection between the local and the global it is worthwhile to consider the present growth of Pentecostalism. This movement can be described as "a form of Christianity adapted to modernity and contextualized into the global culture."[29] With the prominence of healing and speaking in tongues it is natural that the Book of Acts plays a significant role in Pentecostalism. Here, however, two critical notes are in order.[30] First, Luke has a tendency to a "theology of glory" or triumphalism that stands in contrast to other parts of the New Testament but similar to the risk of triumphalism that can be discerned in today's Pentecostalism. Second, it seems that Pentecostals have not developed the full implication of their doctrine for holistic mission. An example is the implicit isolation of sickness from the broader plight of human suffering and injustice. Therefore, healing and tongues should connect the individual Pentecostal Christian and churches with the concern for global redemptive values, for justice and reconciliation, within their eschatological vision of the kingdom.

29. V. Mortensen, "Christianity Is Changing," in *The Charismatic Movement and the Churches*, ed. V. Mortensen Center for Multireligiøse Studier, Occasional Papers 2 (Aarhus: Aarhus Universitet, 2001), pp. 5-9 (7).

30. The first critical remark in J. Nissen, *New Testament and Mission*, p. 61. The second critical remark in Young-Gi Hong, "Church and Mission: A Pentecostal Perspective," *International Review of Mission* 90 (2001): 289-308 (301-2).

The Incarnation — From the Universal to the Particular

The relation between the universality of Christ and the particularity of Jesus raises the question of the appropriate starting point for Christology.[31] While some would start "from below" with the historical Jesus, others would start "from above" with the Christ of faith. Both seek universal meaning and particular application. One position seeks specific historical paradigms in the life of Jesus for Christian action today (e.g., liberation theology). The other stresses that we know Christ as ascended Lord, and this informs our entire understanding of his person and work. What is the relationship between these two starting points? The two positions should preferably not be seen as an either/or question. Theology has to be incarnational. It should take as its starting point neither the Jesus of history alone nor the Christ of faith alone but the incarnate Son of God.

This was made very clear as a dynamic interaction between the gospel and cultures by the report from the World Mission Conference in Salvador 1996 (Section I), "Called to One Hope: The Gospel in Diverse Cultures": "It is the life of Jesus the incarnate, lived out in the realities of a particular context that illuminates the very nature of God's way of salvation, the Gospel." Hence the incarnation of Jesus Christ as testified by John's Gospel is basic to understanding the dynamic between gospel and cultures.[32] This gospel offers an incarnational model of mission. It is also of particular interest when we try to understand the relation between the contextual and universal aspect of Christology.

The universality of Christ does not cancel the particularity of Jesus. The paradox of the incarnation lies in the simultaneity of the particular and the universal. Jesus is the "concrete universal."[33] Jesus was born a Jew,

31. See J. Nissen, "Christology Between the Local and the Global," *Swedish Missiological Themes* 88, no. 4 (2000): 593-609 (604).

32. C. Duraisingh in *Called to One Hope: The Gospel in Diverse Cultures*, ed. C. Duraisingh (Geneva: WCC, 1998), p. 34; cf. T. V. Philip, *Edinburgh to Salvador: Twentieth Century Ecumenical Missiology* (New Delhi: CSS & ISPCK, 1999), pp. 92-96. Section 1 had the title "Authentic Witness within Each Culture." According to C. Duraisingh "'Witness from within' is the only mode of evangelism which corresponds to belief in a God who does not control human history from without but rather enters into it, suffers with it and transforms it by participating in it fully and really" (*Called to One Hope*, pp. 103-4).

33. J. Dupuis, *Toward a Christian Theology of Religious Pluralism* (Maryknoll, N.Y.: Orbis Books, 1997), p. 297.

not a kind of universal man. God's becoming a human person at a particular moment of history in a specific geographical location is an important key to understanding the relationship between gospel and culture.

Encounter with Religions of the World

The Uniqueness and the Universality of Christ

One of the most important issues at the beginning of the new millennium is the encounter between Christian faith and other faith traditions. An urgent task is to formulate a Christian theology of faiths.

To clarify this task it might be useful to distinguish between *plurality* and *pluralism*. This distinction is suggested by the report "Common Witness within a Religiously Plural Context": "Pluralism means that not only are there many religions and beliefs but these religions and beliefs are equally true and valid. . . . Plurality is something all nations have to deal with. It refers to the fact that people of different faiths, ideologies, cultures and ways of life live alongside each other in the same country and as part of the same nation."[34]

For some time it has been customary to distinguish between three principal approaches to other religions: exclusivism, inclusivism, and pluralism. The debate has been largely about which of these three approaches is correct, but now a number of scholars are suggesting that this is a most unhelpful debate and that we need to be looking for a new approach that does not deny the strengths of these three but goes beyond them. The most exciting development at the moment is the suggestion that it is in a deeper understanding of the Trinity itself that we will be led to a clearer theology of faiths.[35]

The most disputed of all issues to do with the religious encounter centers on the uniqueness and universality of Christ. Some of the New Testament traditions seem to have anticipated the contemporary christological debate in a pluralist context. So, for instance, the letters to the Colossians and to the Hebrews both speak of Christ against the background of at-

34. "Common Witness within a Religiously Plural Context," *International Review of Mission* 90 (2001): 346-49 (346). Viggo Mortensen rightly argues that plurality is reigning, but pluralism cannot be the right Christian answer; V. Mortensen, "Nordic Missiology and Ecumenics," *Swedish Missiological Themes* 89, no. 4 (2001): 439-53 (449).

35. Cf. *A Whole New World*, p. 33.

tempts to reinterpret him in ways that harmonize with other religious convictions. There is a remarkable parallel between the beliefs being combated in Colossae and those being advanced by representatives of the "pluralist" position.[36]

The Gospel of John is of special interest in this context. It is addressed to a first-century context of conflicting claims and has particular relevance in our own pluralistic setting today. It is noteworthy that this Gospel has both aspects mentioned in the introduction to this article.

First, *mission as sending.* Unlike Matthew 28:18-20, the mission command in John 20:21 — "As the Father has sent me, so I send you" — is silent about the concrete goal of mission. Mission is to be sent. In John 17:18 we have another version that indicates the disciples are sent into the world. Both forms of the mission command have relevance in today's situation, and so has the fact that John's Gospel is one of the strongest biblical witnesses to the understanding of mission as *missio Dei.*

Second, *mission as invitation.* In the Fourth Gospel Christ is described as God's universal invitation, and John's Christology is marked by a peculiar combination of inclusive and exclusive aspects.[37] This can be illustrated by the "I am" sayings, which are not dogmatic demarcations, but universal invitations to discipleship.

Another example is the prologue in John 1:1-18, which shows that this Gospel from its very opening is cosmic and universal in perspective. The issues are all ultimate: the origin and meaning of creation, the attainment of authentic life, and the search for God. These are elements common to all religious systems. But a Christian interpretation cannot remain at that. The important thing is that John moves from these universal elements to the earthly, historical Jesus. Thus there is a movement from the universal to the particular, from the global to the local, from eternity to history, from the impersonal to the personal. And men and women are called to follow that movement, and thereby realize that Jesus Christ is the unique revealer of the living God (1:18).

36. Cf. J. Andrew Kirk, *What Is Mission?*, pp. 139-40. Instead of the categories: exclusivist, inclusivist, and pluralist Kirk prefers to speak of *particularity, generality,* and *universality.*

37. More in detail in J. Nissen, *New Testament and Mission,* pp. 86-87.

Integrity and Openness

How can we maintain genuine Christian integrity while at the same time being open to people of other faiths? This question is of great importance in the contemporary debate. It seems that a similar question is addressed by Paul in his famous statement in 1 Corinthians 9:19-23, where integrity and openness are held together. The text clearly implies that Paul allowed circumstances and situations to determine the statement of his kerygma to a considerable degree. His mission is marked by a great adaptability to men of different cultures and religions. How can Paul be "all things to all men"? Only by finding a point of reference outside himself. The "law of Christ" (9:21) is the law of love that becomes the authority of Paul's missionary adaptation.

If we want to get an accurate picture of Paul's attitude towards people of other faiths, his openness towards Jews and Greeks in 1 Corinthians 9:19-23 should be counterbalanced by his critique of Jewish and Greek culture in 1 Corinthians 1:18-25. This is another way of saying that the cross is an indispensable part of Christian integrity. Therefore, when we attempt to understand the dialectical relationship between integrity and openness, we must ask the important question: How can our witness to the particularity of the cross, which is so offensive and foolish to others, be shared without a show of arrogance?

Paul's reflections in 1 Corinthians 9 indicate that he as a missionary cannot compel, he can only persuade and appeal; but as a missionary Paul is himself under compulsion, constrained by Jesus' love, the one unfailing missionary motive of all times (cf. 1 Cor. 9:16). Paul does not think of the Christian mission either in competitive or humanitarian terms. "He is not pitting one religion against another or making claims of superiority for his own beliefs. He is presenting Christ, for the sole sufficient reason that he deserves to be presented. . . ."[38] Authentic mission must be characterized by bold humility.[39] In dialogue "our approach must be respectful and

38. D. Webster, *Local Church and World Mission* (London: SCM, 1962), p. 71.

39. In his analysis of Matthew 28:18-20, D. J. Bosch argues that Matthew "wishes his community to know that mission never takes place in self-confidence but in the knowledge of our weakness, at a point of crisis where danger and opportunity come together. Matthew's Christians, like the first disciples, stand in a dialectic tension between worship and doubt, between faith and fear" (*Transforming Mission: Paradigm Shifts in Theology of Mission* [Maryknoll, N.Y.: Orbis Books, 1991], p. 76).

humble. We must not only speak, but also listen, while realizing that we are all on the way to new truths."[40]

Final Remarks

It might be appropriate to conclude this article with a few remarks on the content and form of Christian mission in the coming time. At least two points should be noticed.

Mission in Christ's Way

When the expansion of Christianity is seen as the goal of Christian mission there is a danger of choosing a model that makes mission into something like "marketing," a product.[41] In it mission would resemble the export sales branch of a global corporation, and the prime goal would be like international institutional growth, in which a Western model of religion replaces a local model. Various forms of church growth ideas reduce Christian mission to activities that originate in marketing and consumer studies, not from the pattern of Jesus revealed in Scripture.

When mission in this way is blended with the culture of the missionary, it becomes mission "from above" — or as V. R. Mollenkott says — patriarchal evangelism.[42] According to Mollenkott this form of evangelism is marked by many of the destructive assumptions of traditional Western culture. First of all is the idea that bigger is better, so that evangelism's purpose is to enlarge Christian institutions. Over against this the message of the New Age evangelism (Mollenkott's term for what she deems the genuine New Testament evangelism) is the revolutionary insight hymned by Mary in Luke 1:51-52: God has "put down the mighty from their thrones, and exalted those of low degree. . . ." Since small is beautiful we must seek

40. V. Mortensen, "Mission: Identity in Conflict," in *Identity in Conflict: Classical Christian Faith and Religio Occulta* (FS J. Aagaard), ed. M. L. Pandit, H. Meldgaard, M. Garde (New Delhi: Munshiram Manocharlal Publications, 1998), pp. 219-28 (228).

41. Cf. W. R. Burrows, "Reconciling All in Christ: The Oldest New Paradigm for Mission," *Mission Studies* 15, no. 1 (1998): 79-98 (87).

42. V. R. Mollenkott, "New Age Evangelism," *International Review of Mission* 72 (1983): 32-40.

alternative possibilities to challenge the larger structures, never letting a larger structure assume power that could be exercised by a smaller, more local group.

Some other characteristics might be mentioned. For instance, patriarchal evangelism assumes that competition is necessary and inevitable in society and hence in the church. Also, it assumes that human fulfillment stems from measurable achievements. New Age evangelism, however, stresses God's unconditional love and the infinite dignity of every human being regardless of achievement.

An imperialistic crusader's spirit was foreign to Christ. The ecumenical document "Mission and Evangelism" states that "Churches are free to choose the ways they consider best to announce the Gospel to different people in different circumstances. But these options are never neutral. Every methodology illustrates or betrays the Gospel we announce. In all communication of the Gospel, power must be subordinate to love."[43]

Authentic mission is "mission in Christ's way."[44] It can never be understood as imposing the gospel on other people. Mission is not to be imagined as a "conquest" (winning the world for Christ) or a "sale" (selling the gospel), but as light that illuminates the darkness and as salt that gives flavor (Matt. 5:13-16).

Amid the missions of other religions, Christians remain committed to a mission of love and service in the Spirit of Christ. The meaning of such mission is certainly not exhausted in dialogue, but just as certainly it cannot be lived apart from a dialogical existence. It is no longer acceptable to visualize Christian mission as a kind of spiritual warfare. Such forms of religious violence should be excluded in the light of the very roots of Christian faith. "Maybe we are entering a new phase of mission in which we do not place our own visions and hopes above those of others, but alongside them. We will not exploit the weakness of others and try to conquer them in their vulnerability. As long as inter-religious relationships (and inter-church relationships!) are tainted by threats or even by violence we cannot talk of Christian mission in any meaningful sense."[45]

43. "Mission and Evangelism — An Ecumenical Affirmation," *International Review of Mission* 71 (1983): 427-51 (439).

44. J. Nissen, "Mission in Christ's Way: The Temptation in the Desert and Christian Mission," in *Identity in Conflict,* ed. M. L. Pandit, H. Meldgaard, M. Garde pp. 41-51 (48-49).

45. T. Ahrens, "Theology: A Tool for Mission," in *Into the Third Millennium: Together in God's Mission* (Geneva: LWF, 1998), pp. 57-72 (68).

Reconciliation as Paradigm for Christian Mission

Overcoming violence and building peace will be an important issue on the missiological agenda in the next years. In previous times violence may have enjoyed a kind of unreflective acceptability. "Today, when violence erupts around the globe like a string of volcanoes, or rather like landmines exploding beneath our feet, it is rapidly losing its acceptability. Violence is increasingly recognized as a missiological and ecumenical concern and discussed as such."[46]

A theology of reconciliation is deeply rooted in the New Testament. It can be discerned on three levels:[47] A christological level, on which Christ is the mediator through whom God reconciles the world to himself; an ecclesiological level, on which Christ reconciles Jew and Gentile; and a cosmic level, on which Christ reconciles all powers in heaven and earth.

The importance of reconciliation for Christian mission is particularly evident in Paul's letters. Two texts might illustrate this.[48] The first text is 2 Corinthians 5:14-21. In this passage Christians are called to be "ambassadors of Christ." They have been given "the ministry of reconciliation." This message of reconciliation is for the entire world.

The other text is Ephesians 2:14-16. Here the cosmic reconciliation is concretized in an actual historical fellowship, e.g., the church consisting of Jews and Gentiles. Christ "is our peace; in his flesh he has made both groups into one and has broken down the dividing wall." If, however, the time of the dividing wall is past, behind which God's law stood, how much more is the time of all other walls past, behind which stand only human laws. But the consequences have not been drawn from the broken wall; instead we have misused the Christian message to sanction our own walls of nation, class, and race.

In the coming years "reconciling all in Christ" will be an important paradigm or focal image for Christian mission.[49] Because Christians find themselves in a world racked by social, economic, racial, religious, and na-

46. T. Ahrens, "Theology: A Tool for Mission," p. 64. On reconciliation as an integral part of mission see also J. Andrew Kirk, *What Is Mission?*, pp. 143-63.

47. Cf. R. J. Schreiter, *Reconciliation: Mission and Ministry in a Changing Social Order* (Maryknoll, N.Y.: Orbis Books, 1992), p. 42.

48. Cf. J. Nissen, *New Testament and Mission*, pp. 105-6 and 139.

49. Cf. W. R. Burrows, "Reconciling All in Christ," p. 79.

tionalistic conflict, an absolutely vital task for Christians is to become communities that struggle to bring about reconciliation in both its deepest theological and most basic human senses.

Ecumenism in the Globalization Syndrome

PETER LODBERG

Introduction

In recent years the concept of *paradigm shift* from the natural sciences has been adopted by theology. The first theologian to use the concept was Hans Küng in order to understand the relationship between Christian confessions, which are interpreted as representing different theological paradigms.[1] Later the South African missiologist David Bosch adopted it to understand the different theologies of mission within the Christian churches and the ecumenical movement.[2] In ecumenical theology and practical ecumenism the rapid developments in the world and the consequences for the life of the World Council of Churches are interpreted by Konrad Raiser as representing a need for a paradigm shift for ecumenical institutions.[3] Konrad Raiser's attempt to keep pace with ecclesial, social, and political changes around the third millennium is admirable and in line with the self-understanding of the WCC, that it has a prophetic voice in the world and wants to challenge the churches to live up to their vocation. The WCC has an ambition to speak the truth and see the signs of the day in order to speak out on issues related to the present-day world events.

1. Hans Küng, *Theology for the Third Millennium* (New York: Doubleday, 1988).

2. David Bosch, *Transforming Mission: Paradigm Shifts in Theology of Mission* (Maryknoll, N.Y.: Orbis Books, 1991).

3. Konrad Raiser, *Ökumene im Übergang. Paradigmenwechsel in der ökumenischen Bewegung* (München: Kaiser Verlag, 1989).

More and more it is felt by the leadership of the World Council of Churches that the new world needs new answers, which also involve a paradigm shift in the working style of ecumenical institutions.

Many events in the last ten to fifteen years have called for response from the World Council of Churches. The downfall of the Berlin Wall in 1989, the breaking up of the old bipolar world between communism and capitalism, the forces of globalization, and the fight against international terrorism after September 11, 2001, are events of immense importance for everybody on this globe. The question is, have these events changed anything in the analysis and the responses of the World Council of Churches? How has ecumenism related to these breaking events, and how does ecumenism understand its role in the globalization syndrome? These are some of the questions to be dealt with in this study on the present role and self-understanding of the World Council of Churches as a representative of world Christianity.

Ecumenism and Modernity

The modern ecumenical movement was born in the second half of the twentieth century. The experiences of World War II confirmed ecumenical architects, such as J. H. Oldham, George Bell, and W. A. Visser 't Hooft, in the view that they were right when they contemplated the building of ecumenical institutions. Ecumenism was not only an important matter for individuals and church leaders, but had to involve the churches as collective bodies of faith. To the ecumenical pioneers the issue of church unity was no longer a free choice, but belonged to the very identity of the church of Jesus Christ, who prayed that all may be one (John 17:21). Through conferences, discussions, books, and articles a new ecumenical agenda was set up for the churches, shifting the theological emphasis from a confessional starting point to a christological approach. Not least, dialectical theologians such as Dietrich Bonhoeffer and Karl Barth inspired the reformulation of theology after the collapse of the Corpus Christianum and liberal theology in the aftermath of the two world wars. Ecumenical theology and especially ecclesiology were formulated on the basis of revelation and not on the background of false alliances with culture, state, nation, or people. Dialectical theology offered a welcome alternative and a new start for church and theology, where the critique of religion as false consciousness and an expression of suppressed feelings was considered a new opportunity to redefine the purpose and future of theology. The perspective of ecclesiology was turned upside down. The importance of tradition or confessional heritage was interpreted from a christological point of view. The future of the churches in light of the kingdom of God became more important than their traditions, which often are plagued with divisions and disagreement. According to Edmund Schlink this change of perspective represents a Copernican revolution to the churches, where they had to define common ground *before* they disagreed.[4]

From a christological point of view the issue of church unity was no longer a free choice, but belonged to the very being of church. This is still one of the tasks that the ecumenical movement sets the historical and confessional churches: and it is a difficult task to understand the identity of a confessional church from the perspective of the future, e.g., the perspective of the kingdom of God, and not from the perspective of tradition or history. The questions of what the churches could be and what they have in common are theologically prior to the questions about their heritage and different divisions.

The ecumenical movement has created new images and renewed the theological language in order to capture the new reality of church cooperation, church union, and church unity. Models of church unity have been invented, and the ecumenical vocabulary speaks of "unity in diversity," "reconciled diversity," and "conciliar fellowship." Alongside this tradition organic images have been used to stress the fact that through cooperation the churches come closer to each other and, thereby, to their own true identity as the church of Jesus Christ. Expressions like "the churches grow together," "they are on the way together," "sharing of faith," and "sharing of gifts" point to a new reality of which the churches become part through the participation in the ecumenical movement.

Robert J. Schreiter has called this new theological way of imagining the Christian church *the new catholicity,* because now — at the beginning of the third millennium — Christianity is for the first time in history to be found everywhere.[5] The Christian church is now incarnated in almost all cultures of the world, and its great diversity calls for new forms of communication and exchange that are open for full and equal participation by all

4. Edmund Schlink, *Ökumenische Theologie* (Göttingen: Vandenhoeck & Ruprecht, 1983).

5. Robert Schreiter, *The New Catholicity: Theology between the Global and the Local* (Maryknoll, N.Y.: Orbis Books, 1997). See also his article in this book.

Christians in the many different denominational churches. It is the combination of the worldwide nature of the church today and the challenges raised by the inculturation of faith that is behind the "new catholicity" as a theological parallel to the political and social concept of globalization. The language of globalization is the language of dynamics, flexibility, and change. Just as goods, money, and people are moving around, crossing boundaries on the global market, so theology, according to Schreiter, is flowing across cultural and confessional boundaries. African theology is not only alive in Africa, but is a reality among African refugees in Europe. This could also be said for European, Latin American, or American culture. Thus, forced and voluntary migration has spread cultures around the world and created new forms of cooperation and tension. When people move they bring their religion, so religion is also on the move; alongside with this, theology moves. Robert Schreiter points to the Roman Catholic Church and the ecumenical movement as partners in the globalization of Christianity and Christian theology. Especially, he points to feminist theologies, theologies of ecology, and theologies of human rights as global theological flows, which address the existence, the contradictions, and the failures of global systems. Each theology is located in its own context, but they enjoy a mutual intelligibility within their discourses and to a great extent among them.

The Lutheran World Federation and the World Council of Churches, in combination with confessional and ecumenical sister-organizations on the local level, are institutional expressions of the emerging ecumenical paradigm in the aftermath of World War II. They became member organizations of *churches,* and not of individuals or church groups. Especially, Protestant churches — and later on Orthodox churches — considered membership of international ecumenical institutions to be an important way to enlarge their cooperation and break out of a narrow national or confessional identity. Ecumenism became an important dimension and helped to relativize the national or local culture as the only expression of Christian identity. Following Ted A. Campbell, who understands modernism as the cultural movement to overcome the particularities of traditions, the ecumenical movement became a Christian expression of this broader cultural movement that flourished from the 1880s through the 1960s.[6] Modernism wanted to find a truly global, international culture as opposed

6. Ted A. Campbell, *Christian Confessions: A Historical Introduction* (Louisville: John Knox Press, 1996).

to the divisive national, ethnic, and religious traditions that had prevailed in the past. For the ecumenical movement this meant that unity in Christ was more important than traditional division. A distinctive traditional confessional identity was typically seen as a hindrance to the mission of the church in the modern world. According to Campbell, by the end of the 1960s, ecumenical trends had exerted a deep impact not only at global and national levels, but also at the local church level. "Denominational distinctions by this time were seen much less rigidly than in the past, and many Christians (particularly in the United States) began to see traditional differences as being relatively unimportant."[7]

This may be true for a more confessional pluralistic situation in the U.S. than in Scandinavia, which was — and still is to a certain extent — characterized by a homogeneous Lutheran identity in society. Especially in Denmark, the ecumenical involvement of the established Lutheran Church has been debated over the years and opposed by strong groups related to the traditions of the Pietistic and Grundtvigian Awakening in the second half of the nineteenth century. But the international development and cooperation within NATO, the UN, and the European Union have also called upon the Lutheran Church to recognize an international dimension and fellowship with — firstly — churches in Europe and — secondly — in the Middle East, Asia, and Africa. This work has been carried out by congregations involved in mission and international "diaconia."

Modernism and Ecumenical Social Ethic

The importance of an ecclesiological identity of the ecumenical movement is also stressed from the position of ecumenical social ethic. Thus the Life and World Conference in Oxford 1937 gathered under the slogan, "Let the Church Be the Church." According to J. H. Oldham the essential theme of the conference was the life-and-death-struggle between Christian faith and the secular and pagan tendencies of the 1930s.[8] These tendencies were the mass movements of nazism, communism, and fascism, which had to be counteracted as a matter of Christian faith. As an alternative ideal and model of society J. H. Oldham formulated the idea of "the responsible so-

7. Campbell, *Christian Confessions*, p. 7.

8. *Oxford Report* (London: SPCK, 1937), p. 10.

ciety" and its so-called middle axioms: peace, justice, and order. The model of the responsible society helped the emerging ecumenical fellowship to act in a responsible and common way during World War II and in the years thereafter. The first Assembly of the World Council of Churches in Amsterdam in 1948 decided to stay with the model of responsible society as an alternative to and as a bridge-builder between Eastern Europe and the West, between communism and liberal capitalism. The majority of the delegates tried to distance themselves from a direct involvement in the clash of the two ideologies and concentrated on the difficult road to reconciliation with the German churches and its people and financial and moral support for the refugees on all sides after the war. A special Church Service for Refugees was set up in Germany under the leadership of a Danish theologian and pastor, Halfdan Høgsbro, who had been very active in establishing a similar service to approximately 250,000 German refugees in Denmark under the auspices of the Ecumenical Council in Denmark. According to Høgsbro a precondition for the rebuilding of Europe in the aftermath of the war was the solution of the German question, which included setting aside any national feelings and thoughts about revenge for what the Nazis had done to the occupied countries during the war. Thus, the time was not ripe for a new confrontation between political systems and ideologies, because the immense task was rebuilding Europe and seeking understanding among former enemies.

The price to be paid for this decision was criticism from different sides on the World Council of Churches. The Communist leadership of the Soviet Union prohibited a delegation from the Russian Orthodox Church, because it considered the World Council of Churches to be a puppet in the hands of Western capitalism and the United States of America. John Avery Dulles, in a discussion with Professor Hromádka who defended Christian socialism and the new regimes in Eastern Europe, criticized this region for being too uncritical towards socialism. Documents from this time suggest that the leadership of the World Council of Churches tried to establish a possibility for the different opinions to meet and to discuss outside the political realm, on the basis of a profound common Christian identity. Especially, the Prague Spring in 1968 was regarded by many in the ecumenical movement as an event that showed it would be possible to have socialism with a human face and to reconcile the profound political and economic differences between East and West if people were allowed to decide for themselves. In the period after 1945 and especially after 1968 the churches in

Eastern Europe tried to use the new situation to create free spaces for worship, Christian education, and diaconal work, and in the West there was a feeling of new solidarity with the Eastern European churches.

The developments in Eastern Europe and the strong position of the non-aligned members of the United Nations after the period of decolonization made it possible for the churches in Africa, Asia, and Latin America to raise the question of "social justice" as the most important theological and political question for the World Council of Churches and for an ecumenical social ethic. The theology of revolution was introduced into the World Council of Churches and made an important impact on the fourth Assembly in Uppsala, Sweden, 1968. The struggle against racism and apartheid was regarded as a matter of faith from a theological point of view, which was carried through by Jürgen Moltmann's theology of hope and Ruben A. Alves's theology of liberation. According to Moltmann the new political theology unites the old cosmological theology and the new theology of existentialism in an eschatological understanding of history with the messianic tasks of men and women in society.[9] According to Moltmann it is the task of Christians to interpret the world in the light of the gospel *and* to act accordingly in order to set up signs that can point towards the kingdom of God, which is already at hand. The ideal of an alternative lifestyle confronting the political and economic powers of the world became an integral part of the Christian message in the life of the ecumenical movement. The key word was "the prophetic voice of the Church." The new hermeneutical starting point for theological reflection and Christian action became "the poor." Gustavo Gutiérrez published his well-known books, *Theology of Liberation* and *The Power of the Poor in History*, and argued alongside with Benoit Dumas in his book, *Two Alienated Faces of the One Church*, that the poor belong to the understanding of the mystery of the church, e.g., the poor belong to the understanding of the very nature of the church. The poor become the criteria for the ecclesial identity, and they are the subjects of the church, e.g., not the target for mission or evangelization. It is the poor that evangelize the church and the world, because Jesus said that he would be present in the poor and the oppressed. Thus the new word for "order" and "development" became social justice, and the General Assembly of the World

9. Jürgen Moltmann, *Religion, Revolution and the Future* (Maryknoll, N.Y.: Orbis Books, 1969), p. 218.

Council of Churches in Nairobi, 1975, brought the concern and perspectives together under the headline: "Just, Participatory and Sustainable Society." The Vancouver Assembly of the World Council of Churches in 1983 — and the last one during the Cold War — felt the urgent need for "ethical guidelines" with ecclesiological significance and invited the churches to participate in "a conciliar process of Justice, Peace and the Integrity of Creation." Especially, the churches in the Federal Republic of Germany and the German Democratic Republic played an important role in the conciliar process, and in the GDR the process became the umbrella under which popular and church initiatives related to human rights, peace, justice, and environmental issues could take place in critical dialogue and even in opposition to the East German government, leading up to the downfall of the Berlin Wall in 1989. In the German churches it was discussed whether the opposition to nuclear warfare and the present capitalist society could be regarded theologically as a matter of faith, i.e., a *status confessionis.*

After 1989 — the Globalization Syndrome

The collapse of communism in Eastern Europe symbolized by the downfall of the Berlin Wall represents the beginning of globalization. It represents a change from a bipolar worldview to a more comprehensive global understanding of social and political mechanisms. It remains to be seen what the terrible attacks on the World Trade Center and the Pentagon on September 11, 2001, will mean to global politics. If the process of globalization is stronger than the forces that want to create a new bipolar worldview based on an antagonism between Islam and the West, e.g., the clashes of religious and cultural civilizations, then the events on September 11, 2001, are examples of the fact that globalization changes everybody and all states including the United States of America.

Following the argument of James H. Mittelman, it is possible to understand globalization as a *syndrome* of processes and activities, and not as a single unified phenomenon.[10] Globalization is understood as a dominant set of ideas and a policy framework, and integral to the globalization syn-

10. James H. Mittelman, *The Globalization Syndrome: Transformation and Resistance* (Princeton: Princeton University Press, 2000), p. 4.

drome are the interaction among the global division of labor and power, the new regionalism, and resistance politics. They stand out as central to the transformations in the world order. After the events on September 11, 2001, it is clear that any theory of globalization must emphasize the compression of time and space. The British sociologist Anthony Giddens holds that globalization is structured by social influences absent from the scene. According to Giddens space is increasingly dislocated from place and networked to other social contexts across the globe. "Globalization can thus be defined as the intensification of worldwide social relations which link distant localities in such a way that local happenings are shaped by events occurring many miles away and vice versa."[11]

The ecumenical movement too is challenged to come to terms with the globalization syndrome, where place is disconnected from space. On the one hand, ecumenism is part of the globalization syndrome. The disconnection of place and space had helped churches in many different places to interconnect with each other in new ways. A new interdependence and a rise in transnational and interconfessional cooperation is a reality, and the very idea of church unity points to the world becoming a single place. Ecumenism is an ecclesial and a theological answer to globalization and has helped the churches to adjust to a new political and economic reality. But on the other hand, globalization is not only a one-way development. The rise of religious conservatism and fundamentalism in many different religions and corners of the earth is also part of the globalization syndrome. Ethnic identities with the different religious cultures stress their particular experience of faith within Islam, Hinduism, or Christianity. Thus, the new challenge according to Samuel P. Huntington is the clash of civilizations and not ideologies as was the case in the period after the Cold War. The paradox of the globalization syndrome is that it has been open to the particularities of culture and religion without having any tools to judge and control them — except human rights, which are not shared by everybody in the world. Thus, the globalization syndrome entails the idea of multiculturalism, but at the same time it annuls the very idea of normativity. The challenge is to live with this dilemma and be comfortable with it as an ongoing condition for human life today.

11. Anthony Giddens, *The Consequences of Modernity* (Cambridge: Polity Press, 1990), p. 64.

The ambivalence of globalization is very vivid in the analysis of the ecumenical movement. The World Council of Churches was quick in responding to the issues of globalization. From the beginning of the 1990s it became part of the ecumenical agenda, and according to Aram I, Moderator of the Central Committee of the World Council of Churches, globalization encourages participation on the one hand and generates exclusion on the other.[12] Especially, the poor underdeveloped countries are being involved in the process of the global market economy, but at the same time also excluded from the benefits of the global market and bearing the heaviest debt burden. Thus, according to Aram I the globalization of economy will result in growing inequalities, which will create new socio-ethical problems. He also points to the fact that globalization denies the legitimacy of political institutions and democratic processes. Local governments are weakened, and this situation is generating civil unrest. Instead, Aram I wants a globalization from below, e.g., the kind of process that emanates from within the people and is checked by non-governmental organizations (NGO's) and the democratic processes of civil society.

These references to Aram I clearly show that as a representative of the World Council of Churches, he is dealing with the new challenges of the globalization syndrome by prolonging the old socio-ethical analysis of the ecumenical movement formulated around 1968-75 in order to respond to the present challenges. Nothing is changed in the analysis of the responses — in fact the opposite is the case. Aram I is affirmed in his views by the new social and cultural developments after 1989. It is business as usual in the World Council of Churches.

This impression is confirmed by the Consultation of Churches in Central and Eastern Europe and ecumenical partners on "Globalization in Central and Eastern Europe: Responses to the Ecological, Economic and Social Consequences, 23-29 June 2000, Budapest, Hungary."[13] In the concept paper prepared for the consultation, the present economic and social situation in Eastern Europe is regarded as a time that carries an element of *kairos* in it. The global civilization appears to be the first civilization that is basically atheistic (so President Havel of the Czech Republic), and therefore, despite the positive sides of the present developments, represents a

12. Aram I, *In Search of Ecumenical Vision* (Lebanon, 2000), pp. 66ff.

13. See *Concept Paper for the Budapest Consultation:* www.wcc-coe.org/wcc/what/jpc/globalization-budapest1.html.

situation of *processus confessionis,* i.e., a process leading to a matter of faith. Thus, the concept paper continues an old theological argument related to the confessional stand known in the Reformed and Lutheran tradition as *processus/status confessionis.* It was formulated in the 1970s in the struggle against apartheid, against nuclear weapons in 1980s, and is now being applied to the economic, ecological, and social devastation in Eastern Europe.

The conclusion is that while everything in the globalization syndrome is regarded from the perspective of change, dynamic, and flexibility, the basic analysis and theological concepts in the World Council of Churches as representing the institutionalized form of ecumenism are the same. This could be called ecumenical tradition and shows the stability in ecumenical theory and praxis. Stability and not prophecy, tradition and not reformation characterize the WCC in the globalization syndrome. A paradigm shift has not — yet — taken place despite the outspoken intentions to embark on this way of analysis and organization.

Religion and Globalization

FRIEDRICH WILHELM GRAF

The old *homo oeconomicus* is dead. Many economists have recognized that economic actors are more than just stakeholders interested in safeguarding the greatest possible profits by way of a rational choice. The more rapidly capitalism expands, opening up ever new markets, the more intensively economists discuss the non-economic preconditions of economic rationality. Although they continue to focus to a great extent on consumption and prices, goods in short supply and opportunity costs, they have also begun to reflect upon trust, crisis management, institutional change, cognitive structures, linguistic interaction, and the capital of social skills and abilities. They have become increasingly interested in religious mentalities and the ethical forms of religious communities. Like other cultural scientists, economists have discovered religion as a productive force behind the formation of worldviews that furnish life with meaning, basic trust, and social capital.

How can this new interest in the "soft" preconditions of hard economic processes be explained? Alexander Gerschenkron has shown in his historical studies on *Economic Backwardness* that economic development cannot be understood purely in itself, in isolation from other processes. In order to interpret blocked or successful development, he argues, it is necessary to also consider the general institutional framework as well as mental dispositions such as ideological molds and religious convictions. Since their cultural turn, numerous economists emphasize that profits or the optimal exploitation of a business's economic chances cannot be sufficiently explained by a purely functional modeling of the economic rationality as a rationality of calculation. Certainly, they extol the precise calculability of markets. Yet, now they see more clearly than in the past how the viability of markets depends on the confidence of actors in the relative stability of the basic institutional setting and its underlying conditions.

The same holds for the optimization of maneuvering room, which is conditioned by cognitive maps and belief systems controlling the perception of actors. In accordance with their subjective representations of "reality," actors develop ideas on their leeway and formulate preferences as to how they should choose between the different possibilities. In the 1980s, Viktor Vanberg, James M. Buchanan, and Hansjörg Siegenthaler brought to light the great importance of such theories on everyday life for the processes of optimizing the interaction of economic actors. Actively pursuing economic interests is dependent on an acting subject's awareness of his or her scope of influence and possibilities of successfully asserting his or her interests. Moreover, culturally specific preconceptions also shape the expectations of economic actors, viz. the way in which they view the action of their competitors and picture market processes.

The new evolutionist economists stress that an "internal selection" of ideas, worldviews, and visions of the future as well as varying skills of adaptability and flexibility precede the competition on the financial and goods markets. How, for instance, can a new trust be won in situations of crisis? Hansjörg Siegenthaler offers precise models of such learning processes.[1] Selectors exerting an influence on the markets punish actors who are not, or who are only to a limited degree, able to correct their subjective "pictures of reality" according to experience. Such selectors, he argues, reward those actors who succeed in interpreting the potential action of their competitors more precisely and are capable of reassessing their own options of action. The more learning potential and flexibility an actor demonstrates, the greater his chances will be in asserting himself under competitive conditions. However, the capacity to learn and adapt hinges on the structural patterns of cognitive maps and everyday theories.

It is here that religion becomes relevant to the formation of economic theories. To what extent do religiously shaped cognitive patterns permit the constructive reception and assimilation of experiences that conflict with a subject's assumptions about "reality"? Do they present the

1. Cf. H. Siegenthaler, *Regelvertrauen, Prosperität und Krisen* (Tübingen: Mohr, 1993).

actor with an opportunity to relinquish old views and to revise elements of his or her everyday theories without a loss of identity? Do they foster the "charity" (Donald Davidson) to ascribe meaning to disconcerting things and encourage the ability of discursive communication?

Religions can be interpreted as systems of signs and symbols, mediating coherent and meaningful pictures of reality *in toto.* They present adherents with the chance to digest elementary, negative experiences. Religions disclose to their followers meaningful concepts of time. Whoever knows how to differentiate between time and eternity possesses a cognitive framework that he or she can include in the story of his/her life as a reflective basis, formatively influencing the present and the future. In religious languages, individuals can transcend their finite lives and discover an all-embracing context with meaningful content and form. With a concept of God, the subject of unsurpassable generality, adherents can order chaos, define relatively stable life structures and develop helpful "certainties" for the crises of life. In this way, religion can be construed functionally as a "practice for coping with contingency" (*Kontingenzbewältigungspraxis,* Hermann Lübbe), by virtue of which believers gain a fundamental, ontological confidence.

Discussions about the possible relations between religion and economic development have been underway in Europe since the late seventeenth century. Owing to the developmental lead of many Protestant territories over Catholic countries, theologians and cultural historians were prompted to question how belief influences the way in which people conduct their lives. In these discourses of the Enlightenment over the economic ethics of the main Christian confessions, and the rituals, symbolism, and theologies of their respective mentalities, scholars formulated interpretative models that continue to determine present-day debates on the social and moral foundations of the different types of modern capitalism. Due to their teachings on the worldly profession of Christians, one could read in the eighteenth century that Protestants were far more achievement-oriented, ascetic, efficient, and competent than Catholics in matters of world domination. Because of their religiosity, which, it was claimed, combined authoritarian structures, magical beliefs, and ritualism, the latter were prone to quietism and the passive acceptance of the given.

Possible connections between the "inner-worldly asceticism" of Calvinistic Protestantism and the "spirit of capitalism" also played a central role in the classic studies on capitalism in the sociology of religion at the turn of the twentieth century, piloted by Max Weber, Ernst Troeltsch, Werner Sombart, Max Scheler, and Emile Durkheim. However the capitalistic spirit was "derived" religiously and culturally at this time — some held the Jews responsible for the *habitus* that had nurtured the original accumulation of capital, others pointed to the Puritans — all models linking religious mentality with economic *habitus* reveal a high continuity up to the present-day debates on "capitalism contra capitalism."[2] At issue are always the canon of virtues, guarded by a religious community, its sanctioned way of life, and the possibilities of generating trust in regulations that lie in the religious socialization and the resources of social capital buried in the symbolism of religion. Religious goods of salvation gain economic relevance insofar as they contribute to a certain *habitus.*

All religions are systems of lifestyle. Insofar as religion is concerned with certainty of salvation or, put sociologically, with the transformation of contingency into meaningful determination, it supplies symbolic models of self-interpretation and a world-representation that can help actors respond to critical situations without having to forfeit their self-understanding and worldview *totaliter.* By offering a symbolic identity and reliable structures with which they can order their lives, religious languages can help both individuals and groups to widen their capacity for learning. In situations of profound crisis, where transmitted rules of thought and action are open to question, religion can foster the construction of new everyday theories. It can, however, also bring about the opposite: religious belief can provide a medium for reinforcing pathological traits, where actors do not meet the loss of orientation with a heightened willingness to learn and adapt, but cling to fixed mental constructs, resisting the opportunity to respond to experience with flexibility.

In the current debates on globalization, theorists differentiate between three fundamental types of capitalism. The differences between these types are defined by a particular combination of cultural or religious mentality, institutional order (or organizational structure in industrial relations), and the market. The — at present particularly efficient — Anglo-American capitalism, determined by minimal political intervention and a far-reaching non-regulation of industrial relations, is traced back primarily

2. Cf. M. Albert, *Kapitalismus contra Kapitalismus* (Frankfurt am Main: Campus, 1992).

to Protestant individualism, resulting from the religious emphasis put on the conscience of the devout individual (his direct moral responsibility before God), the self-discipline cultivated by the Protestant sects, and the positive religious acknowledgment of moneymaking. By contrast, Rhineland capitalism, the corporate system of a "social market economy" where the mediation of class antagonisms in institutions of systematic dialogue is raised to the decisive integrative principle, is claimed to be rooted in the profession-oriented Lutheran ethics of public welfare. And, finally, Asia's "crony capitalism," which is strongly shaped by patriarchal family structures, personal relationships, and close moral ties between employees and employers, is seen as the expression of "Asian values," deriving primarily from Confucianism.

Even for the different Latin-American societies and for the transformation processes in the Eastern European countries, the search for developmental potential focuses on the respective religious cultures and their capacities for generating trust, competencies in moral reflection, social skills, and institutional legitimation. In Brazil, for instance, particular attention is given to the Protestant charismatic figures who, in their small but highly structured and authoritarian communities, foster virtues that facilitate a long-term social advancement through education. They make moral demands on their members that run counter to the traditional customs of Latin-American countries: expecting a rigorous abstinence from alcohol and other drugs, a rigid sexual morality, a puritan ethos of efficiency, and the readiness to invest great resources of time and money in the education of their children. However exaggerated this religiosity may seem to the outsider, their lifestyle certainly is extremely disciplined.

In the more recent research into the possible economic transformation of Russia, economists have been looking for an Orthodox-Christian variant of the puritan professional. However, the hope of finding an innerworldly asceticism or *habitus* compatible with capitalism in the religious worlds of Orthodox Christianity has been disappointed. The culture of Orthodox-Christian religiousness has contributed very little to strengthening the communication processes between actors or their trust, promoting traditionalism and a quietist acceptance of the given situation rather than an openness for innovation and entrepreneurial rationality. Having been strongly shaped by traditional anti-capitalistic elements, the culture of Orthodox-Christian religiousness constitutes a strong bulwark against the economic transformation of Russia. The cultural historian Alexander

Etkin has recently shown in an analysis of Russia's sectarian landscape of the twentieth century that capitalistic rationality can only gain acceptance through a reinforced secularization of the cultural elites or the further expansion of sects directed towards Protestant values, such as individual autonomy, rational self-discipline, or free initiative. However, in its authoritarian, protectionist politics of religion, which massively impedes above all the missionary activities of American Protestant groups, the Russian government and Duma strengthen the Orthodox Church whose hierarchy mobilizes resistance to all capitalistic developments.

In the debates on the westernization of Islamic societies and the fundamentalist revolutions of re-Islamization, the question is raised whether an economic *habitus* can be formed that is compatible both with capitalism and with Islamic traditions. It is untenable to claim that, due to the prohibition of interest and binds of the sharia, Islam as such has necessarily remained tethered to traditional, pre-capitalist forms of trade and commerce. Certainly, one can understand Islamic fundamentalisms as a modern-antimodern reaction to the cultural westernization and capitalistic transformation of predominantly traditional societies; such societies react to the shock of an externally induced modernization above all traumatically, with hard-line politics of separation, by revitalizing old values and presenting rigid forms of religious identity. Moreover, in the Islamic communities of Asian countries the new fundamentalisms are primarily backed by those who have not benefited from modernization processes, such as street traders, small shopkeepers, and manual workers as well as migrants who, in search of work, have fled to the urban centers where they are able to earn only an insufficient income in the informal sector.

Nonetheless, Islam does possess a rich and highly flexible symbolic capital that can also be used for purposes of capitalistic modernization. In Western European countries and societies of Eastern Asia, groups of a new middle class have incorporated the Islamic tradition in an ethos of active competitiveness. Their religious belief offers these city-dwellers, who mostly belong to the first generation of social climbers and migrants, psychological security and social support in the face of the diverse risks of their new urban existence. This faith also seems to strengthen their willingness to adopt an inner-worldly asceticism and to develop their capacity for social empathy.

In turn, capitalistic modernization has repercussions for religious cultures. In the main, conflicts engendered by social modernization are mirrored in the internal differentiations of religious communities and in the pluralization of religious milieus. The spectrum ranges from fundamentalisms, which reformulate religious tradition in favor of monolithic identity claims vis-à-vis the Western instrumental, means-ends type of reasoning, through the reform and renewal of religious tradition, which offers new middle-class groups the opportunity of leading a standardized lifestyle in their capitalistically transformed *Lebenswelt,* to syncretisms and conversion processes. On the whole, religious languages possess a remarkably high flexibility. In spite of old conventions in the interpretation of holy scripts, they house considerable potential for internal modernization. The debate on orientalism has shown that many Western opinions on the supposedly constitutive backwardness of Islamic cultures only reflect the old interpretative patterns of the Occident. Just as there was once an Islamic enlightenment, so too will there be societies of an indigenized Islamic capitalism beside re-Islamized communities.

Since the 1960s, there has been an extremely rapid economic change in Eastern Asia that has transformed dramatically underdeveloped and impoverished societies into affluent societies with a relatively wealthy middle class. Research into the mentalities and economic *habitus* of economically successful Islamic groups in these societies has revealed that their power stems primarily from a structurally puritan, achievement-oriented ethos shaped by abstinence, asceticism, perseverance, and a rationalistic lifestyle. In its report on the economic wonder of the "tiger states" in 1993, the World Bank attempted to prove that the miraculous annual growth rate of 7 percent between the 1970s and 1980s and that of 9 percent since 1990 was primarily due to the competitiveness of the middle-class groups who had allegedly worked far harder, learned more intensively, economized more rigorously, and shown a greater willingness to make sacrifices than other social groups. Four years later, the East Asian Development Bank pointed out the formative influence of religious traditions on the formation of this morale.[3]

Traditionally, Confucianism had developed an ethic of self-responsibility in the community. By way of diligent studies and rigid discipline, a good person was expected to develop such virtues as sincerity, loyalty, wis-

3. Cf. World Bank, *The East Asian Miracle* (Oxford: Oxford University Press, 1993); Asian Development Bank, *Emerging Asia: Changes and Challenges* (Manila: Asian Development Bank, 1997).

dom, compassion, honesty, and self-discipline. Originally, this ethos shaped the world of manual workers and the lower middle class, but without difficulty allowed itself to be integrated into a form of capitalism in which families or family associations constitute the decisive organizational unit. The crisis of Asia's network capitalism has now unveiled the dark side of a Confucian-based economic *habitus.* In China, Confucian values serve to a great extent only to stabilize authoritarian rule. Admittedly, Confucian values have helped to strengthen the structure of communal bonds, to generate an excellent work ethic, and to foster the exceptionally high rates of saving in East Asia. Moreover, thanks to the rapid capitalization of their societies, viz. the increase in the share of wage-earners, and their extraordinarily high economic growth rates, the tiger states have by and large solved their poverty problems and witnessed the formation of a new middle class. Nevertheless, these societies are endangered by new social divisions, evincing a politically problematic concentration of capital in the hands of only a few clans, possessing a political culture shaped chiefly by authoritarian powers and, with their rapid boom, having generated grave ecological problems. The shelter of family structures and closely knit communicative networks not only helps to cope with social problems, but also allows for the institutionalization of nepotism and corruption. Such a socio-economic culture can conceal brutal exploitation, help to preserve ailing corporate structures, and foster "morally hazardous" politics, an economically irrational, excessive level of debt, and the lax awarding of loans fraught with risks. In "network capitalism," the transparency of information that is imperative for effective markets is obstructed rather than promoted.

The current debates on these three forms of capitalism revolve essentially around the question of whether one model will emerge victorious in the processes of further globalization or whether the future will be shaped by the emergence of further forms of culturally defined capitalism. Here, the answers of economists are controversial. On the one hand, they refer to the uniformity engendered by global computerization and the improvement of cross-border information networks. On the other hand, they emphasize that people and systems resolve problems using very different strategies and, in crises, have recourse to background "certainties" that are encoded in a specifically religious cultural language. The more they stress the cultural preconditions of economic rationality, the clearer they see how progressive globalization is molded by the emergence of ever new, divergent forms of capitalism. Yet, in view of the pressure to adapt, which under the conditions of global competition is exerted by the economically most efficient capitalism on the other types, critics of the differentiation theorem prognosticate a new homogenization, formatively influenced by either the Anglo-American model or the Rhineland model or a mixture of both.

Scholars of religion cannot settle this dispute among economists. However, they can venture a prognosis: processes of technological convergence and advancing capitalistic revolution will, in all probability, be accompanied by new waves of religious and cultural differentiation. The stronger assertion of the economic rationality will always provoke religiously motivated counter-reactions to the degrading instrumentalization of human beings. The result will be diverse normative conflicts mainly springing from the elementary tensions between old communal values and that of individualistic self-realization. In all societies shaped by modernization processes, the conflicts between secularly minded elites and the poorer, religiously traditional groups of the population will gain in importance.

Capitalistic modernization has always engendered high social costs. Already in the nineteenth century this led many religious people to seek an escape. Also in the future, many believers will seek to revitalize old religious forms of escapism, in an attempt to ward off the predominance of capitalistic rationality. By isolating themselves, these people will build religious counter-worlds that will only intensify the tendencies of cultural fragmentation in their respective societies. And the more one uses the symbolism of religious languages to cultivate a sensibility for the pathologies of modernization, the more attractive religious communities will be that propagate a lifestyle in accord with "creation." At the same time, asymmetric ethics will gain importance, where religious virtuosi adopt a far stricter moral self-discipline than the laity who are forced into diverse compromises with the world. The quicker the change and the greater the erosion of old cultural traditions and institutions caused by global capitalism, the more weight many people will attach to commemorating the past and mourning the loss of cultural treasures using the symbolic language and liturgies of old religious traditions. The third capitalist revolution will, for this reason, give rise to the renaissance of many religious movements. Hard "fundamentalist" religions, which put great demands on believers but offer, in return, a monolithic worldview with the security of unshakable "certainties," are very likely to be particularly attractive. The future of capitalism will not be determined by the great "clash of civilizations," but by a plurality of value conflicts within societies.

Religious traditions also exercise a powerful influence on the moral culture and structure of the institutional order in capitalist societies. Admittedly, the progressive pluralization of religious interpretative systems may well lead to a loss of the churches' influence in the general debates on the relationship between the market and the social or political institutions restricting market dynamics. Nevertheless, being bound to the traditional Christian ethos of brotherhood, the churches will always insist on social duties and corrections of the distribution of income and opportunities generated by the market. Yet, like other religious communities, they must also develop an ethic that goes beyond the understandable concern for the weak and highlights, much more strongly than has been the case in the past, the constructive and affluence-promoting effects of capitalistic expansion. By and large, religion will not become weaker in the processes of globalization, but adapt to the pressure of the economic circumstances. In spite of its functional differentiation, it will continue to exert a powerful cultural influence. For even the creative agents and "flexible people" of global capitalism will require background certainties and remain dependent on symbolic languages that transcend the economic rationality and provide a framework with which to interpret the many new mobility risks and the timeless, elementary experiences of human beings, such as love and grief, birth and death. They will continue to need religious rites and languages in order to represent their cultural identity in times of crisis and change, and be able to resist the pressure to adapt by dint of strong dogmatism. Even the most adaptable proponent of global capitalism remains a contradictory being. Whoever celebrates his success on the stock exchange, resulting from his willingness to take risks, his determination and opportunism, also discovers his fallibility — when he examines the irrational and finite nature of his life.

PART II

Challenges to Ecumenism and Christian Identity

Is Europe Christian? A Challenge to a Viking

VÍTOR WESTHELLE

1. Homage

With the restructuring of the Lutheran World Federation in 1990, Viggo Mortensen became the new director of the Department of Theology and Studies. His challenge was to find ways to articulate theology within a Lutheran world communion with only bits and pieces of the resources up until then allocated within the Federation for the defunct Department of Studies. Viggo rose to the challenge, sponsoring a vision for the practice of theology in a global communion, yet painfully aware of its fragmented character. With Mortensen's leadership the Program Committee for Theology and Studies presented to the Executive Council in its 1995 meeting in Namibia "Ten Theses on the Role of Theology in the LWF," which summarize the vision of the program he skillfully led. Theses 6 and 7 state:

6. In the history of the LWF as a communion of diverse churches, the awareness of the tension between the gospel that holds us together, and the diversity with which we express it, grew as a creative challenge for both the self-understanding of the LWF as a communion and its theological practice.
7. This challenge offers new opportunities for the exercise of theology in the LWF through which the communion will be promoted if, and only if, these characteristics of a theological practice are followed: a) the LWF offers itself as a place for different articulations of diverse

> experiences; b) as a catalyst for innovation within theologies in different contexts; and c) as a guarantor of both the diversity and of the necessity of expressing commonalities.[1]

Possibly it takes a Viking plundering the North Atlantic seas to untangle the relationship that for the last couple of millennia, and particularly the last five hundred years, bundled Christian identity with European civilization. The Nordic corsairs knew, centuries before Columbus, what Spain later claimed as its discovery. The difference is that they did not conquer. Since the symbolic year 1500 Europe steadily raised herself to the center of the world, making its history the universal history, its myth the founding myth of civilization as such. Under these conditions it is almost redundant to ask the question that titles this contribution. Perhaps it would be more proper to ask instead: "How European do we need to be in order to be Christian (the Nazarene notwithstanding)?"[2]

The perspective I bring to this homage to Viggo Mortensen is not one of explaining Europe to Europeans, but to express a fellow feeling, and, yes, an empathy issuing from south of the equator, which has tainted my view of the world. Theologians in the southern and eastern parts of the globe have also been in the corsair business, making their own some of the treasures of Europe while attempting to untangle the Gordian knot that has tied Christianity to modern Europe. So, my reflections here are not an attempt to define the European essence, but rather its perception from the other side of the Atlantic and moreover from the underside of the equator.

2. The Making of a Myth

Taking an insight from the late Nobel Laureate, Octavio Paz (but it is also a lesson to be learned from Grundtvig), that every society is built upon a poem and every civilization upon a myth, what would then be the European myth and how would it be related to Christianity? How do we, looking from the outside, see it? I suggest we look at three emblematic, if not

1. *Between Vision and Reality: Lutheran Churches in Transition* (LWF Documentation No. 47), Wolfgang Greive, ed. (Geneva: LWF/DTS, 2001), pp. 497-98.

2. I write these lines from Tokyo, Japan, where, a month before Christmas, carols, Christmas trees, and all the paraphernalia typical of a European Christmas saturate the environment, though Christianity represents less than 1 percent of the population.

monumental, events situated at the origins of modern Europe (and recognized as such by Europeans since the eighteenth century)[3] to address this question about the European myth: the scientific revolution launched by Copernicus, the religious revolution set in motion by Luther, and the conquest of the Americas inaugurated by Columbus, all happening around the year 1500. These three events combined[4] suggest an image, a picture, that offers the profile of the European myth and its connection with the Christian story. I would like to briefly examine them.

First, the scientific revolution. More than substituting a heliocentric system for a geocentric one, the Copernican turn implied the proposal of a unified system of representations, a common language by which "reality" could be defined on the grounds of reason alone. Science could forge this language without subservience to any other authority or power. Heteronomy was overcome. The knowledge it forged became in itself a power, as Francis Bacon well observed. The history of this revolution is the history of the emergence of the human subject (and points also to its end announced in the increasing effort of the sciences to unify this language; it is the "end of man" insofar as he disappears in the world as representation, incapable of saying his word, of naming his world except in the still existing interstices of cultural fragmentation, though they are plenty). While the scientific representation unifies the world and Europe in particular, while economically and even politically Europe is being brought closer together, ethnic, cultural, and linguistic identities create a countermovement of fragmentation that has brought even war back to the heart of Europe. Yet the belief in this form of rationality, the equation of knowledge and power, and its growing capability of unifying language and shaping a system of representation about the way things are, is quite a remarkable component of the European mythos.

3. Jürgen Habermas, *The Philosophical Discourse of Modernity: Twelve Lectures* (Cambridge, Mass.: MIT Press, 1993), p. 5.

4. To these events one should add also two other facts that transverse all of these events: The mechanical press of Gutenberg, which allowed for a quantum leap in the diffusion of knowledge untainted by mistakes of copyists, and the Renaissance with its freedom, erudition, and praise of human values. See Elizabeth Eisenstein, *The Printing Press as an Agent of Change: Communication and Cultural Transformation in Early-Modern Europe*, 2 vols. (Cambridge: Cambridge University Press, 1979); Agnes Heller, *Renaissance Man* (New York: Shocken Books, 1978); Enrique Dussel, *The Invention of the Americas: Eclipse of "the Other" and the Myth of Modernity* (New York: Continuum, 1995).

Second, the Reformation. With its battle-cry of the justification of the sinner, the Reformation brought about the awareness of the human's totally sinful condition in face of God while at the same time liberating the human to be an agent in the world, unencumbered by any need to work in the world and its institutions the salvation of the soul. Religion became reflective. The subject was able to assert itself independent of heteronomic constraints. This freedom announced the end of the church — insofar as its existence was regarded as the space of grace in and through which salvation could be negotiated — and the beginning of the community, the gathering of free subjects. The ensuing division of Europe along increasing confessional lines, however, did not prevent its own realization that these divisions no longer represented apostasy but accommodation of the expression of the faith to enclaves of different national, ethnic, or cultural identities, as the infamous *cuius regio, eius religio* still symbolizes. There are no heresies after the Reformation. The signing of the Joint Declaration on the Doctrine of Justification a couple of years ago, and the reason that it was in Europe that debate over it was so fierce, seemed to indicate the culmination of a 500-year process of refining an agreement about the human condition. That the process is not over is clear in the Annex to the Declaration, in which standing differences on the interpretation of concupiscence are still noted. However, the religious freedom accomplished with the Reformation and its aftermath still remains as a given that grounds our perception of the European self-understanding.

The third major event was the conquest of the New World, which launched Europe to the center of world history or rather, made European history to be universal history. After the New World was conquered nothing new could come about. The irony in this, however, is that this placing of Europe at the center of world history grew out of this very sense of displacement that also characterized the other two movements. Columbus's justification of the conquering of the New World is of symbolic import: he wanted to amass the resources to conquer the lost "center," the Holy House of Jerusalem.[5] But it was Europe itself that would become the "new" Jerusalem. Hegel in the *Lectures on the Philosophy of History,* after discussing the New World and its conquest by the Old, turns to the discussion of Europe and concludes with the famous statement: "World history goes from

5. See Tzvetan Todorov, *The Conquest of America: The Question of the Other* (New York: HarperPerennial, 1984), pp. 10-12.

east to west, thus Europe is decisively the end of world history . . . although the Earth is spherical, history does not go in circles . . . it is here [in Europe] that the inner sun of self-awareness rises up, which spreads a higher brilliance."[6] There is no possibility of a new beginning, of a new day, for the sun of self-consciousness shines bright and still in the middle of the day. Here the European ventures throughout the world are beyond the possibility of error or of novelty. The end of history is also the end of any further transgression, for a transgression implies the advent of difference and novelty. That is what is meant by the dictum of Casparus Barleus, in the middle of the seventeenth century, reflecting on Dutch travel accounts from Brazil, that there is no sin south of the equator *(ultra equinoxialem non peccavit).* Schleiermacher, taking the consequences of this into the missionary endeavors of European Christianity, confirms this sense of untransgressibility: ". . . new heresies no longer arise, now that the Church recruits itself out of its own resources; and the influence of alien faiths on the frontier and in the mission-field of the Church must be reckoned at zero."[7] When heresy is impossible, so is novelty, so is history.

These are then the symbolic events that mark the articulation during the last 500 years of the European mythos. Copernicus displaced the Earth as the center of the universe and freed reason to be in itself a source of power, the sun of self-consciousness; Luther restored this center by setting the human in relationship *coram deo,* while even radicalizing the *human* displacement on account of the pervasiveness of sin; Columbus displaced Europe itself from the center and end of universal history, yet in the very acknowledgment that it had to conquer and fashion for itself a center that it did not have by annulling any possibility that the ventures into the unknown could make a difference for Europe. These three movements combined are the nucleus of a myth that has woven together European Chris-

6. "Die Weltgeschichte geht von Osten nach Westen, denn Europa ist schlechthin das Ende der Weltgeschichte . . . obgleich die Erde eine Kugel bildet, so macht die Geschichte doch keinen Kreis um sie herum . . . dafür steigt aber hier [in Europa] die innere Sonne des Selbstbewusstseins auf, die einen höheren Glanz verbreitet" (G. W. F. Hegel, *Werke in zwanzig Bänden* [Frankfurt: Suhrkamp, 1970], 12:134).

7. ". . . neues Ketzerisches entsteht nicht mehr, indem die Kirche sich aus sich selbst an den Grenzen und in dem Missionsgebiet der Kirche, was die Ausbildung der Lehre betrifft, für nichts gerechten werden muss" (Friedrich Schleiermacher, *Die christliche Glaube,* 2 vols. [Berlin: de Gruyter, 1960], 1:128; Friedrich Schleiermacher, *The Christian Faith* [Edinburgh: T. & T. Clark, 1989], §21.2, 96).

tianity. It makes for a story that connects a fundamental theme that has been part of the European *imaginary* (to use Jacques Lacan's term for what is more "real" than reality) much earlier than the time of these three symbolic events, but was with them framed into a cohesive mythos, culturally celebrated by the Renaissance and technically supported by the new means of communication that the mechanical press was making possible.

3. History and Responsibility

The end of history, in the sense that no further transgression is possible, as paradoxical as it might seem, is grounded in a fundamental consciousness of transgression, of being deeply guilty, indebted, accountable, and defiled: a condition that only faith can — and has — conquered, liberating reason to work itself into all dimensions of earthly power. This profound dislodging of the self (transgression, guilt, indebtedness, sin) yields then the radical sense of *Schuldigsein,* of being guilty (with all the denotations and connotations the German term implies). The story goes like this: We are not the center of the universe, we have been displaced, we are in a state of being helplessly away from capably addressing our longings by our own selves. Yet, it is exactly this sense of radical transgression, of *Schuldigsein,* that has endowed Europe with a sense of responsibility, for this is also what *Schuldigsein* means. This sense of responsibility is grounded not in any particular act. It is not derivative, but original. When Ernst Troeltsch diagnosed the Lutheran "*Sündenpessimismus*"[8] he did it, not to criticize the mythos, but to lift up what was really a promise, for "original sin turns out to be the greatest treasure of the theologians."[9]

This is an altogether European tale announced by Irenaeus's equation of sin with dare plus childish irresponsibility, confirmed by the medieval blessedness of the sinner in whom alone a greater grace could be shown *(felix culpa),* emphasized by Luther's *Anfechtungstheorie* and celebrated in Milton's *Paradise Lost* when he closes the narrative of Adam and Eve's expulsion with these words:

8. Ernst Troeltsch, *Gesammelte Schriften: Vierter Band* (Tübingen: J. C. B. Mohr, 1925), p. 140.

9. ". . . die Erbsünde sei der grösste Schatz der Theologen." Ernst Troeltsch, *Glaubenslehre* (München/Leipzig: Duncker/Humbold, 1925), p. 311.

They, looking back, all the eastern side beheld
Of paradise, so late their happy seat,
Waved over by that flaming brand; the gate
With dreadful faces thronged and fiery arms.
Some natural tears they dropped, but wiped them soon:
The world was all before them, where to choose
Their place of rest, and Providence their guide.[10]

What the myth expresses is a profound sense of guilt emerging from the depth of individuality and producing nothing less than a unique sense of radical responsibility. Jan Patočka, in his *Heretical Essays,* traces the origin of the European identity to this sense of responsibility that emerges with the Christian overcoming of the orgiastic mysteries with this sense of responsibility. Truth is no longer associated with eidetic intuition, but is bound with responsibility in which "individuality is vested in a relation to an infinite love and humans are individuals because they are guilty, and *always* guilty, with respect to it. We all, as individuals, are defined by the uniqueness of our individual placement in the universality of sin."[11]

Commenting on Patočka's *Heretical Essays,* Derrida has also lifted up the importance of the notion of guilt and its connection to responsibility in European history.

> One might well conclude . . . that this concept of responsibility is Christian through and through and is produced by the event of Christianity. For it is as a result of examining this concept alone that the Christian event — sin, gift of infinite love linked to the experience of death — appears necessary, does that not mean that Christianity alone has made possible access to an authentic responsibility throughout history, responsibility *as history* and history as *Europe?*[12]

Europe is responsible. But this responsibility is placed radically toward the supreme Good that alone can salvage Europe from its sense of radical sin and guilt. It is because the displacement is so radically or absolutely per-

10. John Milton, *The Poetical Works,* vol. 1 (New York: Leavitt & Allen, 1850), p. 400.

11. Jan Patočka, *Heretical Essays in the Philosophy of History* (Chicago: Open Court, 1996), p. 107.

12. Jacques Derrida, *The Gift of Death* (Chicago: University of Chicago Press, 1995), p. 50.

ceived that the positioning of Europe in relation to the rest of the world, as much as to other religious ideas, "must be reckoned at zero," as Schleiermacher boldly stated. This sense of radical responsibility and *Schuldigkeit* vis-à-vis total otherness *(totaliter aliter),* insofar as this is the case, furthermore creates an inability to perceive relative otherness.[13] Derrida's comments are to the point:

> There is thus a structural disproportion or dissymmetry between the finite and responsible mortal on the one hand and the goodness of the infinite gift on the other hand. One can conceive of this disproportion without assigning to it a revealed cause or without tracing it back to the event of original sin, but it inevitably transforms the experience of responsibility into one of guilt: I have never been and never will be up to the immensity of the gift, the frameless immensity that must in general define (*in*-define) a gift as such.[14]

This profound sense of radical responsibility that has created Europe's self-identity, this being in a dissymmetric accountability to the Other, has relegated relative otherness to the fringes of European experience, to be accounted as the exotic, the insane, the wild, the savage, or — as recent historical events attest — plain evil. Europe is responsible, but it will only understand the difference between responsibility and colonialism when it will realize that otherness, toward which responsibility is exercised, is also a finite gift enshrined in the lives of those whom Europe has conquered. This is a talk about angels. Angels are those who represent this borderline between the infinite and the finite, between divine transcendence and the human, all too human realm. "Angel" is the name we give to the experience in which otherness becomes a window to the Other. But angels are often unrecognized, for their otherness is not inscribed in the canons of rationality, i.e., of European, enlightened rationality.

Hermann Borchard, the first missionary sent by the Protestant *(evangelisch)* church of Prussia to Brazil in the third quarter of the nineteenth century, landed there in the middle of an area colonized by German

13. That the question of the relationship between the ground of being *(das Sein)* and the actual relative being *(das Seiende)* is such an important topic in European philosophy from Heidegger through Levinas and Derrida is not a coincidence.

14. Derrida, *Gift of Death,* p. 51.

immigrants. And from there he wrote back lamenting that *es gibt in Brasilien keine Religiosität* ("there is no religiosity in Brazil"). The irony in this is that at that very time and merely a few kilometers from where he was writing, one of the most significant messianic movements, the Mucker movement, led by a charismatic woman of German (and *evangelisch*) descent, Jacobina Maurer, was making headlines in newspapers that called for a full mobilization of the army to literally annihilate it. Apparently, if it was not in his Prussian *Agende*, Borchard could not recognize it; he could not see it.[15]

The others do not exist except insofar as they represent the unconcluded project of Europe itself in relation to its sense of radical responsibility, of *Schuldigkeit* toward the infinite. For example, the early missionary efforts in Latin America would define the Amerindians strictly within the types of people that Europe saw as an internal threat to its own unity: the unfaithful Christians, the Jews, the Muslims. Fantastic theories about the Mediterranean origin of the indigenous peoples are frequently encountered, and even supposed evidences to an apostolic evangelization of St. Thomas are often documented. (The same apostle whose presence in India is also attested to. After all, as Columbus thought, the Europeans had landed in the East Indies, or in what even before Columbus's travel was depicted in 1489 [three years before the European landfall], by the cartographer Henricus Martellus, as the Fourth Asiatic Peninsula.) Similar "documentation" has also been produced to attest to the Jewish or Muslim origin of the American people.[16] The words of Jean-Jacques Rousseau are embarrassingly telling: "After three or four centuries in which the inhabitants of Europe flooded the other parts of the world, and published ceaselessly new accounts of travels and encounters, I am persuaded that we don't know any people but the Europeans alone."[17]

15. Vítor Westhelle, *Voces de protesta en América Latina* (Mexico: CETPJDR/LSTC, 2000), pp. 61-81.

16. See my article "Erobring og evangelisering i Latinamerika: tre missionsmodeller og deres fælles forudsætning," *Mission* 4 (1992): 3-7.

17. In Rudi Laermans, "Heterophobic Halls of Mirrors: Sepulveda's 'Alterization' of the Indians," in *America: Bride of the Sun*, Royal Museum of Fine Arts, Antwerp (Ghent: Imschoot, 1992), p. 23.

4. The Challenge

As I suggested at the beginning, the question about the relationship between Christianity and Europe is not whether and how much Europe is Christian, but how much Christianity has been entangled with European self-awareness. From the perspective of those who have been the object of the European colonial and missionary projects, it is the question of how European is Christianity. And the answer is the following: if European history is viewed as the Hegelian universal history, then Christianity is European to the core and nothing else needs to be said. But if Europe has a particular history and particular also is its science, its religious expressions, its political systems, then Europe's relation to Christianity is problematized, for it implies that the other does not represent only the possibility of apostasy within the ensemble of the European self-portrayal of its Christian identity, but also an evangelical possibility that comes from outside the European self-invention in the areas of science, religion, and politics since the fifteenth century. Obviously, this is a hard decision to make, for the European imprint on the rest of the world for the last 500 years has been so extensive and pervasive that even for non-Europeans to think of themselves in other categories but the ones inherited from Europe is a daunting task. It is a task that requires a belief that another reality is not only the reality of the totally other, but a reality that is utterly of this world, only placed so far from everyday experience that one fails to see it. It is rendered invisible.

Let me propose an analogy to explain what I am trying to approach in answering the question of whether Europe is Christian. I suggest that Europe is Christian in the same fashion as the apostle Thomas was. I am not primarily thinking of the fact that Thomas is regarded as the evangelist who supposedly covered the world from Asia to the Americas, although this is also suggestive. My analogy goes back to the story told in chapter 20 of John's Gospel, which roughly reads: the resurrected Jesus appears to the gathered disciples missing only Thomas. When the others told Thomas about the encounter with Jesus, he did not believe it possible. Thomas needed to see, to touch, to verify that which in his mind and by his experiences was deemed implausible. Thomas doubted. Eight days later, however, when the disciples were again gathered, and Thomas among them, Jesus again appeared and gave Thomas the evidence he needed in order to believe. The point I want to make with this illustration has two aspects. First, Thomas indeed did not believe in what sounded to him like poor evidence, implausible testimonies clearly outside his field of vision, his "scientific" rationality, even his religion, for he was a believing Jew and a disciple of Jesus. This is then the second point. Thomas, doubtful as he was, did not abandon the company of the other disciples. Eight days later he was with the whole group, as his doubt did not affect his fundamental sense of responsibility; and because he was there, faithfully, he encountered the resurrected one. Thomas was responsible and faithful even though he doubted the all too human appearance of Jesus after his death, carrying alive the scars of mortal wounds. The problem with Thomas was not a lack of faith in the all-transcendent Other. Where his faith faltered was in accepting the possibility of another reality that testified to a possibility totally within the confines of this finite world with its bodies and scars. Thomas's sense of *Schuldigkeit* did not entail responsiveness *(Verantwortlichkeit)* to what was outside of the mythos with which he operated.

The Nicaraguan philosopher Alejandro Serrano Caldera speaks of the "return of the caravels"[18] as this promise — that as much as Europe has represented a novelty for the world it conquered, taught, evangelized, and colonized, the rest of the world might become news, even good news, a good angel *(eu-angelion)* for Europe. We owe so much to Europe as to be aware of the responsibility this entails.

18. Alejandro Serrano Caldera, *Filosofia e Crise: Pela Filosofia Latino-Americana* (Petrópolis: Vozes, 1984).

Sanctorum Communio and the Ethics of Free Responsibility: Reflections on Bonhoeffer's Ecclesiology and Ethics

JOHN W. DE GRUCHY

The connection between ecclesiology and ethics, between the church and its moral responsibility in society, was one of the most contested issues in the ecumenical church during the twentieth century. Symbolic of the tension was the gulf that separated those engaged in questions of Faith and Order from those involved in matters of Life and Work.[1] Dietrich Bonhoeffer, it may be recalled, was suspicious of Faith and Order because he felt it focused solely on intrachurch issues rather than on the church in relation to the world at a time in which the struggle for world peace was a priority. Hence his involvement in the World Alliance for Promoting International Friendship through the Churches, a movement related to Life and Work.[2] In his address to the Youth Peace Conference held in Czechoslovakia in July 1932, entitled "A Theological Basis for the World Alliance," Bonhoeffer addressed this tension, as he would later in his more radical essay on "The Confessing Church and the Ecumenical Movement," written at Finkenwalde in July 1935. In both instances he argued that the ecumenical movement needed both a theological basis for its social activism and the ability to speak and act concretely and decisively in relation to the social and political issues of the day.

1. Cf. Peter Lodberg, "The History of Ecumenical Work on Ecclesiology and Ethics," in *Costly Commitment,* ed. Thomas F. Best and Martin Robra (Geneva: World Council of Churches, 1995), pp. 1-12.

2. Eberhard Bethge, *Dietrich Bonhoeffer: Theologian, Christian, Contemporary* (London: Collins, 1967), pp. 146f.

The tension between Faith and Order and Life and Work issues was not just experienced at that high level of ecumenical engagement within the ambit of the World Council of Churches during much of the twentieth century; it reached down deeply into the life of every Christian congregation and synod, often resulting in acrimonious debate and even schism. Nowhere was this more apparent than during the German *Kirchenkampf*, the Civil Rights Movement in the United States, the church struggle against apartheid in South Africa, and in response to the Programme to Combat Racism sponsored by the World Council of Churches. But the issues that have evoked controversy have been more widespread and diverse than these paradigmatic examples may suggest. There is no need to list them here, but simply to mention the debates around such issues as diverse as nuclear disarmament and matters relating to human sexuality immediately bring to mind a whole coterie of moral dilemmas that have deeply divided the Christian church. So while, on the one hand, the twentieth century saw remarkable advances in the ecumenical search to express the unity of the church, it also experienced many divisive forces brought about largely by ethical rather than dogmatic controversies. Of course, as Bonhoeffer discerned, dogmatic and ethical issues cannot be neatly separated out, for every ethical issue is inevitably related to a matter of belief, and every doctrine has ethical consequences. We understood this only too well in South Africa, even if somewhat belatedly. Apartheid was a heresy not just because it was morally repugnant but also because it was theologically indefensible.[3]

Much of my life and work has been at the point of connection between ecclesiology and ethics. For anyone who took seriously the social responsibility of the church within apartheid South Africa, it could not have been otherwise. Of course, there were many Christians and churches that sought to maintain a rigid boundary line between the spheres of church and politics, but as we know only too well, they too were deeply enmeshed in the issues. The extent to which this was so is now well documented in the Report on Faith Communities during the apartheid era prepared for the Truth and Reconciliation Commission.[4] In hindsight, no church es-

3. *Apartheid Is a Heresy*, ed. John W. de Gruchy and Charles Villa-Vicencio (Cape Town: David Philip, 1983).

4. *Facing the Truth: South African Faith Communities and the Truth & Reconciliation Commission*, ed. James C. Cochrane and John W. de Gruchy (Cape Town: David Philip, 1999).

capes from judgment. Certainly not those that gave legitimacy to apartheid, and certainly not those that attempted to be neutral bystanders. But even those who were engaged in the church struggle against apartheid know how deeply we were implicated in injustice. In this respect we were not unlike those within the Confessing Church in Germany who, like Bonhoeffer, recognized the need for a confession of guilt long before the downfall of the Third Reich.

There can be little doubt, further, that those of us who were engaged, however inadequately, in the church struggle against apartheid, drew much of our inspiration from the German *Kirchenkampf*, and especially from the example and theology of Karl Barth and Bonhoeffer. For both of them it was impossible to separate Christian dogmatics from ethics, or the church from social responsibility. How they related these was, to a large extent, determined not just by academic debate, but by critical theological reflection on the praxis of the church both before and especially during the Nazi era. In this paper I wish to explore the issues from the perspective of Bonhoeffer's theological development, showing how from the outset ecclesiology and ethics are related in principle, and how this relationship was shaped during the tumultuous years of the Third Reich. In my opinion, few other theologians have seen the issues so clearly, engaged in them so directly, and influenced ecumenical thought and action so widely.

It should be recalled that Bonhoeffer already in 1933, right at the outset of Hitler's rise to power, was only too aware of the dangers ahead and of the extent to which the church could not remain aloof from the burning ethical issues of the day by recourse to a misappropriation of Luther's teaching on the two kingdoms. Today we may have some problems with his essay on "The Church and the Jewish Question," but we remain impressed by his insistence that the church not only challenge the state to fulfill its true responsibilities, not only aid the victims of state oppression, but also "put a spoke in the wheel itself" by taking direct political action.[5] This anticipated by ten years Bonhoeffer's own involvement in the conspiracy against Hitler in what, to use the phrase from his posthumously published *Ethics,* was an "act of free responsibility."[6] But what, we might well ask, enabled him to make such provocative statements about the political and so-

5. Dietrich Bonhoeffer, *No Rusty Swords: Letters, Lectures and Notes 1928-1936,* Collected Works of Dietrich Bonhoeffer, vol. 1 (London: Collins, 1965), p. 221.

6. Dietrich Bonhoeffer, *Ethics* (New York: Macmillan, 1965), pp. 224ff.

cial responsibility of the church (not just the individual Christian) so early? And to do so at a time when virtually all other theologians and church leaders were either captivated by the charisma of Hitler or fearfully silent?

There are several reasons for Bonhoeffer's stand. Some of these have to do with his own moral formation, which stretched back into his childhood, his upbringing and education. Some of them have to do with his exposure to other cultures beyond the boundaries of Germany, and to his involvement in the ecumenical movement. But we can also see the theological lines being drawn already in his doctoral dissertation, *Sanctorum Communio*, for it is there that the foundations are laid for the development of his theology as a whole, a development that went through phases and significant changes but remained remarkably consistent and coherent throughout. In the words of Joachim van Soosten, Bonhoeffer's conclusions in *Sanctorum Communio* "possess an internal dynamic by which Bonhoeffer himself will be driven to go beyond his earliest work."[7]

Christology is undoubtedly the *cantus firmus* for the development of Bonhoeffer's theology. But the starting point is ecclesiology, the ecclesiology of *Sanctorum Communio*, with its emphasis on the historicity of the church, its empirical facticity, which, despite its sinfulness, is "Christ existing as church-community." And central to this ecclesiology is Bonhoeffer's understanding of ethical transcendence as the basis for genuine personhood and human sociality.[8] So already in *Sanctorum Communio* ecclesiology, Christology, and ethics are brought into creative and inseparable interaction with each other.

But the Christology of *Sanctorum Communio* is not developed and remains subsumed within ecclesiology. It is only later as Bonhoeffer begins to develop his Christology in his Berlin lectures of 1932 that its contours become clear and the focus shifts from the church as such to the world within which the church exists. This does not mean a loss of interest in the church, but rather that ecclesiology is shaped by Bonhoeffer's understanding of Christ as the center of the world. This in turn provides the basis for

7. Joachim van Soosten, Editor's Afterword, Dietrich Bonhoeffer, *Sanctorum Communio: A Theological Study of the Sociology of the Church,* Dietrich Bonhoeffer Works, vol. 1 (Minneapolis: Fortress, 1998), p. 300.

8. Ernst Feil, *The Theology of Dietrich Bonhoeffer,* trans. Martin Rumscheidt (Philadelphia: Fortress, 1985), pp. 8, 84.

his engagement in the *Kirchenkampf* and leads directly to the development of his ethics culminating in the "ethics of free responsibility."

Sanctorum Communio: God's Will for Humanity Restored

At the time of its publication in an abridged form in 1930, Bonhoeffer's doctoral dissertation, written when he was only twenty-one years old, was largely ignored though posthumously hailed as a "theological miracle" by Karl Barth. Later, especially after Bonhoeffer gained notoriety through the publication of his *Letters and Papers from Prison,* students of his theology began to explore the origins of his prison fragments, tracing a great deal back to *Sanctorum Communio.* Eberhard Bethge pioneered the way for this recovery of Bonhoeffer's early theology, and others have built upon his work, notably Clifford Green in his excellent account of Bonhoeffer's "theology of sociality."[9]

Given Bonhoeffer's early interest in ethics, it is noteworthy that Bonhoeffer chose ecclesiology as the subject for his dissertation. But the church had gripped his imagination ever since his visit to Rome as a young student in 1923 and his exposure to the worship of St. Peter's Basilica during Holy Week. Nothing in his background prepared him for this discovery of the church. The major influence on him in the Berlin Faculty, Adolf von Harnack, saw the essence of Christianity in personal faith and moral behavior rather than participation in "the body of Christ." In this scheme of things, the church was a religious community of those who believed, held together by that faith, that is, by the willingness of believers. Harnack's influence was not without fruit, for it was chiefly from him that Bonhoeffer learned to take the results of historical research seriously into account, and it was Harnack who encouraged him to pursue an academic career in ethics. But to Harnack's dismay Bonhoeffer fell under the spell of Karl Barth, and it was largely in response to the challenge of Barth's dialectical theology with its radical critique of religion that he embarked on the writing of his dissertation. He did so under the supervision of Reinhold Seeberg, a

9. Clifford Green, *Bonhoeffer: Theology of Sociality* (Grand Rapids: Eerdmans, 1999). See also Clifford Green, "Human Sociality and Christian Community," in *The Cambridge Companion to Dietrich Bonhoeffer,* ed. John W. de Gruchy (Cambridge: Cambridge University Press, 1999), pp. 113-33.

somewhat conservative Hegelian whose influence is evident in much of what Bonhoeffer wrote, though more so in the original dissertation than in the published version.[10]

Barth initially regarded Bonhoeffer's interest in the church as some kind of hankering after Roman Catholicism rather than an expression of evangelical commitment. But it was through critical engagement with Barth's theology that Bonhoeffer began to discern theologically what he had experienced in Rome: that the essence of Christianity is inseparable from the essence of the church. This was something that Barth himself came to see when he changed tack, setting aside his work on Christian dogmatics in the interests of *Church Dogmatics.* Barth would later acknowledge Bonhoeffer's influence on his own ecclesiological thinking, but at this earlier stage Bonhoeffer was indebted to Barth, who forced him to think of the church not primarily as religious community but as a revelatory event. For Barth enabled him to recognize that it is not our faith which forms the basis for the church, but God's will and grace revealed in Jesus Christ.

> The concept of the church is conceivable only in the sphere of reality established by God; this means that it cannot be deduced. *The reality of the church is a reality of revelation, a reality that essentially must be* either believed or denied.[11]

Understanding the church as an association of individuals denies its character as God's new creation *(sanctorum communio)* in Christ, yet, understanding the church only as a revelatory "event," as the early Barth insisted, denies its historical concreteness.

> . . . the genuinely historical nature of the empirical church. . . . *The history of the church is the hidden center of world history,* and not the history of one educational institution among others.[12]

What drives Bonhoeffer's inquiry in his engagement with Barth is precisely

10. On the relation between the dissertation and the published version of *Sanctorum Communio* see the Editor's Introduction to Bonhoeffer, *Sanctorum Communio,* pp. 9ff.

11. Bonhoeffer, *Sanctorum Communio,* p. 127.

12. Bonhoeffer, *Sanctorum Communio,* p. 211.

the question "where within the reality of the world does the reality confessed by the Christian faith manifest itself and become concrete?"[13] Yes, indeed, the reality of the church is a reality of revelation, but where within the reality of the world does revelation take shape and form? Revelation and history cannot be kept apart even though they cannot be conflated. Hence the logical connection but necessary distinction between the Holy Spirit and the "objective spirit," and between what Bonhoeffer calls the essential and the empirical church.[14] The empirical church is not to be equated with religious community. Rather, "as a concrete historical community, in the relativity of its forms and in its imperfect and modest appearance, it is the body of Christ, Christ's presence on earth, for it has his word." However, once this has been grasped "it is in principle possible once again to define the church as a religious community, namely as a religious community that really has been established by God."[15]

In order to develop his thesis Bonhoeffer draws on current social theory. "Our purpose," he writes at the outset, "is to understand the structure of the given reality of a church of Christ, as revealed in Christ, from the perspective of social philosophy and sociology."[16] Yet, Bonhoeffer makes it clear that he is not engaging in an exercise in the sociology of religion but in theology, only employing insights from social philosophy and sociology to help understand the nature of the church — something that can only really be understood from within. Having made this clear, Bonhoeffer then turns to consider the Christian concept of the person and how this relates to the insight derived from social philosophy that "human spirit generally is possible and real only in sociality."[17] His intention was to refute any notion of an "individualistic social atomism."

Bonhoeffer's understanding of the Christian concept of personhood stands in contrast to the Aristotelian metaphysical model, the Stoic individualistic concept of the ethical person, Epicurean utilitarianism, and the Cartesian epistemological concept of the person. It is an interpersonalist model. The "I" derives its identity from being in relationship to the "You." But what is of critical importance for Bonhoeffer is that this relationship is

13. Joachim van Soosten, Editor's Afterword, Bonhoeffer, *Sanctorum Communio,* p. 291.

14. Bonhoeffer, *Sanctorum Communio,* pp. 216ff.

15. Bonhoeffer, *Sanctorum Communio,* p. 209.

16. Bonhoeffer, *Sanctorum Communio,* p. 33.

17. Bonhoeffer, *Sanctorum Communio,* p. 33.

ethical in character, for the "person exists always and only in ethical responsibility" and it is dynamic, for "the person is re-created again and again in the perpetual flux of life."[18] Indeed,

> the person as conscious being is created in the moment of being moved — in the situation of responsibility, passionate ethical struggle, confrontation by an overwhelming claim; thus the real person grows out of a concrete situation.[19]

The "You" thus presents a "concrete ethical barrier" which the "I" is forced to acknowledge and respond to. This, Bonhoeffer describes as the "*social ontic-ethical basic-relations of persons.*"[20] Everything, then, that "can be said about the Christian concept of person can be grasped directly by the person who is facing responsibility."[21] Why is this so? The answer provided is theological. The "other," the "You" is "an image of the divine You," the one through whom God encounters me. The claim of the "other" upon me is always God's claim, but at the same time it is always also the claim of the "other."[22] This gives priority to ethics over epistemology. It has to do with the "reality of persons encountering one another."[23] But seeing that I can only know this through revelation, the revelation of God's love, and thus can only truly encounter the "other" on that basis, the church as the concrete expression of revelation becomes a necessity. For Bonhoeffer's understanding of the church it is important to recognize, further, that community can be understood as a "collective person," and therefore "with the same structure as the individual person."[24]

From this perspective Bonhoeffer argues there is a "net of sociality" which is "prior to any human will to community."[25] This does not mean that the individual loses personal identity, any more than it means the priority of the social over the personal. It means, rather, that the discovery of genuine personal identity is only possible in community, that is, through "the other."

18. Bonhoeffer, *Sanctorum Communio,* p. 48.
19. Bonhoeffer, *Sanctorum Communio,* p. 49.
20. Bonhoeffer, *Sanctorum Communio,* p. 50.
21. Bonhoeffer, *Sanctorum Communio,* p. 52.
22. Bonhoeffer, *Sanctorum Communio,* p. 55.
23. Van Soosten in Bonhoeffer, *Sanctorum Communio,* p. 298.
24. Bonhoeffer, *Sanctorum Communio,* p. 77.
25. Bonhoeffer, *Sanctorum Communio,* p. 79.

> God does not desire a history of individual human beings, but the history of the human community. However, God does not want a community that absorbs the individual into itself, but a community of human beings.[26]

Community is always a community of wills that is "built upon the separateness and difference of persons."[27] The same is true for the church, except that in the case of the church, it is God's will that brings it into being and sustains it. The church is God's will for a new humanity already present concretely in the world, realized through the death and resurrection of Jesus Christ and actualized by the Holy Spirit.

The reason why there is the need for the establishment of a new humanity is, of course, because the primal community has been broken by sin. Human community is fallen community, community in which relationships have been broken, in which the "I" dominates the "You," resulting not just in distinction but in a separation of wills. "Humanity-in-Adam" is united in its sinfulness, that is, there is an "ethical solidarity," but it is one of ethical failure. It is the "I-You" relation actualized in a sinful way.[28] Such unity or solidarity is not genuine community, but individualistic and fragmented. It is *peccatorum communio.*[29] The overcoming of this requires the church, the *sanctorum communio.* So we return to our earlier observation that the church is not primarily a "religious community," but a "reality of revelation."

> God established the reality of the church, of humanity pardoned in Jesus Christ — not religion, but revelation, *not religious community, but church.*[30]

The way in which this is realized is through the "vicarious representative action" *(Stellvertretung)* of Christ,[31] which was for Bonhoeffer as for his *Doktorvater* Seeberg "the sum and substance of Christology."[32] This, argues, Bonhoeffer, "*is not an ethical possibility or standard, but solely the*

26. Bonhoeffer, *Sanctorum Communio,* p. 80.
27. Bonhoeffer, *Sanctorum Communio,* p. 86.
28. Bonhoeffer, *Sanctorum Communio,* p. 117.
29. Bonhoeffer, *Sanctorum Communio,* p. 121.
30. Bonhoeffer, *Sanctorum Communio,* p. 153.
31. Bonhoeffer, *Sanctorum Communio,* pp. 146ff.
32. Bonhoeffer, *Sanctorum Communio,* p. 155n.88.

reality of the divine love for the church-community; it is not an ethical, but a theological concept. Through the Christian principle of vicarious representative action the new humanity is made whole and sustained. This principle gives Christian basic-relations their substantive uniqueness."[33] The fact that it is not an ethical but a theological concept refers to the impossibility of achieving true community through moral striving rather than accepting it as a gift of grace. But precisely because "vicarious representative action" is the basis of the church's life and existence, so it has become possible again for a community of human beings to live in love for each other.[34] In this way the church as true community is both an end in itself and a means to an end: it is what God wills for humanity as an end, and it is a means to enable the realization of that end.[35] This gives the church its unique sociological structure,[36] one that cannot be fitted neatly into Weber's typology of "church" and "sect."[37]

The social acts that constitute the community of love and disclose its structure reflect the nature of the church as end in itself and means to an end. Church members are both structurally "with-each-other" *(Miteinander),* and members who are active "being-for-each-other" *(Füreinander),* which is precisely what is meant by the principle of vicarious representative action.[38] "Being-with-each-other" goes beyond what is normally meant by this, for it is willed by God[39] and therefore involves "being-for-each-other" through acts of love, namely "self-renouncing, active work for the neighbor, intercessory prayer and the mutual forgiveness of sins in God's name." These involve self-giving on behalf of the neighbor, and significantly in anticipation of Bonhoeffer's own fate, a

> readiness to do and bear everything in the neighbor's place, indeed, if necessary, to sacrifice myself, standing as a *substitute* for my neighbor. Even if a purely vicarious action is rarely actualized, it is intended in every genuine act of love.[40]

33. Bonhoeffer, *Sanctorum Communio,* p. 156.
34. Bonhoeffer, *Sanctorum Communio,* p. 157.
35. Bonhoeffer, *Sanctorum Communio,* p. 173.
36. Bonhoeffer, *Sanctorum Communio,* p. 176.
37. Bonhoeffer, *Sanctorum Communio,* pp. 267f.
38. Bonhoeffer, *Sanctorum Communio,* p. 178.
39. Bonhoeffer, *Sanctorum Communio,* p. 180.
40. Bonhoeffer, *Sanctorum Communio,* p. 184.

This brings us to the heart of the matter, for the "vicarious representative action" of the members of the church not only gives the church its specific sociological character as a "community of love" *(Liebesgemeinschaft)*,[41] but points to the concrete reality of God's revelation. Hence Bonhoeffer's celebrated formula: "Christ existing as church-community" *(Christus als Gemeinde existierend)*, a modification of Hegel's concept of "God existing as church-community."[42] This means, further, that for Bonhoeffer ecclesiology, Christology, and ethics are inseparable because they are connected through the principle of "vicarious representative action," God in Christ being "with" and "for" the human other, enabling the members of the body to be "with" and "for" each other.[43] And because it is already established in Christ prior to any human willing or doing, the vicarious representative structure of the church is real not an ideal, ethical and not metaphysical.[44]

Bonhoeffer's christological-ecclesiological-ethical understanding of "vicarious representative action" *(Stellvertretung)* as developed first in *Sanctorum Communio* in many respects binds his theology together as it develops over the rest of his life. It is precisely this which not only provides the basis for his "ethics of free responsibility" but also for his own deed of "free responsibility." Before we come to that, however, we need to consider briefly the way in which Bonhoeffer's ecclesiology develops during the *Kirchenkampf*, how this is shaped by changing historical circumstances and by developments in his Christology. Our focus here is on the relationship between the church as "church-for-the-people" *(Volkskirche)* and a confessing, voluntary church of disciples *(Freiwilligkeitskirche)*, which sometimes is called to stand against the nation.

A "Church-for-the People"[45]

In his discussion in *Sanctorum Communio* of the relation between the empirical and the essential church Bonhoeffer insists that the "realm of

41. Bonhoeffer, *Sanctorum Communio*, p. 191.

42. Bonhoeffer, *Sanctorum Communio*, p. 189 et al.

43. Cf. Van Soosten, Bonhoeffer, *Sanctorum Communio*, p. 303.

44. See Bonhoeffer, *Sanctorum Communio*, p. 198.

45. This section is, in part, taken from my essay "The Freedom of the Church and the Liberation of Society: Bonhoeffer on the Free Church, and the 'Confessing Church' in South Africa," in *Bonhoeffer's Ethics: Old Europe and New Frontiers*, ed. Guy Carter and René van Eyden (Kampen: Kok Pharos, 1991), pp. 173-89.

Christ" is present to us in concrete historical form as a *Volkskirche* and not as a "voluntary church" *(Freiwilligkeitskirche).* The major reason he gives for this derives from the nature of the proclaimed "Word": "The *sanctorum communio* extends beyond itself and addresses all those who might belong to it even potentially; this is part of its nature."[46] Bonhoeffer is here affirming the responsibility that the church has for the nation in which it is set as a whole. He insists that this is not only because we have no right to separate the "wheat" from the "tares," but because it is of the essence of the church and the nature of the proclaimed "Word" that brings it into being and sustains it.

Nevertheless, Bonhoeffer is aware that the idea of the "voluntary" church is also of the essence of the church. By this he means a church comprised of committed rather than nominal members, the latter being the real danger within a national church. In fact, as early as 1924 when as a student he had visited Rome, Bonhoeffer seriously questioned whether the Protestant church should ever have allowed itself to become a state church, and whether in doing so it did not betray its Reformation heritage.[47] So it is not surprising that Bonhoeffer wrote in his dissertation:

> the sanctorum communio, which by its nature presents itself as a church-of-the-people, also calls for the voluntary church and continually establishes itself as such: that is, the sanctorum communio bears the others, so to speak, who have the latent potential to become "real" members of the church by virtue of the word that is both the author of the church and of the message it preaches.[48]

Bonhoeffer regarded this dialectical relationship between *Volkskirche* and "voluntary church" as genuinely Lutheran. It was not understood, as in the early Barth, as a dialectic between institution and event, or in Augustinian terms, as a division between the "visible" and "invisible" church. On the contrary, such false dichotomies were always rejected by Bonhoeffer, as can be seen in his paper "What Is the Church?" where he insists that the two natures of the church, the human and the divine, coexist as one concrete real-

46. Bonhoeffer, *Sanctorum Communio,* p. 220.

47. Eberhard Bethge, *Dietrich Bonhoeffer: Theologian, Christian, Contemporary* (London: Collins, 1970), pp. 88-90.

48. Bonhoeffer, *Sanctorum Communio,* p. 220.

ity in the world. In *Sanctorum Communio* Bonhoeffer insists that the church is structured in the world in a dialectical way both as "church-of-the-people" and voluntary church and that this derives from the nature of the proclaimed Word. The priority of the Word demands structures that enable the church to exercise its responsibility for the life of the nation as a whole *(Volkskirche),* and this in turn requires that the church be a confessing community of faithful people under the Word ("voluntary church"). Both are visible and public, both are of the essence of the church as a divine-human reality called into being by the nature of the proclaimed Word.

In one of the sections of *Sanctorum Communio* that was deleted from the published edition of 1930 (though included in the dissertation), Bonhoeffer, in affirming that "the church-of-the-people and the "voluntary church" belong together, adds this critical qualification:

> it is all too obvious today that a church is in the gravest internal danger if, as a church-of-the-people, it does not again and again seek to become a community of those who freely confess their faith. There is such a moment when the church may no longer be a church-of-the-people; this moment has come when the church can no longer recognize its "popular" form as the means for becoming a voluntary church, but instead moves toward a complete rigidity and emptiness in the use of forms that are harmful even to its living members. We have today reached a point where questions such as these must find their answer. Today, more than ever, we are grateful for the grace of having a church-of-the-people; but we are also more than ever attentive to the danger of its complete desecration.[49]

Bonhoeffer could not have anticipated the challenge that Nazi ideology would soon present to the Evangelical Church. Then, a moment arrived in which the church was in such danger of desecration that both he and Barth agreed it was a *status confessionis.* But this did not mean that Bonhoeffer turned away from affirming the church as *Volkskirche* in favor of the establishing of a Free Church. On the contrary, he firmly rejected this option. The question is why he did so.

During the initial days of the *Kirchenkampf,* especially after the infamous "Brown Synod" in September 1933, the leaders of the emergent Con-

49. Bonhoeffer, *Sanctorum Communio,* p. 271n.429.

fessing Church seriously considered establishing a voluntary Free Church. The idea was certainly very attractive for Bonhoeffer himself and he explored possibilities for its establishment. Barth was also strongly committed to the idea. But after the Barmen and Dahlem Synods and the launching of the Confessing Church there was a decisive turn away from any proposal for constituting the Confessing Church as a Free Church. On the contrary, Bonhoeffer assertively claimed that the Confessing Church was not a movement or a voluntary association alongside of the national church, but was, in fact, *the* Evangelical Church in Germany.[50] Writing from London on July 12, 1934, to Henriod of the World Alliance in Geneva, Bonhoeffer objects to the notion expressed by Henriod that the Barmen Synod has resulted in the constitution of a church that is distinct from that of the official German church.

> I think you are misrepresenting the legal construction of the Confessional Church in this point. There is not the claim or even the wish to be a Free Church besides the Reichskirche, but there is the claim to be the only theologically and legally legitimate Evangelical Church in Germany. . . .[51]

The irony of this development becomes obvious when we recognize the extent to which the ecclesiology expressed in *Discipleship* is, in many respects, that of the "voluntary" church. The "voluntary" church is of the essence of what Bonhoeffer captured not only in his distinction between cheap and costly grace, but also in his insistence on the boundaries of the church, its separation from the world, and the visibility of the Christian community in the life of the world. It was not for nothing that Bonhoeffer had to defend himself against the charge of having become an Anabaptist!

In insisting on the Confessing Church as the true *Reichskirche*, Bonhoeffer was certainly not supporting the idea of a *Volkskirche* as understood by the *Deutsche Christen.*[52] For the *Deutsche Christen* a *Volkskirche* was nationalist, *volkisch,* and therefore a culturally and racially determined church that served the self-interests of the nation. Bonhoeffer categorically

50. Bethge, *Dietrich Bonhoeffer,* pp. 414f.

51. Dietrich Bonhoeffer, *London 1933-1935,* Dietrich Bonhoeffer Werke, 13 (Gütersloh: Chr. Kaiser/Gütersloher Verlagshaus, 1994), p. 166.

52. On the ambiguous meaning of *Volkskirche,* see K. Scholder, *The Churches and the Third Reich* (London: SCM, 1987), pp. 209, 280, 283.

rejected any such ecclesiology. But he equally rejected the idea of the Confessing Church becoming a purely "voluntary" or Free Church. He insisted that the Confessing Church was not a sect or hole-in-the-corner affair, but the true Evangelical Church of the German people in continuity with the church of the Reformation. It was this church that had the real interests of the nation at heart, not the false "official" church that had sold out to National Socialism. The true church of Jesus Christ had a responsibility to the German nation as a whole. In this sense it was and had to be a *Volkskirche.*

Moreover, the Confessing Church did not have to become a Free Church in order to exercise its responsibility. Its freedom to speak prophetically derived from its faithful confession of Christ to the nation, not from any attempt to be constituted as a Free Church. Nevertheless, to be the Evangelical Church in Germany at this point in history, in order to be for the nation, it had to confess Christ against the nation. In this way the dialectic between *Volkskirche* and *Freiwilligkeitskirche,* and therefore the essence of the church as both national and "voluntary," was maintained. The proclamation of the Word made this a necessity.

Bonhoeffer's knowledge of the Free Churches in Germany naturally determined the way in which he discussed the idea of a *Freiwilligkeitskirche* in *Sanctorum Communio.* Later, as a student at Union Seminary and as a pastor in London, he encountered the tradition more directly and fully in its North American and British setting. There it had developed differently and played a much more significant ecclesiastical and public role for historical and cultural reasons. Bonhoeffer's essay on "Protestantism without Reformation," written in August 1939, and therefore at the end of his participation in the *Kirchenkampf,* demonstrates his developed understanding and grasp of the strengths and weaknesses of this tradition, but also of its contextual character. Moreover, Bonhoeffer had by then clearly shifted away from relating the freedom of the church to a particular form of church structure. This comes out clearly in his comparison of the Protestantism with and "Protestantism without Reformation." Bonhoeffer appropriately sets his comparison in the context of a discussion on "Freedom":

> America calls herself the land of the free. Under this term today she understands the right of the individual to independent thought, speech and action. In this context, religious freedom is, for the American, an obvious possession. Church preaching and organisation, the life of the communities can develop independently, without being molested.

> Praise of this freedom may be heard from pulpits everywhere, coupled with the sharpest condemnation of any limitation of such freedom which has taken place anywhere. Thus freedom here means possibility, the possibility of unhindered activity given by the world to the church.[53]

How different this was not only to the German cultural ethos and the historical agenda of the Evangelical Church, especially within the Third Reich. The difference was rooted, of course, in the distinct ways in which Europe and the United States had historically developed, and which led to very different ways of resolving the problem of relating church and state.

In the land of the Reformation the doctrine of the two kingdoms was operative in such a way that the church was prevented from exercising any politically critical or prophetic function. There the church had a national responsibility as the "church-for-the-people." But its very relationship to the state hamstrung its prophetic role. In the New World, on the other hand, the separation of church and state should have led even more decisively to the withdrawal of the church from the political arena. But, as Bonhoeffer discerned, it actually meant "the victory of the church over any unbounded claim by the state."[54] Indeed, in the United States "the church claims for itself the right to speak and act in all matters of public life, for only so can the kingdom of God be built."[55]

The question Bonhoeffer raises so sharply in this essay is, therefore, whether the cultural and political ethos of a nation, or the formal relationship between church and state, is really determinative for a proper understanding of the freedom of the church. Is the freedom of the church really contingent on being a *Volkskirche* or a *Freiwilligkeitskirche?* For Bonhoeffer this is clearly not so. With emphasis he writes:

> The freedom of the church is not where it has possibilities, but only where the Gospel really and in its own power makes room for itself on earth, even and precisely when no such possibilities are offered to it. The essential freedom of the church is not a gift of the world to the church, but the freedom of the Word of God itself to gain a hearing.[56]

53. Bonhoeffer, *No Rusty Swords,* pp. 99f.
54. Bonhoeffer, *No Rusty Swords,* p. 104.
55. Bonhoeffer, *No Rusty Swords,* p. 104.
56. Bonhoeffer, *No Rusty Swords,* p. 100.

Bonhoeffer sees some real dangers for the church when it understands its freedom as a gift of the state, that is, as a result of some agreement with the world whereby the church becomes either established or technically free, or, indeed, as Bonhoeffer detected in the United States, it attempted to build the kingdom of God on earth.[57] Either way this speeds up the process of secularization whereby the church in fact becomes captive to the world and surrenders its freedom under the Word of God. Thus, Bonhoeffer insists,

> Freedom as an institutional possession is not an essential mark of the church. It can be a gracious gift given to the church by the providence of God; but it can also be the great temptation to which the church succumbs in sacrificing its essential freedom to institutional freedom.[58]

Without recognizing the fact, the church is then in chains even though it regards itself as free. The freedom of the church is not a possibility derived from the state but a necessity derived from the Word of God. The proclamation of the Word creates the freedom and space that the church needs to fulfill its task in its historical context. Hence,

> Only where this word can be preached concretely in the midst of historical reality, in judgment, command, forgiveness of sinners and liberation from all human institutions is there freedom of the church.[59]

Thus the freedom of the church is no longer contingent upon its formal relation to the state, but upon its concrete witness to the gospel and therefore to genuinely human liberation.

When we turn to Bonhoeffer's essay, in his *Ethics,* on the "Church and the World" this relationship between the freedom of the church and human liberation is brought to a head. The dialectic which in *Sanctorum Communio* found expression in the relationship between *Volkskirche* and "voluntary" church is no longer focused on the structure of the church but on its ability to respond to the inclusive and exclusive claims of Christ over the whole of social reality.

57. Bonhoeffer, *No Rusty Swords,* pp. 104f.
58. Bonhoeffer, *No Rusty Swords,* p. 100.
59. Bonhoeffer, *No Rusty Swords,* p. 101.

In the opening section Bonhoeffer refers to one of the "most astonishing experiences during the years when everything Christian was sorely oppressed," namely, the fact that the defenders of the endangered values of truth, justice, and freedom found common cause with those Christians who remained faithful to the gospel.[60] In an Anglo-Saxon context, such as North America, this would not have been a cause for astonishment, quite the contrary. But in Germany where there had been a historical estrangement of the values of the Enlightenment from the Christian church, an alienation exacerbated by developments within the Weimar Republic, it was an astonishing fact. When all other opposition to injustice and oppression were being systematically denied by the state, the church was being forced to become the protector of the values of truth, justice, and human freedom in pursuing its mandate of proclaiming the claims of Christ. For the origin of these values, Bonhoeffer asserts, is none other than Jesus Christ.[61]

This leads Bonhoeffer to his perceptive discussion on the claims of Christ that are at the same time inclusive of all who struggle for truly human values ("He that is not against us is for us" [Mark 9:40]), and exclusive of all who deny Christ in denying such values ("He that is not with me is against me" [Matt. 12:30]). This, as Bonhoeffer argues, is not simply a theoretical position, but one that has in fact taken place quite concretely in the confessing church.

> The exclusive demand for a clear profession of allegiance to Christ caused the band of confessing Christians to become ever smaller . . . then, precisely through this concentration on the essential, the Church acquired an inward freedom and breadth which preserved her against any timid impulse to draw narrow limits, and there gathered around her men who came from very far away, and men to whom she could not refuse her fellowship and her protection; injured justice, oppressed truth, vilified humanity and violated freedom all sought for her, or rather for her Master, Jesus Christ.[62]

The freedom of the church is thus dependent upon her faithfulness in confessing Christ irrespective of what this means in terms of the size of her

60. Bonhoeffer, *Ethics*, pp. 55f.
61. Bonhoeffer, *Ethics*, p. 56.
62. Bonhoeffer, *Ethics*, p. 58.

space in the world. "The greater the exclusiveness, the greater the freedom." The true freedom of the church is an inward freedom derived from "its concentration on the essential."

Yet this exclusiveness must not be allowed to degenerate into fanaticism, any more than the church's openness must lead to the secularization or self-abandonment of the church. The clue lies in the genuine confessing of Christ over the whole of reality.

> The more exclusively we acknowledge and confess Christ as Lord, the more fully the wide range of his dominion will be disclosed to us.[63]

Bonhoeffer thus ends his discussion by denying that this espousal by the church of humanizing values should be understood as an apologetic ploy designed to further its triumphalistic expansion in the world. On the contrary, in faithfully confessing Christ before the world it becomes ever more clear how much these values have their origin in Christ, and therefore confessing him as Lord includes their affirmation in word and deed. It follows, then, that the church does not have to justify its commitment to the struggle for truth, justice, and human freedom; on the contrary, these values have to be understood and therefore justified in the terms of their origin in Christ. At the profoundest level their true meaning can only be discerned in Christ.

> It is not Christ who must justify himself before the world by the acknowledgement of the values of justice, truth and freedom, but it is these values which have come to need justification, and their justification can only be Jesus Christ. It is not that a "Christian culture" must make the name of Jesus Christ acceptable to the world; but the crucified Christ has become the refuge and the justification, the protection and the claim for the higher values and their defenders that have fallen victim to suffering.[64]

In *Sanctorum Communio* it was through the vicarious representative action of Jesus Christ that the church was established; now the focus of Christ's vicarious action has shifted from the church to the world, because

63. Bonhoeffer, *Ethics,* p. 58.
64. Bonhoeffer, *Ethics,* p. 59.

the whole world and not just the church is under the reign of Christ. Thus the discovery of the freedom of the church in the process of affirming those values that liberate from oppression rather than dehumanize is christologically grounded, indeed, grounded in a theology of the cross. For "it is with the Christ who is persecuted and who suffers in his church that justice, truth, humanity and freedom now seek refuge. . . ."[65] In this way, then, the church exercises her public, national task as "church-for-the-people," for it protects those values without which a nation cannot live in justice and peace, and it sides with those who are committed to the struggle for the liberation of the nation from oppression. In doing so, it does not forsake its identity as church, as the community of gathered disciples. In Christ it discovers that its identity as both a confessing "voluntary church" and a public "church-for-the-people" is inseparably bound together not in the self-interests of the nation but as a church-for-others in the service of truth, justice, and freedom. Yet the "other" is now not simply those whom the "I" encounters within the church-community, but the "You" who is on or beyond the boundaries of both church and nation. And precisely at this point in his life Bonhoeffer found himself increasingly on the boundaries even of the Confessing Church, isolated from the church but inexorably drawn into the circle of its "cultured despisers" who were engaged in the German resistance.

The Ethics of Free Responsibility and the Church for Others

Bonhoeffer's essay on "The Structure of Responsible Life" in his *Ethics*[66] brings his understanding of "vicarious representative action" as originally developed in *Sanctorum Communio* into the sphere of social and political ethics. Indeed, it provides the subtext to Bonhoeffer's involvement in the conspiracy against Hitler. The "ethics of free responsibility" is the way in which "vicarious representative action" becomes concrete. Given the close connection between Bonhoeffer's ecclesiology, Christology, and ethics, it is not surprising that this had far-reaching implications for his ecclesiology.

For patriotic Germans within the military, even those opposed to Nazism, the attempt by the conspiracy to assassinate Hitler was unthink-

65. Bonhoeffer, *Ethics*, p. 59.

66. Bonhoeffer, *Ethics*, pp. 224ff.

able. The issue for them was not that of taking someone's life — after all they were mainly soldiers — but of breaking their word of honor. That was the moral dilemma facing the conspirators, and one reason why they welcomed pastor Bonhoeffer into their circle to help them deal with it. It was partly with this in mind that Bonhoeffer wrote his essay "After Ten Years" and why he drafted that on "The Structure of Responsible Life." Submissiveness and self-sacrifice, virtuous as they may be, can be exploited for evil ends. As Bonhoeffer told the conspirators, "civil courage . . . can grow only out of free responsibility of free people."[67] Human beings are responsible to God for their actions, yet there are morally ambiguous situations in which they have to exercise their freedom. Not to do so would be irresponsible, but there is no guarantee that the act of free responsibility is untainted by sin. The truly responsible person acting freely does so without the support of others or ethical absolutes. "It is he himself," Bonhoeffer writes, "who must observe, judge, weigh up, decide and act."[68] Yet, the "free deed knows itself in the end as the deed of God; the decision knows itself as guidance; the free venture knows itself as divine necessity."[69]

We now find ourselves at the heart of Bonhoeffer's own moral struggle, as well as that of the conspirators, that small band of men who were, in their own way, not against but for Christ. Now we are face to face not with the freedom of the church to confess but our personal freedom to act courageously and responsibly. Indeed, to act vicariously on behalf of a church that had squandered and lost its ability to act vicariously and responsibly on behalf of both the nation and the "other." All depended now upon men and women who knew their responsibility and who were prepared to act on behalf of others even if it meant sacrificing their own liberty and even moral righteousness in order to do so. Now it is "the free venture" that becomes necessary and "knows itself as divine necessity."[70] But, as intimated, this act of free responsibility had implications for Bonhoeffer's ecclesiology.

Bonhoeffer's act of free responsibility was a vicarious act on behalf of a church that had failed to exercise its own responsibility. This failure paradoxically began, as Bonhoeffer perceived, when its main consideration

67. Dietrich Bonhoeffer, *Letters and Papers from Prison,* trans. and ed. Eberhard Bethge (London: SCM, 1971), p. 6.

68. Bonhoeffer, *Ethics,* p. 248.

69. Bonhoeffer, *Ethics,* p. 249.

70. Bonhoeffer, *Ethics,* p. 249.

became its own freedom in relation to the state. It stood up for its own cause rather than the needs of the world.[71] In other words, it was a church-for-itself (even if its cause was to protect the integrity of the gospel and its confessions) rather than a church-for-others. From the beginning, the *Kirchenkampf* was about the freedom of the church to be the church, not about the freedom of the church to speak and act on behalf of the Jews and other victims of Nazi terror. The issues debated at Barmen and Dahlem were vital, but the issue not debated was even more vital, namely, the plight of Nazi victims and especially that of the Jews. In hindsight the Confessing Church missed the real point of the confession it was making because it failed to discern the connection between prophetic witness on behalf of human rights and freedoms and the freedom of the gospel and the church. Thus it was that Bonhoeffer turned away from the Confessing Church to engage with others who were committed to human rights, to truth, justice, and freedom — and in the "act of free responsibility" on behalf of the victims surrendered his life.

But this vicarious representative act of free responsibility had another dimension. It was also the acceptance of both the guilt of the nation for its crimes against humanity and the guilt of the church for not speaking out and acting against a criminal state. Already in *Sanctorum Communio* Bonhoeffer had recognized that there was not just a theological but also an ethical meaning to "vicarious representative action." It signified, he wrote then, "the voluntary assumption of evil in another person's stead."[72] As we know, Bonhoeffer had already called for the church to confess its guilt long before anyone else, certainly anyone else in the church. In his essay on "Guilt, Justification and Renewal," also published in the *Ethics*, Bonhoeffer develops this theme with considerable power and insight. Among the many memorable statements we may recall:

> [The church] . . . was silent when she should have cried out because the blood of the innocent was crying aloud to heaven. She has failed to speak the right word in the right way at the right time. She has not resisted to the uttermost the apostasy of faith, and she has brought upon herself the guilt of the godlessness of the masses.[73]

71. Bonhoeffer, *Letters and Papers from Prison*, p. 381.

72. Bonhoeffer, *Sanctorum Communio*, p. 156n.17.

73. Bonhoeffer, *Ethics*, p. 113.

It was in the spirit of Bonhoeffer's call that eventually the *Evangelische Kirche* made its Stuttgart Confession of Guilt, and it was Bonhoeffer, too, who inspired some churches in South Africa in their own confession of guilt for the sins of apartheid.[74]

There is one final consequence for Bonhoeffer's ecclesiology that must be noted, a consequence that derives from his fragmentary prison reflections on Christianity in "a world-come-of-age." The ecclesiology of *The Letters and Papers from Prison* is one that is open to the world. The church is now called to become a church-for-others because "Jesus is the man for others." In this way it would fulfill the intention of the national church as a church for all people, a church concerned about the nation and issues of social justice and righteousness. Yet, at the same time, it would be a church that has given up all the privileges of the traditional national church, with its clergy depending entirely on the free-will offerings of its members.[75] This means, in effect, that the "church-for-the-people" has truly become a "voluntary church," a church that is both comprised of committed disciples and yet open to the world. The church is the community of those who are both "called forth" from the world, and yet who belong "wholly to the world."[76]

In order to retain both its identity and its spiritual power in being-for-others and open to the world, the church practices the "discipline of the secret" *(Arkandisziplin)*, a life of worship and prayer. Indeed, what characterizes the church now is only two things: "prayer and righteous action." Such "righteous action" is, of course, not self-righteous action, but the vicarious representative act, the act of free responsibility, which is modeled on the vicarious sacrifice of Christ on behalf of the world. In other words, the *Sanctorum Communio* is not only constituted by Christ's vicarious representative act on behalf of the world, but the church only remains church as it too acts vicariously for the world and especially for its victims.

74. See John W. de Gruchy, "Guilt, Amnesty and National Reconstruction: Karl Jaspers' 'Die Schuldfrage' and the South African Debate," *Journal of Theology for Southern Africa* 83 (June 1993): 3-13.

75. Bonhoeffer, *Letters and Papers from Prison*, p. 382.

76. Bonhoeffer, *Letters and Papers from Prison*, pp. 280f.

Church Identity in the Nordic Countries — An International Perspective

JENS HOLGER SCHJØRRING

At the turn of the century it seems difficult to identify basic features that have been common to the Lutheran majority churches in the Nordic countries. Moreover, their historic hallmark, the close connection between church and state, is frequently met with suspicion and criticism, not only from inside the Nordic countries but even more from the outside world. For instance, it is questioned whether it is possible to combine the status of a privileged majority church, a national church, with the legal consequences that many citizens today connect with an open society, which is first and foremost defined by equal rights for all religious groups in the population, regardless of their numerical support in the population. Accordingly, the status of a privileged majority church appears to such critics as a survival of past patterns of absolutism and anti-modernity.

Earlier in the twentieth century the Lutheran churches in the Nordic countries were frequently associated with other characteristics, when seen from an international perspective, many of them far more positive. From the outside world — notably from the Protestant churches in Europe — high expectations were directed towards the churches in the Nordic countries, expectations nourished by widely shared images of the Nordic countries as models of the modern welfare state, involving harmonious cooperation between the social policy of the state and the social institutions of the church. This admiration was supported by the assumption that these churches were able to act as bridge-builders in times of conflicting concerns on the international scene.

What are the reasons for the shift from the earlier idealization to the present doubt or criticism? What were the essential features of a common Nordic identity in the earlier decades of the twentieth century? What gave rise to subsequent fundamental changes, mainly in the 1960s? Finally, does anything remain today of the former common ties?

In this article we shall attempt to discuss a few aspects of these far-ranging questions, taking into account that any assessment of the features that the churches in question have in common has to be counterbalanced by due attention being paid to the specific characteristics of each one of the Nordic national churches. And yet, it seems a timely task to collect at least a few stones of the variegated mosaic, and first of all it would be appropriate to analyze the process of transformation that has taken place within the churches in the Nordic countries, as seen against an international and ecumenical background.

The Scene after World War I

Throughout the nineteenth century numerous initiatives were taken towards closer cooperation between the Nordic countries generally and their churches specifically. Immediately after World War I such endeavors found a new, stronger direction, a fact that is in many ways surprising when the historical context is taken into account. Politically the first decades of the twentieth century had seen several painful divisions in the region, to such a degree that it seemed unrealistic to envisage a common international role for the Nordic countries. Norway had broken the union with Sweden in 1905. Similarly Finland had broken its union with Sweden; and moreover, the country was struck by civil war in 1917, a fact that added new complications to its already strained relationship with the neighboring communist Soviet Union, a relationship that was the key political issue for the nation. This challenge added considerable importance to the popular role of the Finnish Lutheran Church as a safeguard for a threatened nation, face to face with modern godless powers. Meanwhile Iceland was on its way to bringing an end to its union with Denmark.

However, there was also room for a common Nordic identity to be realized, especially when challenges from elsewhere in Europe were recognized in their true seriousness. All the Nordic countries had remained politically neutral during World War I, a fact that in itself implied a responsibility for mediation in the midst of the feelings of isolation or hatred, and crises of values elsewhere. The fact that the Nordic nations were able to seek community, or better that the bonds of community proved to be stronger than the indications of division, was in itself a remarkable sign to other regions of the European continent. And the churches were finding a specific, common responsibility in the process of setting up ecumenical initiatives as their contribution to overcoming the damage caused by the previous conflicts. Archbishop Nathan Söderblom of Uppsala, Sweden, had already made several attempts towards mediation during the war. As soon as the armistice was declared these initiatives entered a new phase. At a meeting with colleagues from the other Nordic churches Söderblom defined their common responsibility. In relation to the dominant Christian confessions in other parts of Europe he was determined to define the historical heritage of the Lutheran churches in the Nordic countries so as to be able to identify both their obligations and their possibilities in facing the present challenges. Only then, Söderblom maintained, would it be possible for the churches to play their proper role on the difficult road towards future prospects. He felt, no doubt, that the Lutheran confession, provided it was defined appropriately as a contribution towards "evangelical Catholicity" and in the way in which it had been shaped in the history of the Nordic nations, showed a promising way towards renewal.

He was determined to stay clear of confessional arrogance, claiming that it was a permanent obligation for any church to keep an eye open to the valuable patterns of Christian tradition that might be apprehended from confessional groups other than its own. Allowing for such basic openness, he was convinced that the Lutheran majority churches around the Baltic Sea had a crucial responsibility as propagators of true evangelical freedom. Accordingly Söderblom's position was defined partly by his evaluation of the historical heritage, which he considered a common feature of the Nordic churches, and partly by an international assessment of the actual ecumenical challenge. In this perspective he identified the structural identity common to the Nordic countries, their educational homogeneity, a high degree of individual freedom alongside with a common cultural heritage, a shared religious identity, and a considerable range of areas of mutual cooperation. Söderblom emphasized, "With us in the North the five nations have a rich heritage in common regarding popular culture, just as they are amply developed and accordingly highly individualized in terms of culture and national character, adding to that closely connected in religion and considering mutual cooperation."[1]

The Nordic Churches and the Church Struggle in Nazi Germany

The developments in Germany in the 1930s, politically and theologically, caused the Nordic theologians and church leaders to reconsider their attempts to encourage the building up of ecumenical relationships. The Stockholm meeting of 1925, hosted by Archbishop Söderblom, had been a milestone in the efforts to establish connections and ties across the confessional traditions. The aftermath of World War I, notably the paragraph on guilt in the Treaty of Versailles, directed against Germany, was a permanent stumbling block to a full-scale involvement on the part of German participants in the ecumenical dialogue. Their hesitation became even more noticeable after the Nazi seizure of power, because Hitler's totalitarian grasp of power and his claim of unconditional submission from all citizens involved a corresponding charge of national loyalty from every citizen, a demand that was particularly painful to those who sought to remain faithful to international concerns.

Against this background there were serious issues on the agenda as international representatives convened for an ecumenical conference in August 1934, hosted by the Danish bishop Valdemar Ammundsen acting in cooperation with the Anglican bishop George Bell. It is an indication of the deeply rooted ties existing between the Nordic churches that Bishop Ammundsen invited colleagues from the Nordic countries to a preparatory meeting, prior to the principal international conference. Evidently the challenges arising from the German church struggle were focal for the Nordic consultation, and — no less obviously — the delegates felt an obligation to reconsider their historic relations with the churches of the Reformation in Germany, at the same time taking into account their more recently established connections with the churches in the Anglo-Saxon countries.

Their difficulty had several aspects, and the Nordic theologians faced the danger of being caught in a pincer movement. On the one hand they

1. N. Söderblom in *Nordens Kirker og nordiske Aandsstrømninger efter Verdenskrigen,* ed. Alfred Th. Jørgensen (Copenhagen, 1921), p. 21. (My trans.)

felt compelled to distance themselves from an interpretation of state authority that gave unlimited power to the political leadership while at the same time preventing citizens from expressing their dissent. The challenge for Lutheran theologians became even more urgent considering the fact that leading Lutheran theologians in Germany were being ostentatiously outspoken in their support of the Nazi claim to power. On the other hand, the Nordic theologians expressed basic disagreement with the "dialectical theology" developed in Germany, first of all because they considered the dialectical distinctions between divine revelation and everything earthly as a serious threat, leaving all that is human, in its widest sense, as something merely relative and ambiguous. Such a distinction, they felt, would involve a total separation of social ethics from the gospel.

In an attempt to find a way out of this impasse they aimed at a mediating view of creational orders, arguing that the Christian attitude had to be both positive and polemical. Such a balanced position, they claimed, was a way of making an appropriate reappraisal of the teaching of Luther in a modern context. Moreover, they regarded this direction as a direct consequence of their own heritage, connected with the specific way of interpreting the relationship between church and state current in the Nordic countries. Not only was it an urgent task to resist the powers of secularization and to promote interaction between the church and popular culture, but from an international perspective it was no less important to promote support for minorities and all kinds of suppressed groups. The Nordic theologians maintained unanimously that exactly such differentiation was a key experience of the democratic, liberal tradition in the Nordic societies.[2] In terms of any effect on the historical course of events the deliberations of the Nordic theologians remained utterly void, without influence on attitudes inside Nazi Germany. Bishop Ammundsen, who hosted the conference, was well aware that an effective opposition against Nazism would have to evolve from inside Germany. Notwithstanding the failure to

2. For reports from the 1934 meeting see the Nordic ecumenical journal *Kristen Gemenskap* (1934): 134ff. For a more detailed analysis see the comparative Nordic volume *Kirken, Krisen og Krigen,* ed. Stein U. Larsen and I. Montgomery (Bergen and Oslo: Universitetsforlaget, 1982), pp. 259ff. with articles about each one of the countries involved under the headline "Fronten mot fascismen" (The front against fascism). See finally Jens Holger Schjørring, *Ökumenische Perspektiven des deutschen Kirchenkampfes* (Leiden: E. J. Brill, 1985), pp. 66-70, 103-6.

exert direct influence on events, the inter-Nordic dialogue remained a crucial experience for the circle of participants and beyond.

New Challenges after 1945

Seen in a European perspective the Nordic countries remained relatively isolated from the devastations caused by World War II, especially when compared with countries like Russia, Poland, and Germany. Yet, some of them had also endured terrible sufferings, especially Norway and Finland, whereas others were left without damage (Sweden). This contrast in itself constituted a challenge to the traditional ties within the North, and a further strain was added, as contrasting political attitudes became connected with internal embarrassments in inter-Nordic relationships. Accordingly, the aftermath of World War II turned into a period of rebuilding in more than one sense, also in Northern Europe. The churches were deeply affected by this situation, a fact that became visible when bishops from all the Nordic churches came together for the first time after the war in August 1945.

The Swedish archbishop Erling Eidem had taken the initiative, continuing the tradition established by his predecessor during World War I, or more correctly a tradition reflecting an even longer historical continuity, since in the sixteenth century Sweden had already assumed the position as leading safeguard of Protestantism in Northern Europe. During World War II Archbishop Eidem had been in contact with other international church leaders, among them the archbishop of Canterbury, preparing for ecumenical efforts towards reconciliation and cooperation, as soon as the war would end.

It is in itself an indication of the strains on inter-Nordic relationships at this historic turning point that Archbishop Eidem's well-meant intentions were met by strict rejection from his colleague in Norway, Bishop Erling Berggrav. Whereas Sweden had remained neutral and therefore untouched by the warfare, Norway had been occupied by Nazi Germany, and the Norwegian church had been thrown into a church struggle in 1942. Bishop Berggrav had been the leader of the opposition against the suppression by Quisling's government, an achievement for which he, his country, and his church had won international reputation.

However, Norway's sufferings during the war were counterbalanced by the admiration the nation received after 1945. Sweden's advantages as an island of undisturbed prosperity in an ocean of unrestrained military savagery were now darkened by feelings of suspicion, especially from the Norwegians, claiming that Sweden's neutrality had been anything but idealistic. Instead, their neighbors to the west considered Sweden's so-called neutrality to be the result of shallow deliberation, ensuring short-term gains for their country at the expense of their neighbors. Such feelings were nourished especially by the bitter feelings of Norwegians, because Sweden had been selling iron ore to Nazi Germany and permitting military transport for Hitler's army to pass through Swedish territory. Against this background, Berggrav was unwilling to resume inter-Nordic relationships after the war, as if it was appropriate simply to resume business as usual. He was anxious to meet with his colleagues from the Nordic sister churches, including Erling Eidem, but he was against a venue in Sweden.

Accordingly, the Danish bishop Hans Fuglsang-Damgaard was given authority to act as convenor and host at the meeting that took place in the last week of August 1945. The reports of the talks in the bishop's palace in Copenhagen reflect the feelings of joy, expressed by all the participants. This conference was for most of them their first opportunity to travel after the war. The relief of being able to go abroad after five years of isolation was further nourished by the satisfaction that the resumption of traditional Nordic ties of friendship was the first signal on the way to the return of normal conditions for international cooperation.

Accordingly the atmosphere contained joy and expectation, but, as it turned out, it also contained indignation and bitterness. Bishop Berggrav asked for permission to speak out and directed vehement criticism against his Swedish colleagues. Referring to the interpretation of Sweden's position, as it has just been indicated, he also pointed out that the Swedish bishops had failed to intervene when the bishop of Gothenburg had expressed unfair criticism of the Norwegian church in its attitude of resistance. Berggrav did not pause a second before turning towards the representatives from Finland with similar accusations. His resentment was due to the fact that Finland had followed a strategy of cooperation with Nazi Germany in order to survive in its life-and-death struggle against Soviet aggression. Berggrav could well understand the main reasons for this policy, but he resented the relationships between the Finnish church and the official church government in Berlin.

The Finns, on their part, had expected more empathy from their

Nordic colleagues, not least because they themselves had been left without support during the Winter War, in spite of preceding rhetoric about the unconditional solidarity of their Nordic sister nations.

The hosting moderator, Hans Fuglsang-Damgaard, had to mediate, a task that in itself was far from unproblematic, since the Danes had looked upon Norway with admiration while at the same time feeling ashamed on account of their own policy of cooperation with the Nazis. At the same time Fuglsang-Damgaard felt compelled to express understanding for the ambiguities that arose from Finland's position. The report mentions that all the representatives finally expressed their understanding for the specific difficulties the Finns had faced.

This disagreement had barely been settled, before a new and sensitive topic came up for discussion, this time bringing Denmark into the crossfire of criticism. The bishop of Iceland, Sigurgeir Sigurdson, blamed the Danes for having shown so little understanding of the Icelandic policy when the island had declared its national autonomy as an independent republic in 1944. The Danes had reacted with offended self-pride, showing no expression of self-criticism as a former colonial power and no empathy for the Icelandic intentions.[3]

When such an emotional day of reckoning is evaluated from an international perspective, a few comments seem appropriate. It is itself a remarkable sign of rooted friendship on a deeper level that such moments of disagreement could be revealed without causing lasting enmity. On the contrary, all the representatives recognized that it was now inevitable to give some vent to all these accumulated resentments, in order to be able to go on with other topics on their agenda. Moreover, this internal Nordic inquest was itself a necessary prelude to subsequent endeavors towards future joint international efforts. Facing the new international agenda the common Nordic identity and determination of the participants was often emphasized without the slightest indication of the previous difficulties behind the scenes.

Ecumenically the Nordic churches were given a leading role in the aftermath of World War II, an assignment they could take up only because they had themselves proved able to openly discuss their internal differences.

3. About the meeting in Copenhagen, see *Nordiske folkekirker i opbrud. National identitet og international nyorientering efter 1945*, ed. J. H. Schjørring (Aarhus: Aarhus University Press, 2001), pp. 11ff.

A Vision for Nordic Community

It may be appropriate here to include a voice from a different viewpoint, a vision concerning a commitment to a Nordic pioneering effort for the sake of European rebuilding, considered afresh against the background of the disaster of European civilization and the need for a new vision. The author was neither a church leader nor an academic theologian, but a Danish literary critic, a teacher rooted in the Grundtvigian tradition of adult education. His name was Jørgen Bukdahl.

Bukdahl was familiar with political ideas, church life, culture, and art in all the Nordic countries. Accordingly he was well equipped to present an overview of this historic heritage with the purpose of giving a precise analysis both of present challenges and future prospects. Bukdahl's style was far from that of a learned investigation, conceived in the ivory tower of a university professor. Instead, he was conscious that in his essay he should reflect popular culture, thus taking into account a basic feature of the peculiarities of Nordic culture, that is to say its anti-hierarchical, egalitarian character. To Bukdahl it is an undeniable fact that it is possible and appropriate to speak of "the North" in the singular, in the first place because careful historical orientation will clarify this expression, in the second place because recent events have elucidated the same fundamentals.

In order to enable his readers to evaluate the historical context at the point of writing, i.e., 1947, Bukdahl presents a number of preliminary remarks. For instance he poses the question, whether it is not totally misleading to speak about the values of the North at a point of history when the whole of Europe is trying to come to life again after the barbarism of the Nazi ideology, not least its racist fanaticism with its inherent claim to "Nordic" superiority and its contempt for other peoples, whether of Jewish, Slav, or Mediterranean origin. No, Bukdahl replies. Precisely because of such appalling abuse of true Nordic values, it is imperative to present a truer picture. The Nazi ideology, he maintains, was "a forceful primitivism, dressed in steel," but without even a touch of spirit or liberty. Similarly concerning nationalism, Bukdahl readily admits that it was national chauvinism that had been behind the military aggression that turned key areas of European civilization into a battlefield. But he points to the Nordic countries themselves as examples of a balanced interaction between national identity and a determination to move to a peaceful realization of international community. Either side of the dynamic correlation presupposes equal participation from the other.

National fanaticism is nothing but suppressed, unredeemed national consciousness, either turning into inward strain or outward aggressiveness. Legitimate expressions of national identity, however, will encompass a dynamic that can set free a power for magnanimous community. Bukdahl is perfectly aware that his exposition of Nordic identity may be interpreted as if it were nourished by self-pride. Self-criticism is absolutely urgent, he underscores, pointing to the values of open debate and adjustment as prerequisites for true community in society. In that sense Nordic values are far from being colored as a sentimental idyll. Referring to common images of "the North," he rejects the mistaken idea that the North could be determined only as "the homeland of the Sagas and Eddas, the romantic hyperborean, wooden churches, national costumes, folk dance, midnight sun." Instead he points to such key features as the rise of the common people to political participation, the empowerment of ordinary people, endeavors towards social justice without flagrant class division, and towards national awakening, insisting that precisely these features have implied incentives that point to international community.

Accordingly historical lessons show the importance of avoiding false alternatives and of facing necessary both-ands. Bukdahl tries to clarify this perspective through his application of the bridge as metaphor. The bridge has to rest upon pillars, reaching into firm soil. This refers to the vertical dimension of national cultures, nourished from deep roots of historical heritage. Each one of the six branches of national culture within "the North" embraces such rootedness, deepened in the course of centuries-old national history. The bridge, however, also has a horizontal dimension, the spans connecting with other nations and cultures and pointing to wider horizons.

If this metaphor is taken seriously, according to Bukdahl, it will ensure that the North will not get caught up in self-sufficiency or chauvinism. Rather, it will teach us to see "the North" in interaction with Europe as a whole. Moreover, it will safeguard an appropriate measuring rod, as we set out to estimate the individual characteristics of each one of the Nordic nations as compared with their common features and with the history of European civilization as a whole. By the same token this also implies the response to the challenge of totalitarianism, Bukdahl continues, with obvious reference to the actual circumstances in Europe in 1947. To him there can be no doubt that an unprejudiced evaluation of the history of ideas in Europe will indicate Christianity as a primordial source, but notably implying also a synthesis with the most valuable aspects both of Jewish and of Greco-Roman heritage.[4]

With hindsight, more than fifty years later, this vision may be said to reveal a poetic beauty of its own, in many ways even a prophetic tone. Yet, seen from another angle Bukdahl's vision reflects an unrealistic optimism on behalf of Northwestern Europe. The rude awakening became evident during the subsequent decades inside Europe itself, but also considering the relationship between Europe and other continents.

At the time of publication, however, Bukdahl's viewpoint was one shared by many, including ordinary citizens who did not possess his command of rhetorical eloquence. His position reflected a mainstream way of thinking in the Nordic countries, as can be proved by many pieces of evidence, a few of which will be mentioned.

The conviction of a deeply rooted heritage marked by ideals of freedom and equality, of a popular culture with everyman's access to art and poetry, of a balance between national identity and dedication to international community all indicated a close connection between church and people. In a certain sense this confidence was the logical consequence of a historically rooted conviction, one that was consequently more or less premodern, though Bukdahl personally was sufficiently educated to acknowledge the challenges of modernity. Yet, the vision, especially when shared in less elaborated versions, was bound to slide into a confrontation as the process of secularization and the decline in consciousness of tradition gained momentum soon after the war.

The fact that the Nordic countries were simultaneously pioneering in establishing a functioning welfare system led to their becoming "icons" for many other societies, not least in the southern hemisphere, when new states emerged as a result of the process of decolonization. We shall have to examine whether this status as model could remain tenable in the long run.

At this time political leaders from the Nordic countries were given the role as chairpersons and mediators in several international political organizations such as the United Nations. Similar responsibilities were con-

4. Jørgen Bukdahl, *Norden og Europa. Et Essay* (Copenhagen: Aschehoug Dansk Forlag, 1947).

ferred on Nordic church leaders and theologians in ecumenical organizations. For instance, it is a speaking evidence of the widespread expectation that the churches in the Nordic countries would prove able to act as bridge-builders in the whole process of reconciliation and rebuilding, not to mention the particular challenge of assisting the Protestant churches from the German-speaking world in seeking a constructive coexistence with the churches in the English-speaking world. This task was imperative in ecumenical organizations such as the World Council of Churches and the Lutheran World Federation, reflected for example in the fact that Professor, later Bishop Anders Nygren of Lund, Sweden, in 1947 was elected the first President of the Lutheran World Federation.

It needs to be mentioned, though with all necessary brevity, that the postwar period saw many other examples of inter-Nordic community and determination to take joint responsibility in the world outside. For instance, the "Union for the North" *(Foreningen Norden)* became a significant factor in several areas of public life, acting as a forum for inter-Nordic exchange at many levels. The folk high school movement experienced a revival with an explicit Nordic note. In sports, most competitions during the initial postwar years were arranged between Nordic participants. Students frequently conducted part of their studies at another Nordic university, and there was a constant flow of exchange between university professors.

More evidence might be added. Suffice it here to ask a critical question for the sake of balance: Why was it that such instances of Nordic community faded away after a decade or two?

Transition in the 1960s

In the sixties many churches in the western world were shaken by fundamental changes. The churches in the Nordic countries were no exception, but the dynamic of transformation took a specific contextual form, leading to a pattern of Lutheran Church order previously unseen, though certainly not to the termination of the community between Nordic churches, as will be apparent from a number of examples.

The transformation was the result of a broad range of changes, mostly originating from outside the churches themselves. Among the characteristic evidences were a higher degree of geographic mobility, which gradually reduced the importance of parish boundaries as given entities, not to speak of the weakened consciousness among parishioners regarding their tie to the parish church. Moreover, the conflict of generations had obvious repercussions for the churches, a fact that could be observed at the assemblies held by the World Council of Churches in Uppsala 1968 and the Lutheran World Federation in Evian two years later. The impact resulted in new forms of conference with less influence given to the inner circle of authorized officers and with greater access to the floor for grass-root representatives. The clash of confronting viewpoints was frequently accompanied by demonstrations that sometimes may have been experienced by conservatives as a fairground performance. But an investigation of deeper roots will reveal signs of a thorough transformation. It needs to be added that the official churches and faculties of theology mostly kept outside the immediate and spectacular confrontations, a tendency that was seen by some as a proof of the power of age-old church structures to resist the fashions of the day, by others as a failure to be sensitive to the necessity of adjustment.

The effects of this transition have not yet been sufficiently analyzed, but from an international perspective it seems obvious that precisely the Lutheran majority churches in the Nordic countries were rather unprepared to face these challenges. A possible explanation for this may be found in the fact that their preceding history had been marked by continuity, and by their belonging to societies marked by economic equality and cultural homogeneity. Hence a privileged church in a nation-state was bound to feel uncertain in encountering the rise of powerful international organizations alongside of national authorities. Equally, national churches in many cases were initially hesitant concerning cross-confessional cooperation.

Within this complex international pattern of transformation specific features can be observed in the Nordic churches.

Loosening of Traditional Ties Between Church and School

Throughout the twentieth century a development took place that led to more and more consistent breaks in the connection between church and school. This tendency is part of the common pattern also to be found in the Nordic countries, allowing for varying features in concept and timing, sometimes strikingly different from one country to the other. The common trend shows the leading role of the social democratic parties, mostly in union with other leftist political groups, demanding a school liberated from the previous guardianship of the church. Concessions were given step by step, beginning with the termination of pastoral participation in religious instruction, termination of daily prayer and proclamation, the possibility of dispensation from attending religious instruction, with subsequent steps such as equal, "objective" attention to non-Christian religions in higher class-levels. As already indicated the process mostly took place as a long-term development, without a complete discussion of its extensive implications. In the 1960s, however, the "goal" could be said to have been reached in Sweden from the point of view of the governing Social Democrats, and so a more exhaustive debate could start.

It is not possible here to address all the details of this far-reaching transformation. Our interest is restricted to the final challenge, which appeared for the churches as established churches still claiming to represent the vast majority of the population in each of the nations implied. It cannot be doubted that there was an inner logic behind the development, even a necessity when considered against the background of the full-scale dynamics of transitional forces that characterize our part of the globe. Accordingly it is a waste of energy to deplore the loss of previous clerical access to exert direct influence on the state school system. The relevant deliberation has to do with the historical perspective, and arises from the fact that the special characteristics of the Nordic societies, their homogeneity, was based upon the national churches *(folkekirker)* together with the state schools *(folkeskoler)* and the close interaction between these institutions.

Hence a new challenge for the churches has emerged since the 1960s, which with still more urgency demands a strategy for a new type of religious instruction, taking into account that the baptismal catechism has to be conceived as part of a lifelong process of learning and therefore also as comprising elementary instruction for the parents of the baptized, or better for all adults.

It should be conceded that important initiatives have been taken in this area. Yet it must be admitted for any full-scale assessment of the situation that the churches have acted without the determination to address the challenge with due seriousness. Consequently, it is a basic feature of the churches today, still allowing for a certain degree of variety, that there is discrepancy between two statements: on the one hand the status of the established churches, which are deeply rooted in the national heritage and represent the original characteristics of the population; on the other, the appalling lack of basic insight and understanding for Christian teaching on the part of a vast majority of the members of the national churches, whether due to a general indifference or to a doubt about all binding values.

Structural Adjustment Regarding Church and State

A dominant person in postwar church politics was the Danish state secretary for church affairs Bodil Koch. Her main accomplishment was her successful reorientation in the church political strategy of her party, the Social Democratic Party, to the effect that the party gave up its former long-term target of reducing religious belief to a mere conviction of the individual, "a private issue," combined with the breaking up of the state-church system. On top of her contribution to this historical change, Bodil Koch put forward a proposal in order to ensure an adjustment of the structures of the church. For instance, she pointed to the necessity of establishing better possibilities for the church to be present in the rapidly growing suburbs of the cities. Moreover, she suggested the possibility of opening up other forms of pastoral service than those restricted to the parochial system, for instance in major public or private institutions, or within the voluntary Christian organizations. Moreover, she suggested a more permanent structure for the participation of the Danish Lutheran Church in international, ecumenical institutions. However far-sighted her vision appears in retrospect, she failed in the short run. A conservative attitude among pastors and theologians proved stronger than her suggestion for a reorientation. It is true that most of the specific proposals have since been taken up and to some extent even realized, but this has taken place without any consistent re-evaluation of the whole situation. Instead the specific items of restructuring have been taken up one by one, leaving coherent conceptual reasons aside.

In the neighboring Nordic countries, however, a gradual transformation has emerged, in some cases as a result of a strategic re-assessment, in others without consistency or inner consequence, in yet others more occasionally. Nonetheless the tendency has been the same, namely to ensure a higher degree of inner self-determination for the church, its independence of a seemingly more and more omnicompetent state administration. This tendency has proved strongest in Norway and Sweden (here with emphatic attention to the purpose of ensuring equal rights for all citizens, regardless of their religious convictions and adherence to any given religious organization), but also to some extent in Finland.

At present the effects of this development seem to leave the Danish church (formerly pioneering in inventing new, liberal forms of church politics) as the most conservative of the Nordic churches in terms of the preservation of structures handed down from past decades. Accordingly it seems likely that the general similarity regarding church order will be fading in the years ahead, unless new initiatives should emerge.

Weakening of Nordic Community in Theology and Ecumenism

In theology the period since World War II has been marked by a gradual shift of orientation for Nordic theology. A dominant dependency on German Protestant theology has been replaced by a growing influence from various types of theology in the English-speaking world. Such characterization needs to be considered with due attention to modification, in the first place because many forms of Nordic theology before and after 1945 were still marked by specific national characteristics, secondly because there had been important connections with theology and church-life in the English-speaking world before 1945, and thirdly because important ties with German branches of tradition persisted after 1945. Allowing for such premises, however, there is indeed a transition. An illustrative incident of the process was the first international conference for Luther-research, held in Aarhus in 1956. The venue was chosen because a local professor, Regin Prenter, an internationally acknowledged representative of Lutheran systematic theology, was chairperson for the theological commission in the Lutheran World Federation. In a certain sense the secretary of the same commission, Vilmos Vajta, could be said to represent a similar tradition. He had come to Lund from his homeland Hungary in order to write his doctoral dissertation under the guidance of the distinguished Luther-specialists at the faculty in Lund, Anders Nygren and Ragnar Bring. Together with Gustaf Aulén and Gustaf Wingren these theologians became internationally influential, often mentioned under the heading, the "Lund school." Vajta's topic was "Luther on Worship: An Interpretation" (English version 1958), a monograph that became a standard work in the postwar period. Seen in a wider perspective it was evident that Scandinavian Luther-interpretation was reckoned as distinctly different from that of German Lutheranism, and yet in permanent interaction with it. But it was the call of the hour in 1956 to reintegrate German Luther-research into the international discourse, and undoubtedly the Scandinavian colleagues were considered well equipped to guide this mediation. Accordingly, from then onwards, international Luther-research could only be carried forward with equal attention to the German- and the English-speaking world, with the Nordic countries in a mediating position as bridge-builders. As years went by, however, English was gaining momentum as the lingua franca, even within Lutheran theology. This transformation became most markedly obvious in Sweden. For one thing, the Lund-school from about 1960 onwards gradually lost its influence inside Sweden, whereas a new paradigm, mainly coming from Uppsala, became influential with a radical turn away from Lutheran systematic theology in the classical sense to a more descriptive theological method, more connected with religious science. Second, confessional orthodoxy was forced to retreat. This development in Sweden had no direct parallel in the other Nordic countries, but its dynamic was one indication among others of the fact that the earlier ties within theology were growing weaker. As a general tendency, it was difficult to identify a common understanding of the mutual connection between confessional identity and ecumenical participation. The Danish church, especially, has been hesitant about ecumenical fellowship, a fact against which the international background has proved significant, since the ecumenical dialogues came into the center of theology from about 1970 onwards. While the ecumenical initiatives earlier had been conceived with the participation of leading Nordic representatives, and indeed without important reservations, it has subsequently become a contested topic, at the point when ecumenism was claiming a constituent responsibility for the church universal. Conservative theologians have protested against the alleged domination by leftist political attitudes in the World Council of Churches and have formed a conservative, confessional counterweight. Until the late 1980s the Danish church had no official board to ensure its participation in the ecumenical movement, and when finally an ecumenical board was established it was accompanied by repeated reservations. Suffice it therefore to state that defining the proper balance between confessional orthodoxy and ecumenical openness in the Nordic churches has become a highly sensitive issue.

Concluding Remarks

This historical sketch has led us to a critical assessment of the Lutheran churches in the Nordic countries. Considering their privileged status as majority churches in prosperous countries with a rich cultural heritage nothing but an unvarnished evaluation would be appropriate.

We have seen that as national churches they have contributed substantially to the growth of the Nordic community, leading subsequently also to international and ecumenical involvement. This general direction, however, has to be conditioned by two qualifications. In the first place, it needs to be repeated, as we have already indicated in the case-studies, that there have been considerable variations regarding the interaction of the countries involved, and regarding the individual countries during the course of the last century. In the second place we have stated that the common identity reached a maximum in the aftermath of World War II, in spite of painful internal disagreements, or perhaps it would be more correct to say because it proved possible to get beyond these conflicting themes and look forward jointly to new challenges ahead. Yet, since the 1960s the common Nordic identity seems to have been caught in a process of decline.

Among the symptoms we have seen are

a. tardiness concerning the adjustment of church structures to changes in the societies
b. failure to maintain a common course regarding ecumenical involvement
c. failure to face the challenges arising from growing multiplicity, not least cultural and ethnic.

Having taken the critical aspects of the assessment into account it is relevant to take stock of the treasures that have been preserved.

At present the national churches in the Nordic countries have specific prospects and responsibilities, especially viewed from an international perspective. This is true, because the societies in our part of the world are marked by so many signs of rapid change and such a loss of tradition that it is both a gift and an obligation for the churches to be havens for the historic heritage. Efforts towards this end are urgently needed, and the task seems realistic especially in countries where majority churches have been an essential part of that heritage.

Moreover, precisely because they are privileged, the Lutheran majority churches should be able to face the task of opening a dialogue with people of other faiths, whether these are living inside the nation in question or in other parts of the world. In a situation of globalization it is more necessary than ever for the churches to take seriously their obligation to be contextual in the positive sense of the word and at the same time to be conscious of belonging to the church universal.

Lutheran Ecclesiologies Today — Custodians of the Past or Guides to the Future?

ELSE MARIE WIBERG PEDERSEN

> I therefore, the prisoner in the Lord, beg you to lead a life worthy of the calling to which you have been called, with all humility and gentleness, with patience, bearing with one another in love, making every effort to maintain the unity of the Spirit in the bond of peace. There is one body and one Spirit, just as you were called to the one hope of your calling, one Lord, one faith, one baptism, one God and Father of all, who is above all and through all and in all.
>
> Ephesians 4:1-6

In the Transit Hall

In this article I shall take my point of departure mainly in studies done by the Lutheran World Federation (LWF), of which 133 Lutheran churches covering all continents are now members. Although the LWF does not comprise all Lutheran churches in the world, this meets two ends. First, the LWF is the closest one comes to approaching the question of Lutheran ecclesiologies. Second and not least, Viggo Mortensen was the director of the LWF's Department for Theology and Studies from 1991 to 1999, a period in which he reformulated the social-ethical agenda of theological and ecclesiological issues. Here problems such as ethnicity, environmental ethics and bioethics, peace, and justice were taken under scrutiny as a way to developing well-structured societies and churches that would also take seriously the role of women.

In this same period Lutheran churches around the world asked themselves what it means to be Christians, and specifically what it means to be Lutheran Christians? What should be accentuated as special characteristics of a Lutheran church on the threshold of the third millennium? The Lutheran churches all over the world have been undergoing a major transition process due to a variety of factors, and, most importantly, they have finally realized the fact that they are different, embedded in different societies as they are. Thus, the so-called Third World postcolonial countries are first and foremost, at varying pace, changing from conservative and feudal to modern and democratic societies. European countries having, allegedly, already made the change from Christian to secular societies, are now facing a rapid change into multireligious and multiethnic societies and, as a reaction to that, perhaps going through an actual de-secularization. North Americans, on their turn, are facing the competitiveness of an overwhelmingly intensive market orientation in an increasingly secularized society. All in all, great social or cultural changes are bringing pressure to the role of the church in society, and the church is challenged to react.

But the church is not challenged only by the immediate society in which it is located. The global community is also affecting what happens in the church. In different ways all the Lutheran churches are influenced by globalization that, positively or negatively, is reflected in their view of the world as a market and in their attempts to work out new models of being church. In the North Atlantic countries Christianity has been superseded by the multireligious supermarket, perhaps because in its highly secularized form it has left a vacuum to be filled. This has of course to do with globalization's easy flow of communication. Furthermore, Christianity's move from the so-called First World to the so-called Third World, where the radical evangelical movements are rapidly growing and thus challenging the "old" churches, has put the Lutheran churches on the alert. Particularly the European continent, the cradle of the Reformation and part of two millennia of Christian church history, seems to be emptied of its Christian ecclesiological essence, whereas there is some kind of spiritual surplus to be detected in the postcolonial continents that were old Christianity's and Lutheranism's mission fields. Is all this a strong reaction to something? It appears as such, and it should be left open as to whether the picture will change again in the near future. Perhaps it already has begun to change in Europe after September 11, 2001, in the form of a sincere re-Christianization in response to the claims of other cultures and religions. At any rate, these ongoing transformations remind us that the world really is one, and that actions and movements in one part of the world affect what happens elsewhere.

Whatever their type of transition, all Lutheran churches seem to see it from the perspective of crisis. It is important, though, to remember that such transitory situations are not new phenomena but are inevitable changes of an ever moving world. I believe that the Lutheran churches have finally realized that the "attacks" of new times are not disappearing whimsies but remaining facts, and that is exactly why they now view their transformation under the perspective of crisis. For when the process of transition is taken up positively and seriously as a crisis, namely as a time for decision and change, then the churches begin to take seriously the Protestant principle *ecclesia reformata semper reformanda.* Then the churches are no longer simply custodians of the past or the *status quo* but make in-depth endeavors to be critical and timely in such a way that they are able to point to the future of God.

Communio — Vision or Reality?

From its initiation the Lutheran World Federation in various ways has given attention to finding the theological balance between identifying and maintaining the Lutheran tradition and the more recent critical concerns, mediating between continuity and change. The LWF being first, at Lund in 1947, defined as "a free association of Lutheran churches," the organization found its common doctrinal basis in "the confessions of the Lutheran Church, especially in the Unaltered Augsburg Confession and Luther's Catechism, a pure exposition of the Word of God."[1] However, after much consideration and inspiration from the churches of the Southern hemisphere and from ecumenical circles, the LWF moved towards an ecclesiology centered on the concept of *communio.* After ongoing discussions from 1979, the LWF at the Curitiba Assembly in 1990 decided to define it-

1. See Michael Root, "Affirming the Communion: Ecclesiological Reflection in the LWF," in *From Federation to Communion: The History of the Lutheran World Federation,* ed. J. H. Schjørring, P. Kumari, and N. Hjelm (Minneapolis: Fortress Press, 1997), p. 217.

self (in article III.1. of the new constitution) as "a communion of churches which confess the triune God, agree in the proclamation of the Word of God and are united in pulpit and altar fellowship."

The question, also posed in the ecumenical context, was and is now what it means to be a communion. The LWF had to ask how these very different Lutheran churches could be a visible communion. Considering that the churches were even more diverse in the 1990s than they had been in 1947 yet claiming deeper unity, what were the identity and self-understanding of the member churches that justified such a claim to unity? To answer these important questions, a series of ecclesiology projects were launched. Following a more theoretical and dogmatic study on the church as communion,[2] an international team of theologians from five different continents undertook a more empirical and ecumenical study on the Lutheran churches' self-understanding.[3] Based on consultation meetings with representatives from the local and regional churches in alternately Asia, Africa, Latin America, North America, and Europe, this latter study had as its clear aim to widen the scope, so that the church as an actual and acting institution was seen in relation to the surrounding society: What part does the church play within a given society? Does the Lutheran church, wherever it is, understand itself as a communion, i.e., as a grouping of people who hold something in common, so much so that it acts as a community? Furthermore, if that is the case, does it hold that communal something up against the society in which it is placed, in a counter-cultural perception (church as salt); or does it rather hold that communal something as a calling to be like the society in which it is placed (church as mirror)? The findings of this work led to the conclusion that all churches reflected a lack of deeper and more comprehensive understanding of communion, the church's communion often reduced to mere ethnicity and nationality, while the mission and *diaconia* of the church were understood without the vision of *communio*.

In light of the multicultural and pluralistic societies that the Lutheran churches worldwide are part of, the significance put on ethnicity, a cultural or national uniformity, at the expense of the universal gospel and its promise that Christ will be all in all, was a rather shocking discovery to

2. *The Church as Communion: Lutheran Contributions to Ecclesiology,* ed. Heinrich Holze (Geneva: Lutheran World Federation Documentation, 42/1997).

3. *Between Vision and Reality: Lutheran Churches in Transition,* ed. Wolfgang Greive (Geneva: LWF Documentation, 2001).

make. Not least, if we take in consideration that there is a coherence between the modern pluralistic society and the priesthood of all believers claimed by Protestants. In many ways the principle of the priesthood of all believers has been a contributory factor in promoting the claims for freedom of religion, freedom of conscience, and freedom of speech in modern society. Thus, without pretending to explicate the complex *Wirkungsgeschichte,* the Protestant claim to freedom of conscience is reflected in modernity's individualism and democracy in contrast with any type of theocratic feudalism. Furthermore, in a certain way Protestantism anticipated the pluralistic society as it rapidly split up itself in a variety of denominations and confessions, a process that again promoted the claims to freedom of religion as well as the individualization and privatization of Christianity. What we witness now is that, while defending their pure doctrines against each other, the various denominations and confessions forgot the unity, apostolicity, and the catholicity of Christianity. In their preoccupation with confessionalism, the Protestant churches, Lutherans notwithstanding, overlooked the positive side of their heritage of pluralism. I see it as a vital question whether the churches should take up in an integrative fashion the pluralism, inherent in Christianity from its genesis and reinstated in Protestantism, as their task. What if the churches, instead of regretting and condemning pluralism and individualism, took up the challenge in responsible dealings with the richness of life and the plurality of values? If acting in such an integrative fashion by opting for the freedom of a Christian, the churches would be able to take seriously the people of God as a communion of responsible individuals.

In the following, I shall explicate one point where I find Lutheran ecclesiology to have moved considerably forward towards, though not having reached the goal of, full communion. I am thinking of the inclusion of women in the ordained ministry, which was perhaps the most significant achievement of Lutheran ecclesiology during the twentieth century, and indeed on the part of the Christian church as a whole. By thus incorporating the other half of humanity and community into the full *communio* of the church, Lutheran churches have taken an important step towards true catholicity and are keeping the vision of faith and the idea of *communio* in its full, multidimensional sense alive.

The Gospel Came to Church

In 1530, Luther wrote to the clergy assembled in Augsburg and asked: "Are you the church? Prove it then in words and fruits!" In several of his writings as also in the Augsburg Confession, Luther expresses a strong opposition to the hierarchical feudal church that had taken God in Christ hostage while forgetting the people of God. Building on his *sola scriptura* principle, Luther pointedly emphasized the freedom and equality of all Christians. This comes particularly to the fore in his expositions of the ministry of the church, at which point he is a strong adversary of the papal church's hierarchy. Hence, one of Luther's doctrines that most positively was not only a re-enforcement of Scripture's charter of equality and freedom (Gal. 3:28) but also a principle pointing to the future was the doctrine of the priesthood of all believers. His rediscovery of this participative model of ecclesial life to which all are called to serve God and creation according to their specific gifts (1 Cor. 12–14) is central to most modern theology and ecclesiology.

On April 28, 1948, three women were ordained pastors in the Evangelical-Lutheran church in Denmark. Even though some few women had already been functioning as nonordained pastors since the 1920s (or at least "only Lutheranly" ordained, without the assistance of a bishop), this was the first time the modern Lutheran understanding of ministry was fully implemented in a large Lutheran church.[4] However important this historical event is, what attracts attention here is the preceding debate, which reflected the schism between a more Catholic understanding of tradition and ministry on the one hand, and a Lutheran understanding of Scripture and ministry on the other.[5] The opponents of women pastors, in contrast with central Lutheran principles, referred to tradition by employing such formulations as "the old church" or "the several hundreds of years of old apostolic tradition" and to "the catholic church" (including the Tridentine). When pointing to potential ecumenical problems these formulations rather functioned as an unmediated mantra, and the mainte-

4. The small Lutheran Church in the Netherlands seems to have ordained a woman already in 1929. Cf. *Lutheran World Information* (August 2000), p. 15.

5. For a more comprehensive exposition of this and the debate on women's ordination in Denmark, see *Se min kjole. De første kvindelige præster historie (See My Dress: The History of the First Women Pastors in Denmark)*, ed. Else Marie Wiberg Pedersen (Copenhagen: Samleren, 1998).

nance of an old custom overshadowed the tradition of the gospel. The proponents of women's ordination, on the other hand, pointed to the spirit of freedom and equality of the gospel, and to the Bible as a message always spoken into the concrete situations of any given time. In the words of the respected ecumenist, Bishop Valdemar Ammundsen, Galatians 3:28 is "a fundamental Christian idea" expressing that

> within the new Christian humanity, all are religiously equal without any advantages based on race, nation, social position and sex. From a Christian perspective it is desirable that outer arrangements are shaped through the interplay between this fundamental principle and the practical matters of life.[6]

Therefore such *adiaphora* as *who* can hold the ordained ministry would always be a question of time and place. That the understanding of ministry is a question of tradition more than of Scripture, and that both tradition and Scripture are matters of continuous interpretation, is manifestly stated by the professor in Old Testament (and member of the Conservative Party), Flemming F. Hvidberg. Drawing on the central Lutheran teaching of Scripture, Hvidberg underscores how the Bible is not to be read as a law book or an encyclopedia transmitting some "abstract, theoretical infallibility." The Bible is something much bigger, namely the gospel message *(kerygma)* spoken into every concrete historical time, as in biblical times so also now. Concurrently, tradition must be regulated in a timely way and not become a set of frozen, ahistorical rules allowed to block every ecclesiological renewal. Thus, according to Hvidberg, Lutherans cannot be tied to the "Catholic history of the past," but must look to the Reformation's doctrine of the priesthood of all believers that "maybe ought to be implemented in another way than it has been hitherto, for example within the area with which we are now concerned."[7] In other words, to be true to

6. Letter of October 21, 1924; Archive of the Danish Parliament.

7. Parliamentary speech on January 10, 1947, in Parliamentary Proceedings 1946-47, col. 2031-42. See also Augsburg Confession (AC) 7 and 15, *Apologia* 7-8 and 28 on traditions versus Scripture. In the latter article on ecclesiastical power, the usually diplomatic Melanchthon sharpens the argument when he strongly emphasizes that "human traditions are useless as acts of worship, and that therefore neither sin nor righteousness" depends upon such matters, and that imposing such traditions invented by bishops is a burdening of the church and making "a trial of God" (Acts 15:10). The climax of his argument against the

tradition the church and its doctrines have to change all the time, otherwise it does not consist of living stones but fossilizations.

From the Danish debate on women's ordination, at its height from 1918 through statutory legislation in 1947 until the first official ordinations in 1948, it is important to note the central part played by the gospel. Theologically this should be seen in the wake of the rediscovery of Luther's writings, and ecclesially in the aftermath of two world wars. The shocks of these two wars, and the soul-searching they necessitated, forced Europeans to change their worldview considerably, often influencing both state and church polity. In the first half of the twentieth century, it had become increasingly apparent that democracy had to be further developed, embracing full acknowledgment of the people as a whole, irrespective of sex and class, as responsible citizens and as responsible and responsive church members.

What was at stake ecclesiologically was the message of both liberty and equality central to the gospel. As to equality, stress was put on the equality of all baptized believers and the coherent Lutheran understanding of baptism as the true ordination, thereby liberating the ordained ministry from its Babylonian captivity to an exclusively sacramental understanding of ordination tied to a hierarchy of especially sacral males *(officium sacerdos)* safeguarding salvation to the almost dispensable laity.[8] Hence, to accentuate the egalitarian principle of Scripture, the ordaining bishop, Hans Øllgaard, on April 28, 1948, preached on the empty tomb, on the women who were the first witnesses to Christ's resurrection and who were thereafter commissioned to pass on the testimony of Christianity. The bishop concluded by poignantly citing the New Testament's charter of freedom: "There is no longer Jew nor Greek, there is no longer slave or

---

Confutation, that what is central to the church is the Word of God which is "efficacious when it is delivered by men" (per homines [not *vires*] efficax esse), is accompanied by this citation from Paul: "Stand fast in the freedom with which Christ has set you free, and do not submit again to a yoke of slavery" (Gal. 5:1). Melanchthon concludes that even ordinances ordained by the apostles were changed by time. See *Bekenntnisschriften der Evangelisch-Lutherischen Kirche* (Göttingen: Vandenhoeck & Ruprecht, 1979), p. 401.

8. For Luther's understanding of ministry, see for example *De captivitate Babylonica ecclesiae praeludium (On the Babylonian Captivity)* (1520), WA 6, 484-574; *Dass eine christliche Versammlung oder Gemeinde Recht und macht habe, alle Lehre zu urteilen und Lehrer zu berufen, ein und ab zu setzen, Grund und Ursach aus der Schrift (That a Christian Gathering or Congregation Has the Right and Power to Judge All Doctrine and Call, Install and Oust Ministers, Grounded on Scripture)* (1523), WA 11, 401-17; *De instituendis ministris (On Ministry)* (1523), WA 12, 180.

free, there is no longer male and female: for all of you are one in Christ Jesus" (Gal. 3:28). The gospel had come to church, as one of the ordained women so felicitously remarked.[9]

As to freedom, what became the absolutely decisive pivotal point for the implementation of female ordination was the freedom and responsibility of the parishioners (or congregations) to call and elect not only a male but also a female pastor. In other words, it was a matter of distributing power to all church members, ensuring their true participation in *communio* and entrusting all baptized believers with the freedom to call pastors as well as to become pastors through the right calling (the *rite vocatus* of AC 14). The gospel had come to church, and the Lutheran understanding of ministry as a *ministerium verbi,* not tied to the person in office but to the Word of God, was taken seriously in a Lutheran church after some 400 years.

One Ministry of the Whole People of God

Since then a growing number of Lutheran churches have followed this path towards full *communio,* also in ministry. Denmark was followed by Sweden in 1958, by Norway in 1961, by the Lutheran Church of America and the American Lutheran Church (now together the ELCA) in 1970, Brazil in the 1970s, and by Iceland in 1982 and Finland in 1992 — to mention but a few. Of 133 member churches in 2001, forty do not ordain women, whereas six churches are discussing ordaining women and four, while not ordaining women, accept ordained women from abroad. Furthermore, women are being elected bishops by (slowly) increasing numbers.

However, there is a long way to full equality when we regard the Lutheran churches as a whole. The numbers mentioned above, and the ecclesiology study done from 1997 to 2000,[10] show that too many churches still disregard their female members and treat them as secondary creatures only to be tolerated as lay persons or, when they ordain women pastors, regard them as not being on a par with men. This situation prompted the LWF to take up the question of women and the ministry of the church as

9. Johanne Andersen, "Som vi oplevede det. Erindringsbilleder" (As We Experienced It: Images of the Memory), in *Se min kjole* (see above note 5), p. 233.

10. *Between Vision and Reality: Lutheran Churches in Transition* (see above note 3).

an extremely important and urgent issue in the inter-Lutheran and ecumenical discussion on communion.[11] Thus, back in 1983 the LWF published a report affirming the Augsburg Confession's article 5 on the ministry of word and sacrament, the ordained ministry having its origin in Christ or God: there is but one ministry and vocation of the church, and in a Lutheran perspective "the pastors perform their ministry of word and sacrament as *instruments* of Christ." Through this formulation the understanding of ministry as a Christ representation (the Roman Catholic concept of *in persona Christi* being claimed to demand only male representation) is translated into the much more comprehensive understanding of ministry as an *instrument* of and for Christ. In order to prevent a total clericalization of the church and a total sacralization of ministry at the expense of an ethically conceptualized ministry, the old definitions of church as "a holy priesthood" that is "to offer spiritual sacrifices acceptable to God through Jesus Christ" (1 Pet. 2:5) and of the people (the term *laity* derives from the Hebrew for people, *laos*) as "a royal priesthood" (1 Pet. 2:9) are reinstated. The logical question therefore is: If the whole people of God, ordained through baptism, are not the instruments of Christ, who then?[12]

In 1984, the Assembly in Budapest, based on these study reports on the understanding of ministry in the member churches, decided to keep ministry considerations a programmatic concern in the LWF. Two goals were set: (1) to urge member churches that do not ordain women to take steps toward such action, and (2) to urge member churches that do ordain women to enlarge equality in service. When the LWF made the theological concept *communio* a Lutheran hallmark at the Curitiba Assembly in 1990, it stood even more to reason that a central factor in this relation was the question of ordination only among males. Expressed differently, it became glaringly clear that the ordination of women is intrinsic to a "*communio* ecclesiology" constituted through baptism if it wants to transcend the level of paying mere lip-service.

11. See "Lutheran Understanding of the Episcopal Office," "Women in the Ministries of the Church," and "The Lutheran Understanding of Ministry, LWF Studies (Geneva: Lutheran World Federation, 1983). These works were strongly inspired by the "Lima Declaration," *Baptism, Eucharist and Ministry,* Faith and Order Paper 111 (Geneva: World Council of Churches, 1982) that — together with the previous Accra paper (Geneva, 1974) which made the question of women's ordination a *status confessionis* — gave the Lutheran churches their further ecumenical impetus.

12. "The Lutheran Understanding of Ministry." See above.

In 1993, the Lutheran World Federation therefore published a study report on ministry, focusing on the much debated ministries of women and bishops. The report very clearly states that there is no need of developing a specific doctrine of ministry for women. Lutherans already have a theology on the one ministry, the participative and inclusive notion of the priesthood of all believers, founded on the doctrine of justification through faith, baptism being the constitutive factor:

> Lutherans do not have or need to develop a theology of female ministry. Rather we have a theology of ordained ministry developed in relation to an understanding of the ministry of the whole people of God and grounded in the Reformation understanding of justification through faith. The question of who may be ordained arises only after we agree on the theology of ministry. The primary question must then be: is there any basis in our theological understanding of ordained ministry which prevents us from ordaining any baptized person who has the needed gifts and whom we are convinced is called by God? On the basis of our present understanding of Scripture and of the gospel, we are convinced that the ordained ministry must be open to both men and women.[13]

Carrying the concept of communion constituted through baptism beyond the convenience of abstraction, the LWF report goes straight to the core and questions any separations within the church based on social and cultural distinctions. In keeping with 1 Peter 2:5-9, Romans 12:1, and 1 Corinthians 12, the message is that in any church *communio* in which baptism plays a significant role, such distinctions, particularly the distinction leading to an exclusively male ordination, must be problematized. In accordance with the arguments for women's ordination found in the Danish debate, the report emphasizes Christ's reflection of the value system of his time, Galatians 3:28 as the grand charter of freedom (expressing the total theology of Paul and the other New Testament writers), and the mission of the church, its task to preach the gospel, as decisive factors that all point to an inclusive and open understanding of the ordained ministry evident from the "present understanding of Scripture."

Scripture being the matrix, one should also be aware that in relation

13. *Ministry, Women, Bishops,* LWF Studies (Geneva: Lutheran World Federation, 1993), p. 12.

to the question of female ordination the *sola scriptura* principle can be an impasse. Therefore it is imperative that churches make endeavors to find the ecclesiological and sociological reasons for actually ordaining women rather than finding biblical reasons for not doing so, not least because these reasons seem to be justified by an appeal to prevailing cultural values.[14] The 1993 report does not consider this problem. However, what is particularly liberating about this report is the fact that it lifts up the debate of female ministry from the traditionally and culturally embedded convictions, and places it within the dialectics between history and eschatology. Precisely because the church is an eschatological reality existing in this world as a sign of God's kingdom, and because it is given the mission to witness to that kingdom in word and deed in this world, we must already now break down the barriers contradicted by the kingdom of God. Although we must not confuse the church with the kingdom, it is nonetheless illegitimate to postpone the eschatological dimension of the church to some fluffy otherworldly future. For God's kingdom already has broken into history through the incarnation of Christ who so manifestly preached the breaking down of old barriers, and through the sending of the Holy Spirit to all the world. Therefore, barriers such as race, class, economic status, caste, or sex, all contradictions of the human community, should have no place in a church understanding itself as a sign of God's kingdom. On the contrary, it is imperative that the church challenge such hinderings. The great achievement of this argument is that, in a sober theological way, it inverts the well-known objection to equality within the church — that Galatians 3:28 is to be understood as having validity only in God's kingdom, not in this world's church. No, says the report, this objection is false if the church, truly eschatologically understood, is instituted as the sign of the kingdom. This does not mean that there are no sexual (biological) distinctions, but these are on par, created by God as they are, and should as such creational distinctions be welcomed in the church as a gift and a blessing to all humanity rather than treated as a curse put on half of humanity.

What really characterizes the "only-half-of-humanity" party's argument for nonordination of women, merely implied by the LWF report, is its having stiffened in a rigid distinction between history and eschatology, on the one hand, and in a blurred identification of the biological sex (fe-

14. This was the forceful insight of the 1983 report "Women in the Ministries of the Church." See above.

male) with a fixed ontological and cultural gender (woman), on the other hand. Away in the "only-half-of-humanity"'s theology is the distinction between creation and fall, between the godly creation of two different sexes and the human fall of both sexes equally. Away are the sacramental and eschatological dimensions of the whole *communio* of all believers as a body consisting of members with so many creational and spiritual differences (Rom. 12 and 1 Cor. 12). The authors of the 1993 report, however, accentuate the fact that a genuine and contemporary Lutheran ecclesiology requires the gifts of both sexes in the ordained ministry: "A church which today limits its ordained ministry to males blurs its nature as eschatological sign." This statement is further emphasized by the following unequivocal statement on the ecumenical implications of a Lutheran understanding of the ministry of all believers:

> Any ecumenical conversation involving Lutherans about the church or its ministry will have to face squarely the fact that when another Christian World Communion recognizes Lutheran ministries, it will mean recognizing ministries exercised by both women and men.[15]

Finally, in accordance with its forerunner, the 1983 report, it is stressed that precisely in light of the Lutheran emphasis on the one office of ministry, the integration of women in the church should also include the office of bishop. Once the ordination of women has been implemented, there are no further in-principle questions to be raised.

Backlash — Two Scriptures, Three Successions

In spite of the promising steps taken by the LWF and most of its member churches since the late 1940s, we still witness opposition to recognizing women's participation in full communion, and, as mentioned earlier, the LWF still receives members who do not ordain women. On an in-depth examination of the arguments against the ordination of women employed by this opposition, it is very difficult to find any theologically tenable substance.[16] It is almost intrinsic to the question of women's ordination that

15. *Ministry, Women, Bishops*, p. 17.

16. In 1994 the Lutheran Church of Australia became an associate member of the

the sober theological arguments to be found in other areas of theology seem to vanish into non-theological considerations.

One might ask: Why does the debate on ministry completely change in character depending on what sex is in question? Often, the very moment the term *woman* is mentioned, the debate is no longer about the in-principle meaning of ministry, its essence and functions, but exactly about the *who* of ministry — and this in a Lutheran church to which the person in ministry should be without importance. It becomes less interesting to discuss the theological content of ministry than to discuss an alleged inferiority and marginal position of women in relation to ministry. The focus is moved from ecclesiology and theology to a highly debatable anthropology, according to which males constitute a particularly favored race that really has to complete the work of creation and salvation which God apparently was only able to do half of. This is a dangerous theology that makes the male God and God male while reducing God's creational and salvific order to male chauvinism.

As stated earlier, the arguments by the opponents of women's ordination are usually claimed to be founded on *the* Scripture and even more so on *the* tradition, both perceived as absolute and immutable categories. However, this perception soon blurs and in reality the two categories are intermingled with each other as also with other factors. I shall now show how such an "absolute" understanding of Scripture and tradition leads, not to *sola scriptura,* but to two lines of Scripture, and not to a live and continually changing tradition, but to at least two or rather three frozen traditions of apostolic succession. First, scripturally perceived there is the fact that a strictly Lutheran understanding of Scripture is guided by a total understanding of the New Testament gospel which, in Luther's words, is "a talk about Christ, that he is the son of God and has become man for our sake, is dead and risen, made Lord of all things."[17] According to Luther, there is but one gospel, though written by many apostles, and the four different gospels as well as the various epistles are poorly understood if they

---

LWF. In this church, in 2000, a resolution to ordain women was narrowly defeated at the church's national convention despite the fact that a two-thirds majority of its theological commission in the preparation had recommended there being no theological barrier to such an ordination. Cf. *Lutheran World Information* (August 2000), p. 15. This is fully in line with the Danish debate (see above) where the theological consultants saw no theological hinderings whatsoever to the ordination of women.

17. Luther, *Ein kleyn unterricht, was man in den Evangeliis suchen und gewarten soll* (1522), WA 10, I:1, 9. (My trans.)

are read as law books. This is the *sola scriptura* principle, to read the New Testament as one gospel telling the story about Christ. By contrast, the opponents to women's ordination hold a *sola pars scriptura* principle, a particular reading of Scripture according to which only a certain compilation of Bible citations has validity for women, particularly Genesis 2:18; 1 Corinthians 11:7 and 14:34; Ephesians 5:22; and Titus 2:5 — and indeed by allegedly substantiating female inferiority and a coherent exclusion from pastoral ministry. On the other hand, for males quite another compilation of Bible citations has validity, particularly Genesis 2:16-17 and Genesis 3; Galatians 2:9; Ephesians 5:22-33; and James 3:1, all claimed to give full divinity, the full Christ representation, to males and hence the exclusive right to the ordained ministry.

The appeals to these citations are not only partial but also very problematic, taken totally out of their context as they are. They do not convey any salvific core, and sometimes they even contradict each other, as for example Paul's apparent prohibition of women's speech in church (1 Cor. 14:34) in contrast with the charter of equality and freedom (Gal. 3:28) and his clear assumption that women actually do say prayers and prophesy (1 Cor. 11:5). Consequently, 1 Corinthians 14 cannot simply be understood as implying an in-principle denial of women's active participation in the worship of the church. Furthermore, it must be stressed that such an in-part reading of Scripture, without the gospel as the guiding rule, logically results in two lines of Scripture reading: one law for males and another law for females.

Second, from a strictly Lutheran theological perspective, ordination is not a sacrament and not absolutely necessary for ministry, although a pastoral ministry is recommended for the sake of order (so for instance AC 5). As has already been explicated, the concept of priestly ministry in a Lutheran context derives from baptism and thus applies to all Christians. It is the ministry of the Word, independent of the person who preaches. Therefore it is a backlash in relation to Luther's understanding of ministry as well as to the *ecclesia semper reformanda* when Lutherans give specific claims to ordination — and even more so when claim is made to a specific ordination for males. If such specific ordination for males, closed to female pastors, should be implemented, the result would be two types of ordination totally detached from baptism. Let me illustrate through an example from Denmark in the 1990s. In a letter to the bishops a small group of conservative theologians demanded a special, sacramentally conceived ordination and the freedom to "not in act [the handshake of *koinonia/communio* in Gal. 2:9] recognize the ordination of female pastors," whom they consider "heterodox" along with "the bishops and others who call women." It is vital that we notice the texture of this claim and its justification. Not only is the claim diametrically opposite to the Reformation's understanding of ordination. Also the justification of it, with its allegation of apostasy, is more in line with Donatism than with AC 7 and 8. When the group, as we can see, converts the freedom of conscience to the freedom not to recognize fellow Christians, and continues by terming the ordination of women an interruption of the apostolic succession of the old church, we reach the point of absurdity. The group totally ignores the fact that the Evangelical-Lutheran church in Denmark (plus in Norway and Iceland) had already broken with a historic episcopal succession in 1536, while holding apostolicity to belong to the whole church through the gospel. The aim is quite clearly that of obtaining a "higher" ministry freed from female pollution, and would in reality be the reintroduction of an ecclesial hierarchy not to be taken as a parallel to the threefold ministry of bishop, priest, and deacon. Hence, what these conservative theologians propose is that, if they must tolerate a ministry for women, the ordination of women should be to a subordinate ministry of deacons solely, without the right to administer sacraments.[18] The logical result of such a position is that we would have at least three lines of succession, hierarchically ordered: one of historic episcopal succession, a second of "orthodox" Lutheran males, and a third of "heterodox" males and females.

I have spent time and space on this problem because the attitudes sketched can be detected in various forms in recent ecumenical texts ratified by Lutherans who seek *communio* with other confessions. Thus, in 1993 another reminder that women are considered a problem in relation to ministry was published. The otherwise beautifully designed *Porvoo Common Statement* between the Anglican and Lutheran churches in Britain and Ireland and in the Nordic and Baltic countries has a flaw. Thus the Joint Declaration *per se*[19] does not mention female ministry, but the com-

18. See E. M. W. Pedersen, "Når præsten er 'køn'. Om de såkaldt teologiske argumenter i debatten om kvindelige præster" ("When the pastor is 'sex/y.' On the so-called theological arguments in the debate about women pastors), in *Se min kjole*, pp. 206-14.

19. See *Together in Mission and Ministry: The Porvoo Common Statement with Essays on Church and Ministry in Northern Europe*, ed. David Tustin and Tore Furberg (London: Church House Publishing, 1993), pp. 30-31.

ments to one of its paragraphs unfortunately do, and not in an overwhelmingly sophisticated way as I shall demonstrate.

The purpose of the statement is to obtain common understanding, a closer communion, and the pursuit of a wider unity through the acceptance of one another's ministries, especially that of bishop, without reordination. All in all the statement *per se* endeavors to de-dramatize the battle of differing theories of episcopacy and the coherent question of the apostolic succession. In that respect the statement is successful, as it ties ministry to an understanding of the church as sent (apostolic), not treating ministry as an arbitrary locus but as the ministry of the church. But while claiming to open the way to a reconciled, common ministry (the administration of word and sacrament and a common confessional foundation) by "welcoming . . . persons episcopally ordained in any of our churches to the office of bishop, priest or deacon to serve, by invitation," the very formulation on ordained ministry opens the door slightly to the underlying problems as it continues: "and in accordance with any regulations which may from time to time be in force" in the receiving church (clause b.v). On the surface this sounds promising. What an openness! But what is hidden in this formulation is revealed in the commentary:

> Clause b(v) makes clear that the interchange of ordained ministers must be "in accordance with any regulations which may from time to time be in force." This implies a realistic acceptance of certain restrictions which already apply within our communions, e.g. regarding the ministry of women bishops (and those ordained by them) or women priests in particular places . . .[20]

This is a high-priority regulation. Only thereafter follow requirements of "reasonable fluency in the local language, appropriate professional qualifications, state employment regulations, taking of customary oaths, etc." — in that priority.

At least three objections should be raised to such conditions in relation to women ordained and ordaining. First, the fact that all ministers ordained by a female bishop are included is absurd, because its logical consequence is that pastors ordained by a male bishop, but previously ordained pastor by a female bishop, are also excluded from being welcomed in the

20. *Together in Mission and Ministry*, pp. 30-31.

"open" communion. We thus witness the acceptance of, not only the threefold ministry mentioned, but indeed of a hierarchically ordered twofold, if not implicitly threefold, succession — a parallel to the aforementioned claim to specific ordination by Danish conservative theologians. The tragic irony is that the statement of openness is in a way dissolved by the comment of exclusiveness, in a certain way turning it into a *contradictio in adjectu.* Second, such a condition related to women pastors and bishops and all ministers ordained by them ought to be superfluous in a statement utilizing the terminology of acceptance, respect, invitation, and welcoming. However realistic the exclusion of women is in certain churches such as the Lutheran church in post-1989 Latvia (and to some extent Estonia), why does a joint declaration between churches of which the majority actually do ordain women take such considerations? No doubt, such churches will simply not invite ordained women. So why make it a matter of a declaration claimed to seek communion? In a declaration obliging itself to contribute "jointly to ecumenical efforts of others," what about the communion of the local church and its efforts to reflect catholicity?

Third, it is disgraceful that (still on the threshold to the third millennium) the sex of the ordained minister or bishop stands out as more important than something so important as the appropriate qualifications of a minister. At any rate, it is highly questionable in a statement seeking to think ministry positively anew as it does, and certainly in conflict with its aim. Hence in the very "Foreword" to chapter IV: "In seeking to unlock our churches from limited and negative perceptions, this chapter spells out a deeper understanding of apostolicity, of the episcopal office, and of historic succession as 'sign,'" linking it again to a mission context.[21] But by virtue of the priority of conditions (to b.iv), ministry is again locked into limited and negative perceptions from which the statement aimed at unlocking it. Also, focus is put on a certain understanding of episcopacy and the person in office much more than on the whole people of God as communicating the gospel, lay and ordained ministry together in the totality of ministry of word and mission of the church. Consequently, the person in office is made more important than the function of office, and we can really look forward to the past. Is there no other way to true ecumenicity and full *communio?*

21. *Porvoo Common Statement,* p. 4.

The Way to True *Communio*

Lutheran churches took the most positively ecumenical step since the sixteenth century when, during the twentieth, they finally opened the ordained ministry to women and included them in full *communio.* This inclusion is a sign of full respect to all of God's creation, both as a mandate to that half of humanity who happened to be born female to be called and ordained and as a mandate to the whole people of God to call and elect. The central foundation of this inclusion has been the gospel and the unity in Christ.

In contrast with this, there has been a preoccupation with episcopal ministry in various ecumenical dialogues and statements such as the Porvoo Statement in recent years. These have taken place as serious attempts to seek ecumenicity and should of course be welcomed. However, in light of the previous exposition, one might ask if not too much weight can be put on agreements on the episcopal office on behalf of the priesthood of all believers, and on the threefold ministry *(munus triplex)* on behalf of the one ministry, that of the gospel. Many ecumenical formulations and cooperation projects have been shaped according to the slogan "toward communion in witness, church life and diacony," in practice meaning that some time (in an eschatological future) we may obtain communion when we have agreed theologically on baptism, eucharist, ministry, and justification. But first, so it goes, there must be an agreement on episcopacy and on moral (and sexual) questions, and real communion is drowned in the ocean of *adiaphora.*

What if instead communion is about the common belief in Christ and the actual witnessing, celebrating, and living together in the churches? We must consider whether a truly Lutheran and ecumenical ecclesiology is an ecclesiology from below, a church constituted as the communion of all believers and centered around word and sacrament. We must contemplate the possibility that the minimalist definition of concrete church unity formulated by AC 7 expresses a viable ecumenical ecclesiology that focuses on the absolute center of being church. Taking this center as its point of departure might strengthen communion. I contend that the more we focus on gospel and the less we focus on right doctrines and codices the sooner we can accept each other irrespective of sex, race, and class. In this respect the Lutheran churches should remain true to the Reformation standard and not give in to the trend of re-traditionalization, the point of which seems to be a commitment to the "Great Christian Tradition," as in the debate on women pastors. The danger of traditionalism is that it takes God captive of only one interpretation of the God relation. Therefore to traditionalists the people of God with all their individual differences and nuances are threatening, because to them church is an ideology, built on a set of frozen rules, the provenience and theological rationale of which are never thoroughly questioned.

If the churches are only preoccupied with being custodians of old traditions, development will stop, as history so magnificently illustrates. Thus in the Roman Catholic Church, which after Vatican II had breathed new life and hope into its members, a re-traditionalization resulted in a loss of hope for renewal.[22] Where people hoped for a female ministry they received a ban on even discussing the issue. Where people hoped for an opening of the church, they got limited communion as well as limitations in relation to other sacraments for various moral reasons. Instead of opening the church to people, frozen traditionalism yielded to an exclusion of people who derogate from the norm, in such a way that they despite baptism and belief are not welcomed as active participants in full communion. Such a view of the church as an abstract idea, whether represented by a pope and *Codex iuris canonici* or a bishop and a national church law, while having a logical consequence, results in the *de facto* estrangement of the church leadership and the disintegration of the communion.

Critique of (post)modernity with its liberty, individualism, and pluralism has become a captivating axiom for so many. However, I am not sure that liberty, individuality, and plurality are such threatening factors to the life of the church. On the contrary, the inventiveness and inspiration from multiple creative individuals might be an impulse to the church to gain new life. Of course an individualism identical with totalitarian egotism should be avoided. But individualism, a term having so many different contextual meanings, may as well be the capacity for being open to other individuals and their specific gifts so that these individuals together may form an open communion. Perhaps the real threat to the life of the churches, the reason for their crisis today, comes from within and not from the seculum. Perhaps the real threat to the churches is a totalitarian under-

22. In the following sketch I am drawing on Martin Chase, S.J., "Gudsfolket — hvem er med?" (The People of God — Who Are In?), in *Gudsfolket i Danmark* (The People of God in Denmark), ed. E. M. W. Pedersen (Copenhagen: Anis, 1999), pp. 92-93.

standing of unity or collectiveness, a yielding to ethnocentric or episcocentric uniformity that de-sacramentalizes the individual members and thus empties the church of sacramentality. Perhaps if the churches want to be taken seriously by people, they should take the *communio fidelium* seriously, giving it back its God-given sacramentality. The future of the churches lies with the whole *communio,* with the mutually responsible ministry of lay and ordained in their freedom to serve, call, and be called. In this respect, Lutheran ecclesiologies have a basis on which to build their vision.

From Solidarity to Accountability: The Responsibility of the Church to Women

MUSIMBI KANYORO

I am a lay theologian by the design of my church. Although I hold two doctoral degrees, one of which is in Ministry, and have studied the Bible and theology, I have nothing to contribute to the theology or ministry of my church simply because I am born female.

The Evangelical Lutheran Church in Kenya has defined my role and my place and bars me and all other women from preaching, reading the gospel text in the church, or even standing in the pulpit. As for contributing to theology, ministry, and leadership of the church, that is completely unthinkable in my church in the year 2001. Like other women in similar situations, I believe the church is poorer for denying to utilize my training, calling, and talent in the service of the people of God.

Yet, I am also one of the few lucky ones who have been embraced by the global church and invited to the table to participate as a theologian, preacher, Bible translator, and child of God in the ecumenical and international context. Though in the local church I am only a woman, at the ecumenical international church I have experienced immense hospitality. Here I preach to millions of men and women and teach Scripture to pastors and lay persons. I lead Bible studies for whole assemblies and I feel completely human. I realize in this context that I am a forgiven sinner, invited by God to commune with all other people and to obey the mission command of telling the gospel to all that they might indeed know that Jesus Christ is Lord.

Many of the subjects in the international work of the ecumenical movement speak directly to women because they feel directly concerned by them. In fact, most of the activities cannot be thought through, planned, or carried out without the dimension of personal involvement. This gives the way of working a vitality that constantly overcomes phases of weariness and resignation. It is this direct involvement that constitutes the vitality of feminist theology as well, because it is an immediate expression of personal suffering under humiliation, injustice, contempt, etc., and also of anger and hope in defiance of all other experiences. It dares to put visions into words in the certainty that they can become realities.

What Is Church and Where Is Church?

The two realities above locate for me the question: What is church to me and where is church to me? Surely it is easy to conclude that for each one of us, church is where we are free to experience God and to celebrate God in our lives. Church is not a structure or an institution or a group of particular people. Church is the place where Christ continually calls us to listen, to wait for the Spirit, and to go out and do the gospel works guided by the Spirit of God. Church is a place where we feel at home and yearn to go — for nurturing, for confession, and for celebration with others in our human community. Yet, I remain keenly aware of the contradictions that exist in the church universal and in individual churches such as my own, the Evangelical Lutheran Church in Kenya. How can I still claim to be part of the church that continues to reject women's God-given talents? What do I do as a woman who believes with all my heart that whatever I have and whoever I am, it is by the grace of God — and my church does not believe that with me? Where is church for me? Do I live with the church and in the church or do I leave the church?

My own experience and that of many other women have totally convinced me that there is a case for putting the church on trial for its subordination of women. When the church does not see women in their full humanity, it slips into inaction and fails to protect women from abuse and violence in society. I use this strong judiciary language not to despise the church, which I love, but to hold the church accountable. Women who love the church have for centuries asked the church to be church because we love the church and want to belong in the church. If we did not care for the church, it would be easy to leave, but women have waited in the church and dialogued with the church for ordination and participation for years because the words of the gospel invite both women and men alike. Over these years women have developed skills to dialogue with the church. Women continue to dialogue both by words and in silence.

Most important, we stay in the church because we have learned to trust the gospel of hope. Women who have felt hurt in the church stay because we hope that things can change and will change. You cannot see hope unless you believe what the Bible says about hope. "Now, hope that is seen, is not hope. For who hopes for what is seen? But, if we hope for what we do not see, we wait for it with patience" (Rom. 8:24).

In Christian theology, hope is ultimately hope in Christ. Our hope is in the Christ who for centuries we have been claiming Christ to be. The hope is that in Christ and through Christ, all of us stand a chance of somehow conquering sin and death, which cause us pain and suffering. The hope is that at some unforeseeable time, and in some unimaginable way, Christ will return with healing in his wings. But living out this hope beyond an intellectual framework is really difficult for those of us that are challenged by our experiences in the church. What should we do when we hope for justice and peace, and even make attempts to work for the elimination of injustice and to be peacemakers, only to find that the forces of war, injustice, and death are too strong to counteract? What do we do when we hope for wholeness and yet find our own lack of wholeness is so great that our vision of wholeness is distorted? Where will the courage and preparedness to face the pain of self-examination and change come from?

Subordination of Women in the Church

To be subordinate is to be considered of less value. The subordination of women is expressed in defining roles and reserving some roles as superior, as belonging to men alone. Those aspects of mission and ministry seen to be of lower value are ascribed to women. Unfortunately we as women bought into this ranking and believed indeed that our roles were of less value, even when they were the most needed life-giving elements of the church.

Everyone knows that in local congregations women share in many ways in church life, both as individuals and in groups. They are irreplaceable in many of the church's activities. We can observe some growth in confidence where many congregations have surmounted their prejudices against women in the ministry because of positive experiences with women ministers. This could serve as an encouragement from the local level to bring about more participation by women in decision-making processes at all levels.

But where there is bias, women's gifts are silenced. Women have for instance for many years raised funds for mission and yet have not been regarded as missionaries. The vocabulary in vogue for this division of roles is "gender discrimination."

Gender discrimination is alive and well in the church. Gender refers to the social relationship between women and men. Gender is shaped by religious, ethnic, economic, and cultural factors, whereas the sex of a person is defined by physical factors. What is considered to be "womanly" and "manly" varies widely between different times and places, whereas the purely biological distinction of being female or male is universal.

The Authority of Scripture

In the past thirty years women have spent much energy and scholarship in rediscovering the scriptures through reading the Bible in their own context or with their own eyes. Women have studied the Bible individually, in small groups, at church and ecumenical gatherings, and in institutions of learning such as seminaries and universities. They have discovered for themselves Jesus the Christ whose death and resurrection symbolize new life and new beginnings. This hearing and knowing God has resulted in the reconstructing of the Bible stories through literary and historical criticism. Women have brought their individual and collective imagination to bear on Scripture, reading between the lines and looking for the women lost or silenced in the pages of the Bible.

One of the stories that came to me through women's theologizing is the story of Jephthah. He was a warrior who sacrificed his only child for the sake of success (Judges 11:1-40). Dispossessed of any birthright by his half-brothers because his mother was not a legal wife, Jephthah became an outlaw. Yet the elders of his clan recognized his abilities in a time of need and made him their leader during territorial disputes with neighboring groups. So intent was he on gaining victory over the Ammonites that he vowed to God to sacrifice the first person who would greet him on his return home if he made it from the war. His military campaign was successful, but as he came to his home he was met by his daughter, his only child "coming out to meet him with timbrels and with dancing" (NRSV). Realizing immediately the implications of this action he blames her for causing him trouble rather than first accepting responsibility for the vow that he has made.

The honor of the vow is of greater weight than the life of his daughter. The child is ready to sacrifice herself for her father's vow and asks only that she be given two months for lamentation with her companions. "So there arose an Israelite custom that for four days every year the daughters of Israel would go out to lament the daughter of Jephthah the Gileadite" (NRSV).

Today women are sacrificed to uphold the honor of the church fathers. This happens when churches refuse to take responsibility for the patriarchal theology that has been passed on and on for generations. It happens when churches like my own refuse to utilize our gifts and talents just because we are women and someone told them that we have a different role. It happens when theological institutions in many parts of the world refuse to teach or even refer to books written by women and from women's perspectives. It happens when feminist theology is dumped as not real theology and those who learn or teach it are not regarded highly in the church or in theological institutions.

Men and women in the church who dare to speak, read, and believe the Bible must accept that the gospel calls for radical change of our hearts and minds in order to embrace the good news of the kingdom. The vision of inclusiveness in Christ is offered in Galatians 3:28: "There is no longer Jew or Greek, there is no longer slave or free, there is no longer male and female; for all of you are one in Christ Jesus" (NRSV).

The subordination of women in society easily becomes translated into the sub-Ordination of women to ministry in the church. It is a cause for celebration that the Evangelical Lutheran Church of Denmark no longer questions (I hope) the presence of women in ordained ministry, including the office of bishop. This is a clear recognition of shared roles for men and women within the life of the church. Yet we know that this position was arrived at with considerable effort and caused many pains on the way. Ordination of women does not signify the equality of women and men, but it does symbolize the obedience of men and women to the scriptures, which point to God as the creator of both men and women.

But even when such steps have been made, assumptions made about what "all women are like" are not matched by what "all men are like," when considering how women serve in the church. At best, women are expected to be a combination of Martha and Mary when exercising ministry, and criticized for falling short of this ideal while men's inadequacies in combining the roles are easily forgiven or assisted. In Africa, until today, pastors' wives are trained to support their husbands, but not vice versa even for those churches that ordain women.

The division of work along gender lines, which is seen in society also, finds its way into the church. How many men take on the unseen maintenance of the community of the church, rather than being choir leader or pastor? What happens when they do — is this seen as something routine or something special? Does the fact that the majority of the members of a congregation are women mean that they are the main source of funds for church work? Can women have a proportionate role in deciding on how those funds are spent?

Women Call the Church to Accountability

Over its two-thousand-year history Christendom aroused unquenchable hopes for women and, at the same time, it has been guilty of many omissions and wrongs. It was the call for a renewal of life that set ecumenism in motion. The churches recognized the partiality of sticking to their own little areas with their own sorrows and joys and started looking — some cautiously and fearfully, some with passionate longing — for a way of working ecumenically. Ecumenical work in churches has greatly promoted the voices of women, while ecumenical bodies such as church councils or international denominational organizations have enabled cultures and people to challenge each other.

I saw much change in the church during my ten years with the Lutheran World Federation, ten years that coincided with the Ecumenical Decade of Churches in Solidarity with Women, initiated by the World Council of Churches. For ten years, 1988-1998, women in the churches set out to discuss the local churches' attitude towards women. Discussion took place at local, national, and international levels. I preached at the festival that marked the end of the Ecumenical Decade of Churches in Solidarity with Women. More than 1000 women and a handful of men met in Harare, Zimbabwe, prior to the World Council of Churches' Assembly (November 27-December 3, 1998). The Decade Festival was both a celebration and a time to evaluate what we had seen and heard when the church was asked to stand in solidarity with women.

From Cameroon to California and from Chile to China we as women of the church agreed that the ten years had, without question, created solidarity of women with women and of women with the church. But our hope for solidarity from the church was not fulfilled. It is the results of that decade that moved me from the language of "solidarity" to that of "accountability." Why did I do that?

Women's Humanity an Issue of Accountability

The church as a community entrusted with the communication of the gospel is called to be a sign of *the* kingdom of God, which is present wherever the liberating, saving, and transforming power of Christ is incarnate. There, the question of women in the church is not a marginal issue, but one that touches the core of the church's identity and mission. When the women's movement in general and feminist theology in particular challenge the church with regard to its attitude to women, they ask how far the church is ready to exist as a sign of the kingdom of God here and now. The struggle for the acceptance of women is at the same time a struggle for the trustworthiness of the church's proclamation. For the communication of the gospel does not happen only through words but also through actions, structures, and relationships. It is expressed in theology, liturgy, and worship, in proclamation, history, and access to the ordained ministry. Women in the church often lament that what is said in public documents is not commensurate with their experiences in their churches. They ask the church for accountability to the humanity and dignity of women.

New Creation in Christ: An Issue of Accountability

The Christian message is about becoming a new creation before God. In the new creation, the structures and relationships of the fallen world give way to the new covenant, to a new acceptance and to new relationships. In the new creation, Jews and Gentiles, poor and rich, women and men, young and old, people of different races, castes, or social standing have the possibility to be called children of God and enjoy all the privileges and responsibilities this new relationship entails. In the new covenant it is not the social customs or oppressive structures that give us our first and foremost identity, but God's acceptance of us as children and heirs of the divine. This love and acceptance of God revalues the concept of the "other" totally. In the new creation, the "other" is no longer a possible object for exploitation or oppression, but a point at which God and human beings meet. When Christ said that we encounter him in the smallest of our brothers and sisters, he made each of us a potential meeting place between God and human beings. Is this not challenging enough for the church to become accountable to women and in so doing to God?

The familiar truth from the Bible and tradition that men and women are justified sinners, creatures who are sons and daughters of God with responsibility for God's and our world, leaves no room for gender injustice. Our institutional relationships — social, political, ecclesiastic, and economic — are therefore subject to the criticism of these fundamental aspects of the biblical message. It is before these that they must be judged.

The equal participation of women and men in the body of Christ is one way in which Jesus has shown us how to make the body of Christ known. We are being asked to expand our personhood. Women need to share the responsibility implied by membership in the body of Christ with men and vice versa. Together we can envision the sacramental presence of the body of Christ moving us from the center like concentric shapes, ever expanding and extending. As a pebble that is dropped into the water ripples, so we can hope to enable the body of Christ to ripple throughout the world, if only we can move our actions beyond mere solidarity to accountability. Solidarity invites; accountability compels. The gospel is compelling because it is urgent and it is good news. It is truth and it is life. Why not choose the gospel and discover what God wishes to give us together, men and women, for the care of all creation?

Church studies to evaluate the stand of churches on ordination of women provided the cornerstone for changes that countries like Denmark experienced in a long and painful transition. These studies in particular showed and continue to show how closely the relationships between men and women are connected to the urgent problems of our world today. Writing after September 11, 2001, I cannot help noting how the Taliban's denial of rights to Afghan women opened up our understanding of certain forms of "club mentalities." The harvest of club mentalities can be expensive as we have seen and continue to see in the wars being waged by men who isolate themselves in clubs.

Participation: An Issue of Accountability

Participation is affirmation. Denial of participation is a clear indication of subordination because it refuses to recognize the gifts of those denied participation.

Lack of women's full participation at the local level often means that they will also be absent at all other levels of church. Since relatively few women have leading positions in their churches, they frequently are not nominated as representatives or delegates to important forums. They are considered to be "not effective enough" for the follow-up work because they are out of decision-making structures. The consequence of the lack of women representatives as voting delegates at church and ecumenical assemblies is that there is only a tenuous link between the congregations, in which women constitute the majority, and top-level ecumenical bodies.[1] Only a very small number of women have leadership positions at the upper decision-making level.

In addition to these practical obstacles, in many parts of the world there are still some fundamental reservations about women's sharing to any great degree in ecclesiastical responsibility. They are based to a large extent on biased interpretation of the scriptures and cultures.

Finally, we must mention another complex structural factor, which applies to the situation of the majority of women on the world scale. The international tasks of the churches require a high level of education. The education level of women in many parts of the world as well as lack of family welfare services often prevent women from participation. The self-help programs of the women's desks in the churches and the work on lead-

1. When I worked in the Lutheran World Federation as the Programme Secretary for Women in Church and Society, promoting affirmative action in favor of women was part of my responsibility. From time to time, Viggo and I would argue about this, whether it was not a way of also subordinating women by not choosing them according to their qualification. But years of working together as men and women from all over the world helped us see beyond our cultural inhibitions.

ership training have increased the awareness of women to ask for this infrastructure correction and to demand participation.

Separate areas of responsibility, which still tend to predominate, are an obstacle to an exchange of experiences and insights. Common areas of responsibility in which women do not constitute a minority could serve to liberate men from the unconscious constraints of a view of work that has restricted their awareness of other dimensions of life. This would seem to us to be a prerequisite for "community."

Accountability to Women's Talents

Our hypothesis expresses the hope that more men and women will experience liberation. The unity of the church's ministry exercised by the whole people of God must be made visible to all dimensions of life. The acceptance of our reconciliation with God through Christ, despite our dubious tendencies and our confused history, can enable us to repent.

Let me end this essay by reverting to the message of hope, which has indeed grounded me in the church.

Jürgen Moltmann has stated that "[h]ope is the distinctive contribution of Christian faith to our world in the midst of ambiguous and even hopeless circumstances that plague human existence."[2] For several years I worked in the area of Bible translation in rural villages in several African countries. I was always amazed that rural illiterate people who heard the Bible read to them appropriated the words of Scripture immediately and assumed that the Bible was written directly to them. These people taught me that Christian hope is about appropriating the message of hope, by faith. To have faith and to hope means to engage hour by hour with life in such a way that our deeds express that which we hope for, while acknowledging the realism of disappointment, frustration, anger, brokenness, and even despair. The challenge for the church is to dare to hope, and in daring, to wrestle with all that seeks to deny us hope and disempower us by creating roles that exclude gifts needed in the mission of the church.

2. *Hope for the Church: Moltmann in Dialogue with Practical Theology* (Nashville: Abingdon, 1979), p. 10.

The Church, the Churches, the Orthodox Churches, and the World Council of Churches: Notes on "Ecclesiology and Ethics" in Conciliar Debate

ANNA MARIE AAGAARD

In September 2000, the world exhibition "Expo" in Hannover, Germany, featured some events involving representatives from the World Religions. Round table discussions had Jews, Christians, Muslims, Hindus, and Buddhists converse on religious support of human dignity and the mounting global poverty as a challenge to the religious communities. Contributions to social development and peace among peoples and nations were on top of the agenda. The correspondent from an influential German newspaper found it all merely moderately engaging. His review of the world exhibition's "day of religions" quickly turns to the German Evangelical Churches' pavilion which had a glass case with a statue of the crucified Christ at its center.

> It is obviously not all the same to the religions whom they put at the center of worship and whom the faithful address in their prayers. . . . Suddenly one discovered talk about God in the flow of church leaders' talk about human dignity and peacemaking and the urgently needed combat of poverty and oppression. . . . [The Orthodox metropolitan Augustinus] seemed, strange to say, to insist on glorifying God for the sake of human dignity. . . . "Watch and pray" he told his colleagues from other churches and religions, before they again turned to the world.[1]

1. *Frankfurter Allgemeine Zeitung,* September 13, 2000 (Heinz-Joachim Fischer). My translation.

Without any reference to recent debates, the newspaper entry captures basic lines of demarcation in the ecumenical discussions of ethics and ecclesiology. A short essay cannot deal adequately with the tensions grasped by the correspondent. My aim is much more modest. I shall, first, sketch the positions that dominate the largely unknown and/or ignored ecumenical debate on approaches to ethics and policy decisions on moral matters. Second, I shall present the contours of some typical views and attempt to have the brief presentations indicate the Orthodox impact on the conversations.

Approaches to Ethics

From the early 1990s study reports reminded the member churches of the World Council of Churches (WCC) that ethical reflections are social practices marked by their social location and the context of the respective communities within which they are situated. The reports argued for moving the ecumenical debate on Christian ethics to moral formation of the faithful, affirming that the church not only has, but is, a social ethic.[2] "Watch and pray," as the Orthodox Church leader admonished at the Expo gathering while placing the merely "inner-worldly chatter of the religions" on a side track.

The history (and most of the current practice) of ecumenical social thought and action shows, however, that churches involved in conciliar ecumenism predominantly are concerned with political ethics. They try, consistently, to respond to damages to life that are either dividing humankind or affecting it as a global whole. The underlying assumptions take the primacy of the state in modern life for granted, constrast "politics" as a social fact with religion, and are concerned with right relations (however they are conceived) between particular churches and a "political realm" supposed to represent society as a whole. But — and now I am back at the lone Orthodox voice at the Expo round table — there is nothing distinctively Christian about an ethical approach based on expertise in the systems of society and their functional interrelations.

2. *Ecclesiology and Ethics: Ecumenical Ethical Engagement, Moral Formation and the Nature of the Church*, ed. Thomas F. Best and Martin Robra (Geneva: WCC Publications, 1997).

> "Pragmatic realists" and "liberation ecumenists" only differ in relation to the subject of political change and the analysis of present conditions. Both have an instrumental or functional understanding of the role of the church in society. . . . Ecumenical social ethics is (still) political ethics and not the Christian ethics of ecclesial communities trying to be a witness through their way of life.[3]

While some participants in the ecumenical conversations stress the formative role of a Christian community committed to particular practices, traditions, and forms of communal life, other churches and ecclesial traditions typically borrow from Kantian, utilitarian, or intuitionist heritage and present moral knowledge as available to all rational agents irrespective of context. The latter view involves a moral realism implying that moral truth must be established by appeals to standards that transcend the particularities of a specific story-shaped community.

Yet other participants in the ecumenical debate argue that there can be common moral ground (moral perception and agreement) across cultures and traditioned communities without a common moral theory. Distinctive Christian convictions about world, history, and human beings may be tied to particular forms of ecclesial worship, teachings, and communal life, but (this is the argument) these convictions can only claim to be persuasive outside the Christian tribes, if they are embedded in "a theology of nature" that can account for the experiences of a degree of moral agreement across traditions. Ontological realism thus comes with an epistemology that ties the knowledge of moral truth to cultures, beliefs, language, and communal practices.[4]

3. Peter Scherle, "All in One Boat? The History of Ecumenical Social Thought and Action: A Case Study of the WCC," unpublished draft, s.a. (1995), II, pp. 20 and 22. Cf. *Der Überblick* 3 (2001) section "Kirchen und Konflikte," pp. 95-102. Further, Martin Robra, "Methodology in Approaching Moral and Ethical Issues," in *Methodology in Approaching Social and Ethical Issues*, Special Commission on Orthodox Participation in the WCC (2001), pp. 35-39, and Anna Marie Aagaard, "Ecclesiology and Ethics," *Studia Theologica* 55, no. 2 (2001): 157-74.

4. I have borrowed the description of this neo-Barthian position from David Fergusson, *Community, Liberalism and Christian Ethics* (Cambridge: Cambridge University Press, 1998). On the Barthian tradition in the WCC, cf. Konrad Raiser, *Ecumenism in Transition* (Geneva: WCC Publications, 1991).

Ecclesial Ethics

As old certainties about the knowing, autonomous subject and history as a single, coherent plot began yielding to an awareness that human beings inhabit different cultures, meanings, and narrative plots, some mainline churches initiated reviews of their habitual approach to decision-making on moral matters. Typically, policy decisions in mainline Protestant denominations were pronounced by experts and church leaders, who were convinced of the efficacy of communication by argument and a single system of truth based on universal reason. Because it was difficult to see any difference between these policies, which had been drawn up without any sort of communal consensus, and those of secular institutions, these policies were, however, largely ineffective both in shaping a common Christian witness on burning moral issues and in linking Christian faith with the public sphere.[5]

The verities of modernity separated ethics from koinonia, theory from practice, and moral life from community, but towards the end of the twentieth century some churches began to recover Christian ethics as the body politics of being church. The ecumenical conversations on "ecclesiology and ethics" helped articulate, in 1993, the mounting conviction

> that the community of the disciples rather than the individual Christian is the bearer of the tradition and the form and matrix of the moral life. . . . Koinonia in relation to ethic does not mean in the first instance that the Christian community designs codes and rules; rather that it is a place where, along with the confession of faith and the celebration of the sacraments, and as an inseparable part of it, the Gospel tradition is probed permanently for moral inspiration and insight, and where incessant moral counsel keeps the issues of humanity and world alive in the light of the Gospel.

The assumptions were that "faith has always claimed the being of the church as itself a 'moral' reality. Faith and discipleship are embodied in and as a community way of life . . . the church not only has, but is, a social ethic, a koinonia ethic."[6]

5. Cf. Lewis S. Mudge, "The Church and Social Witness: Pastor, Congregation and Public Leadership in the Reformed Tradition," in *Methodology in Approaching Social and Ethical Issues*, Special Commission on Orthodox Participation in the WCC (2001) pp. 1-14.

6. *Ecclesiology and Ethics* (cf. note 2), pp. 9 and 4-5.

The utterances may mirror the beginnings of postliberal Protestant theologies, but the fact is that the ecumenical attempts at articulating new versions of ecclesial ethics were rather prompted by the WCC's Orthodox "undercurrent,"[7] which gained fresh vitality after the fall of the Communist regimes. From Orthodoxy conciliar ecumenism borrowed the phrase "liturgy after the liturgy" as a marker of a distinctively ecclesial ethics connected with socio-linguistic communities in which believers become a "peculiar people" by learning to see all of reality through the lenses of "creation" and "the reign of God" and acquiring the virtues needed to make wise judgments and follow "the Way." Christian moral life is thus conceived as the practice of a liturgical existence, a continuous worship of the triune God (cf. Eph. 5:19-20).[8]

The ecumenical articulation of ecclesial ethics as a "liturgy after the liturgy" made ecclesiology inseparable from ethics:

> All Christian traditions . . . have a particular way of linking liturgical practice, theological reflection, assessment of the issues of world and humanity, and formulations of moral judgment. The Orthodox tradition privileges God's *philantropia* (love for humanity) as the approach to ethical questions. The approach is rooted in Scripture and the living Tradition. We need to realize that the highly divisive issues (e.g. Christian attitudes to human sexuality, the status of women, and the content of social justice) can only be addressed through a dialogue which draws on the particular relations between Scripture, Tradition, experience and reason as used within the different ecclesial traditions.[9]

Ecumenical conversations across the East-West divide are beginning to

7. The phrase "under-current" is borrowed from Peter Scherle's analyses (cf. note 3).

8. Cf. Jon Bria, "The Liturgy after the Liturgy," in *Orthodox Visions of Ecumenism*, ed. G. Limouris (Geneva: WCC Publications, 1994), pp. 216ff. The phrase "a peculiar people" is borrowed from Rodney Clapp, *A Peculiar People: The Church as Culture in a Post-Christian Society* (Downers Grove, Ill.: InterVarsity Press, 1996).

9. Special Commission on Orthodox Participation in the WCC, Report Sub-Committee III (2000). Slightly edited. Cf. "The Ecumenical Dialogue on Moral Issues: Potential Sources of Common Witness or of Divisions," a Study Document of the Joint Working Group, *ER* 2 (1996): 143-54. (The Joint Working Group deals with matters of common interest to the Vatican and the WCC.) Anna Marie Aagaard and Peter Bouteneff, *Beyond the East-West Divide: The World Council of Churches and "the Orthodox Problem"* (Geneva: WCC Publications, 2001).

show signs of distancing themselves from "one-issue shouting matches" between proponents of conflicting ethical views. Some voices do advocate that the Christian churches may have a deeper impact on their social environment by sustaining their own peculiar politics of forgiveness rather than by seeking consensus solutions to the problems of contemporary humanity. The Russian Orthodox Church's remarkable position paper "Bases of the Social Concept of the Russian Orthodox Church" (2000)[10] has helped the dialogue by countering criticisms that an ecclesial ethics as a way of life with distinct virtues, formation, and witness necessarily must succumb to a retreat from the realities of the world. The position paper is distinctively Orthodox in its readings of Scripture and Christian tradition. It is distinctively Russian Orthodox in its understanding of the church as a moral community with relations to a particular state and cultural history, and it is distinctively contemporary in its choice of issues (e.g., ecology, drugs, copyright, bioethics) that are probed in the light of the faith. Ecclesial ethics means "thick" contextual descriptions of a particular practice. As an initiation into the unlearning of the idolatrous common sense with which societies continue ethnic and economic privileges, ecclesial ethics develops ways of seeing and speaking of the world — from rainbows to globalization processes and armed conflicts — that may be recognized as distinctively Christian. Faithfulness rather than success is demanded of the church's witness.

The Prophetic Voice

Ecclesial ethics has generated a number of criticisms, but three charges are invariably repeated: the charges that ecclesial ethics succumbs to relativism (epistemological objections), to fideism (sociological objections), and to tribalism (political objections). In dealing with these charges some monographs have used ecumenical material or reflected on the ecumenical implications of an ecclesial ethics which asserts that tradition and community are coextensive, but the WCC's ecumenical debates have not addressed the criticisms in any systematic way. Ecumenical gatherings have, however, reiterated that a community-based ethics inevitably will silence the churches' "prophetic voice."[11]

10. http://www.russian-orthodox-church.org.ru/en.htm

11. Lately during the WCC's Central Commission, February 2001.

Although it is far from clear what a "prophetic voice" might denote, it is possible to read the critical utterances as referring to the major objections to ecclesial ethics. First, prophets talk *at* the faith community. Keeping a "prophetic voice" thus means keeping a distance between what God does in creation and redemption and what human beings in the Holy Spirit are empowered to do. Faith and discipleship are not intrinsically ecclesial. The criticism claims that the circularity between the truth of any story and the sort of community it generates is overblown in ecclesial ethics. The Protestant doctrinal *extra nos* must be kept, and translated into Christian ethics it ensures a distance between the church's performance and the way things really are because of the God-story's priority to and independence of our story.

I read the position as the ecumenical parallel to objections charging ecclesial ethics with relativism. References to "a prophetic voice" function in ecumenical parlance as theological resorts to an external vantage point that makes it possible to judge between versions of Christian life. The references to a God-story over and above the church comply with Western modernity's insistence on having the justification of moral principles set off from their origination in order to avoid solipsistic self-validation of ethics.

Second, prophets seek — and find — alliances outside the faith community, and thus "the prophetic voice" challenges the tribalism of the church. The following lines capture some of the issues at work, and at stake, in ecumenical calls for the churches' prophetic voice:

> there is . . . a danger for the ecumenical movement to be deserted because of its absence of relevance to the issues of our time. . . . There are many, among the laity particularly, who would wish the ecumenical movement to deal with the whole inhabited world more than with the world of the churches.[12]

The quote sets the world of the churches over against the whole inhabited world with its issues relevant to human persons, and it makes an emphasis on the churches equal ecclesiastical navel-gazing. Assuming such fundamental polarity between world and church presupposes secular modernity's belief in a wider and deeper and broader community than the com-

12. Special Commission on Orthodox Participation in the World Council of Churches, Documents from the Meeting of Sub-Committees I and IV (WCC, March 2000).

munity in the body of Christ and a more unified world than the world that holds together in and because of Christ. Secular groups and movements may, consequently, be better positioned than the churches to witness to a human community with no other limits than the whole human race.

Both past and present ecumenical social thought and action[13] testify to the perceived connections between retaining a prophetic voice and forming functional alliances with non-church agents outside the churches. The implied criticism charges ecclesial ethics with tribalism and fideism, and the objections emerge from the need to secure a public role for the Christian witness in secular society. Against the tenets of an ecclesial ethics embedded in cultural-linguistic traditions the objections assume a social fact (state; civil society) that can be contrasted with religion. The Christian story does not absorb the world; the story does not go all the way down. On the contrary: it is possible to contrast church and world and yet have churches and Christian organizations make a common cause with secular groups and agencies.

Most versions of this position presuppose the Western political arrangement and its subsystems plus a history of Christian influence on shaping the common good.[14] Somewhere between a merely tribal ecclesial culture and premodern privileges for the church there is — in democratic pluralist societies — the possibility of Christian presence in the secular, public sphere. This conviction will often result in charging ecclesial ethics with an inability to uphold a public role in society and thereby contribute to silencing the prophetic voice of the church in public affairs (the political objection to ecclesial ethics).

I contend, however, that the charges of fideism carry the weight also in objections that perceive ecclesial ethics as necessarily sectarian. A "fideism

13. Peter Scherle (note 3) documents the history. A description of the recently formed Ecumenical Advocacy Alliance (December 2000) speaks of strengthening the prophetic voice of the Alliance and the impact of ecumenical witness on contemporary social, political, and economic problems. In order to achieve the goal, the organizational planning includes "keeping our distance from the institutional logic of the ecumenical organizations that, in the majority, are based on church membership and membership in a community." *Das Schweigen brechen. Aktionsbündnis gegen AIDS* (Hamburg: EMW, 2001), p. 47 (my own translation).

14. E.g., *Church and World: The Unity of the Church and the Renewal of Human Community,* A Faith and Order Study Document, Faith and Order Paper 151 (Geneva: WCC Publications, 1990).

objection" may be construed in different ways, but generally it implies that for religious beliefs and practices to be intelligible it must be possible to account for them in terms of reasons and explanations external to "the Way." The objection further implies that for moral principles to be moral their justification or moral validity must be separated from their origin. Why would people listen to the prophetic voice of the churches and be able to understand the witness, if it was not intelligible to rational creatures? Why would the social witness of the churches be able to impact society and create alliances (if not conversions), if it was not perceived as expressing a common moral ground?

Contributions to the ecumenical debate on "ecclesiology and ethics" do *not* assume that Christian beliefs can be reformulated within the idioms of secular culture. The ecumenical "fideism objection" to ecclesial ethics is of a more complex kind. It charges ecclesial ethics with the lack of a proper foundational basis that upholds a distance, not a separation, between the church and human beings determined also outside the church by the God of the Christian story. There can be genuine moral perception outside the church and a common moral ground with people of other faiths, and such commensurability between cultures is not the result of contingent, historical overlappings. It is grounded in the foundational faith that God speaks to the world in ways other than the church. There is an Archimedean point (not external to the faith the church proclaims, but primary to the witnessing church) that makes it possible to uphold both Christian distinctiveness and a common moral ground with people outside the church. The Archimedean point may be articulated as a form of christianized natural law, as "law" or orders of creation, or as the eschatological kingdom present; but basic is the assumption of church and world as "always antecedently being involved in one conversation."[15] Ecumenical insistence on the prophetic voice of the churches may not always signify a sustained and coherent theological thinking (far from), but even in their simplest articulation the calls for prophetic alliances imply that it is possible to speak simultaneously to church and world on moral issues; it is possible to avoid tribalism and fideism and include secular groups and movements in the pro-

15. Cf. Robert Jenson, "The Hauerwas Project," *Modern Theology* 8, no. 3 (1992): 285-95; Lewis S. Mudge, *The Church as Moral Community: Ecclesiology and Ethics in Ecumenical Debate* (New York: Continuum/Geneva: WCC Publications, 1998), esp. chapter 6: "Horizons of Meaning and the Household of Life."

phetic role of the church. It is possible, because the Word (the Creator Spirit; the reign of God) is mediated also in non-ecclesial ways. What is primarily done by God is only secondarily received — actively or passively according to the denominational divides — by the church.

Configurations Matter

In 1995 the Joint Working Group between the Vatican and the WCC issued a study on "The Ecumenical Dialogue on Moral Issues."[16] A summary claims

> For those pathways of moral reflection and deliberation which churches use in coming to ethical decisions, the churches share the Scriptures and have at their disposal such resources as liturgy and moral traditions, catechisms and sermons, sustained pastoral practices, the wisdom distilled from past and present experiences, and the arts of reflection and spiritual discernment. Yet church traditions configure these common resources in different ways.

A very recent collection of statements on "Methodology in Approaching Social and Ethical Issues"[17] verifies that many churches do use the same resources for fashioning moral formation and arriving at moral discernment. The Evangelical Church in Germany (EKD) establishes "memoranda" as orientation for the faithful by drawing on Scripture in the light of doctrinal and spiritual traditions of the Reformation (e.g., the law-gospel dialectics). The established principles for acting in society also draw on philosophy, empirical sciences, and the history of German church-state relations. The Russian Orthodox Church shapes its teaching on moral matters by reflections on Scripture in the light of doctrinal, moral, pastoral, and cultural tradition. Findings of the arts and sciences (e.g., philosophy, history, law; medicine, psychology, and bioethics) impact the moral discernment. The methodology used by these two churches resembles the methodology followed by, for example, the Presbyterian Church USA.

16. Documented in *ER* 2 (1996): 143-54.

17. Special Commission on Orthodox Participation in the WCC, Background Materials (WCC, 2001).

Shared resources are obviously not the ecumenical problem. It is the configuration of the resources that differs, "even when similar attitudes and outcomes often emerge." The conciliar oikoumene is faced with "common sources and different pathways of moral deliberation."[18] Differing ecclesiologies and doctrinal traditions will keep the churches apart and divided, even when these same churches react in a similar way to abortion, armed humanitarian intervention, and economic globalization processes. And divisive, conflicting views on specific moral matters will not be solved by ecumenical consultations on single moral issues.

The following examples of differing configurations must substitute for a sustained argument for prioritizing doctrine and ecclesiology in the ecumenical dialogues on moral issues.

a. Individual Vocation

In the context of continued bilateral dialogues between EKD and the Romanian Orthodox Church, Bishop Rolf Koppe has provided an introduction to the basic ethics guiding the EKD's engagement with secular German society. Koppe describes the adopted approach to ethics and ecclesiology under the rubric of "vocation" and claims,

> The specific place of the human being within the social order, i.e. in his or her "office" or "vocation" in the world, determines to a large extent the scope and nature of his or her ethical responsibility. . . . ([A] generally acknowledged and widely recognizable Protestant church ethic does not exist, if by this is meant an elaborate casuistry). . . . But there are characteristics of a Protestant ethic which are essential: fostering the ability to become a real person, able to live in community and to act within the tension between plurality and integration, reflection and action, community and institution. . . . [In] Protestant thinking, it is the individual human being who is the acting subject. [But] . . . the believer lives, and makes decisions, as one who partakes of Christ — as a mem-

18. Cf. The Joint Working Group study (note 16). Problems do arise, however, if churches claim to build moral teaching exclusively on Scripture and ecclesial authority and neglect the impact that other resources make on their moral discernment. Cf. "Homosexuality: Some Elements for an Ecumenical Discussion," *ER* 1 (1998).

> ber of a local congregation or of the church in a broader sense — in the community of the people of God.[19]

This view makes individual "vocation" the configurating glue of the moral life. It places church and world, faith and "works," law and gospel, witness and service, ecclesiology and ethics in distinct, although not separated, spheres. In the perspective of the ecumenical "ecclesiology-ethics dialogues" it follows that the distinctive identity of this version of Protestantism becomes located in a law-gospel dialectic's ability to affirm the secular nature of the world and to empower individual responsibility and autonomy in ethical action. The Christian community and its life is not the area in which the moral life is lived out. Moral life is the worldly "vocation" of the individual Christian, and the role of the church is not "to do politics" but to enable politics by "advocating values which serve the well-being of all, including the poor, deprived and powerless, the next generation of creation which has no voice of its own."

Social ethics as political ethics rallying individuals, believers and non-believers, around specific tasks of reducing perceived damages to life — the position makes sense of the moral experience of contemporary Germans. The individual must make moral choices and cannot find evaluative commitments by tending to the question of personal social identity. The moral agent is sovereign, and the sovereignty is backed up not only by the agent's (German) historical social vocabulary, but by Protestant doctrinal convictions that make the single human being stand alone before God as a justified sinner abstracted from all social relations and practices.

b. Building Up the Body of Christ

Ethics is, on the contrary, an ecclesial, corporal matter in the Orthodox tradition. Decisions on moral matters involve informed use of complex resources, but these resources must be configured so that language, practices, and virtues will be aiming at building up the body of Christ:

19. "Fundamental Protestant Principles for Acting in Society," provisional translation of "Evangelische Grundlagen für das Handeln in der Gesellschaft," in *Methodology in Approaching Social and Ethical Issues*, Special Commission on Orthodox Participation in the WCC (WCC, 2001), pp. 29-34.

> The church is the assembly of believers in Christ, which He Himself calls every one to join. In (the church) "all things heavenly and earthly" should be united in Christ, for He is the Head of "the Church, which is His body, the fullness of Him that filleth all in all" (Eph. 1:22-23). In the Church the creation is deified and God's original design for the world and man[!] is fulfilled by the power of the Holy Spirit.

The opening sentences of the Russian Orthodox position paper on social ethics leave no doubt that the Christian story absorbs the world. The narrative leaves nothing out, but encompasses all reality from alpha to omega, from beginning to end. But the Christ-centered narrative does not by and in itself figure all of cosmos and history in. The claims of the story to universal significance mean that the story must be inhabited and constantly shown to be able to absorb all human enterprises and all reality. Separated from a living, believing church that turns to Christ, confesses its sins, accepts forgiveness, and engages in becoming the *eucharistia* it celebrates, the story becomes empty fables. The God-story and the worshiping community are mutually constitutive. Unembodied, the Christian narrative loses its claim to authority; it is the ecclesial body of Christ that mediates and practices the reality and the purposes of all of cosmos, of life and human nature, of history and society.

Affirming the nexus between the Christian narrative and the church as its paradigmatic setting does not make Christian living or "liturgy after the liturgy" identical with applying a fixed, ahistorical story to the stuff and conundrums of everyday life. Narrational foundationalism is not the danger of current Orthodox theology, but the absolutizing of a specific history-bound conceptual language employed to draw out the ontological and strict *theo*logical assumptions of a historical story that interprets all other stories. The danger is a fixed, privileged, and possessive doctrinal language so enmeshed in the story that the story cannot make meaning of all stories (of history's changing events, conflicts, and the fragmented world), because the Christian narrative has become unable to interpret anything but its own fixed and privileged ecclesial setting.

Where Orthodox theology keeps tending to the provisional character of the conceptual language that in-forms the Christian community's practices and readings of world and societies, a Christian way of life may be interpreted as the *struggle* to live transfigured or resurrection life:

> There is no final, rigid, arbitrary pattern to this process. . . . First and foremost we will seek to keep before us all the time that our ultimate goal is conformity and communion with the Triune God, that all our ethical decisions — in order to be correct — must be in harmony with and contribute to growth for the fulfillment of the image and likeness of God in persons and to the realization of the Kingdom of God.

Ethics deals with the never finally achieved task of reading the world and living the "liturgy after the liturgy" in such a way that "all things heavenly and earthly" become transfigured and thus build up the body of Christ. Everything else would be to abandon the Christian claim that there are no more fundamental readings of the world and no other exemplary community than the practices that build up the body of Christ — the "fullness of Him who filleth all in all."[20]

Reflecting on ethical conflicts in terms of Anglican understanding of the body of Christ, Rowan Williams refers to living in the body of Christ as "profoundly hard work." It involves remaining in communion with people judged to be "dangerously deluded in their belief about what (is) involved in serving Christ," because only *in* the body of Christ can disagreements, considered to be betrayals of hearing and showing the truth, be enfolded in learning to live Christ's gift of self-giving, healing holiness.

> An ethic of the Body of Christ asks that we first examine how any proposed action or any proposed style or policy of action measures up to two concerns: how does it manifest the selfless holiness of God in Christ? And how can it serve as a gift that builds up the community called to show that holiness in its corporate life? . . . if I am serious about making a gift of what I do to the Body as a whole, I have to struggle to make sense of my decision in terms of the common language of the Faith, to demonstrate why this might be a way of speaking the language of the historic schema of Christian belief. This involves the processes of self-criticism and self-questioning in the presence of Scripture and tradition, as well as engagement with the wider community of believers.[21]

20. Cf. Stanley S. Harakas, *Toward Transfigured Life: The Theoria of Eastern Orthodox Ethics* (Minneapolis: Light and Life Publishing Company, 1983).

21. Rowan Williams, "Making Moral Decisions," reproduced in *Methodology in Approaching Social and Ethical Issues,* Special Commission on Orthodox Participation in the WCC (2001).

No one will confuse this vocabulary and way of thinking with current Orthodox reflections on ethics, but Rowan Williams's emphasis on an ethic of the body of Christ does point to cracks in the walls dividing the Christian East and West. Configurations matter, and thinking about moral life and making moral decisions in terms of asking about the building up of the body of Christ will at least situate ecumenical discussions of moral life in the context of traditioned understandings of church as the body of Christ. Configured by the understanding of the body of Christ, the emerging ecumenical debates on "ecclesiology-ethics" may prove more fruitful to ecumenical understanding than the inherited "political ethics" debates that combine highly diverse readings of Reformation heritage with varying degrees of commitment to residual(?) liberal individualism. This may be a non-spectacular ecumenical strategy, but I am convinced that it is what is possible just now. And the possible may not be nothing, unless one (falsely) reduces the distinctiveness of Eastern and Western doctrinal traditions to mean conceptually irreducible traditions of incorrigible beliefs.

PART III

God Challenging the World

Transformation as Mission

PHILIP HEFNER

Transformation is a theological mandate that flows equally from the gospel, from our understanding of the basic nature of the church, and from our participation in the situation of our times at the beginning of the twenty-first century. Viggo Mortensen has perceived this multifold significance of transformation. He has contributed to our interpretation of transformation and has also committed himself to shaping and empowering it. It is appropriate that this tribute to him should include concentrated reflection upon this fundamental reality of our time. Mortensen's life and work have dealt with several aspects of transformation, so it is natural that this essay will also be multidimensional, including perspectives from theology (including ecclesiology), the natural sciences, and historical-cultural analysis.[1]

Theological Foundations of Transformation: Mission as Faithfulness to the Gospel of God

Transformation is fundamental to the gospel that stands at the center of the Christian faith and thus at the core of the church's proclamation. Con-

1. Portions of this essay have appeared in Philip Hefner, "The Church as a Community of God's Possibility: The 1996 Hein-Fry Lectures," in *Currents in Theology and Mission* 25 (August 1998): 245-319.

sequently, if we are to be faithful to the gospel, we will understand transformation as fundamental to our mission.

The Theological Context for Transformation: Creation and Creator God

Theologically, our understanding of transformation is rooted in our doctrines of creation and the Creator God. Transformation is the central image of God's work for us as individual Christians and for the church. Transformation is God's process of bringing forth the possibilities that are ours by virtue of God's will and grace. Transformation cannot stand alone, however. It must be viewed in its dynamic interconnection with the total picture of reality that coheres in our faith. This means initially that transformation is the work of the Triune God, carried out in the widest possible cosmic scope — God's work, in other words, in the entire world, in ourselves as humans, and in all that exists as God's creation. God alone is the source and generator of all that is. Our very existence, as well as that of the entire cosmos and planet earth, is grounded finally in nothing else but the intention, the freedom, and the grace of the Creator God. We and our world owe our existence to God's will that we exist, and the kind of world that we live in must also be the world that God intended. We affirm this God-intoxicated view of the world in the Creeds, when we confess that God is the "maker of heaven and earth, of all that is, seen and unseen." The church has traditionally spoken of this affirmation in the technical term, "creation-out-of-nothing" *(creatio ex nihilo)*, thereby asserting that God and no other being or power or source has brought forth the natural world. The word "creation" means just this: *Nature as the work of God, out of nothing else.*

Our world, therefore, and we ourselves in it, are constituted by God's action of bringing us to the future that God intends for us. All of cosmic history, human history, and our own personal lives are defined by this vast work of God perfecting the creation that God initiated in the first place. We are what God has created, and our future is the future God holds for us. The church must be placed in this context, and whatever happens in and to the church, whatever the mission of the church is, it must also be placed within this context of God's creation and God's will for the creation's future. When we relate the church to Jesus Christ, who is the Son of God, the

Logos of God, the second person of the Trinity, we are at the same time affirming that whatever the church is about, whatever its mission, it has to do with the eternal will of God for the creation.

The revelation in Jesus Christ speaks to us centrally and concretely of the shape of God's transforming work. Jesus lived a life of availability to God's possibilities; his earthly life portrays for us the substance of such availability. The crucifixion underscores the sense in which God's possibilities seem to be impossibilities when judged by human criteria. In the resurrection we receive the word that God's possibilities can indeed become real in the very world of flesh that God created and in which we live out our earthly existences.

God the Holy Spirit accompanies the creation at every moment and in every situation, and it is this Holy Spirit that makes the resurrection life actual in every moment of our lives. Transformation in the here and now is, strictly speaking, the work of the Holy Spirit.

This grand view of the world in God's hands, as creation under the power of the resurrection, is an essential presupposition of ecclesiology and of our concept of transformation. This view is also the foundation for our trust, our faith in the process of transformation and the church itself as a participant in this process. There is no basis for trusting our own lives and the processes of our transformation and of the church unless we also can believe that somehow all of this is rooted in God, and in the freedom, intentionality, and love of God that we find in Jesus Christ.

Such a theological grounding is not simply an affirmation of what is, with no critical edge. Quite to the contrary, the affirmation of God's triune work as I have just set it forth is both indicative and imperative, both vision for our lives and critique of our lives in the church. The life we live and the church's life are not only resourced, but also governed by the grace of God's creation work. The church not only *is* a signal community within God's work of fulfillment, it also *must become* that community, and it is held accountable by God to hold itself to that vision. The church is not only already vivified by the power of the resurrection, it also must realize more fully what resurrection under the conditions of flesh really entails. The church not only proclaims the gospel of God's transforming work in Christ, it must also be transformed in its own life. The grand view that Christians hold of reality not only gives us confidence in the church and its place in God's salvation work, it also provides a basis for criticizing and norming the church's life. It is God's creation work and will that give rise to possibilities, and it is that same work and will that govern possibilities and give them life.

Transformation in the Christian Tradition

Transformation and the Encounter with Jesus

Transformation is fundamental to the Christian tradition. It is at the heart of our conviction that something fundamentally new can be brought about by God's gracious will and work. We would not be here today as Christians if we did not have the witness and the tradition of actual transformation already wrought in the encounter with Jesus of Nazareth. In their relationships with the man Jesus, the apostolic men and women and children found a transformation that changed their lives. It convinced them that doors were open that they had either never dreamed of before or that they considered to be irrevocably closed. They came to envision futures that were no option for them before they encountered the man from Nazareth.

Residing as it does at the heart of our experience of Jesus and of the apostolic witness to him, this actuality of transformation grounds our Christian affirmation that Jesus is the Christ, the Messiah, the *Logos* of God, who finally stands in our faithful interpretation as the second person of the Trinity. These declarations of who Jesus is and of his significance are expressions of faith that the transformation experienced in him is grounded in ultimacy, that its source is a self not our own, God's power of transformation.

Transformation in the New Testament

Transformation is not an add-on to the Christian way of interpreting life and the world. Without transformation Christian faith would not be what it is. Hence it is at the heart of salvation, redemption, and sanctification. The New Testament speaks of these realities as Creation and New Creation, the First Adam and the Second Adam, birth and rebirth, the Old Man [sic] and the New Man [sic], this age and the new age, a New Heaven and a New Earth. In each case, the most precious gift of God, central to our faith, is spoken of as the transformation of what is into what shall be, through the grace and power of God — God as Creator, God as Redeemer in Christ, and God the Giver of Life as the Holy Spirit.

A closer analysis of the New Testament would reveal that each of its writings aims at the transformation of the reader. Paul envisions the transformation of the believer from bondage to the Law to the freedom of justification. Mark's Gospel hopes for transformation from self-centeredness and fear to the empowerment that God's reign brings, whereas Matthew focuses upon transformation from the hypocrisy that is grounded in a false interpretation of Israel's Law to the integrity that flows from repentance and a truer obedience as set forth by Jesus. Luke speaks of the transformation from oppression to compassion and mercy; John is governed by a desire for the transformation of the blindness that fails to see God's presence in life to the light that is able to discern eternity under the conditions of history, in Jesus Christ. Even this cursory summary of a few of its writings suggests that the New Testament is thoroughly grounded in, perhaps we could say driven by, the dynamic of transformation. Further, we could understand the message of Christ in the New Testament by careful attention to how each of its writings interprets Jesus Christ in terms of how he brings about this transformation.[2]

Transformation and Theosis

The monumental contribution of Eastern Christianity by the fourth century C.E. is its clear sense that human life cannot be adequately understood if transformation is not placed at its core. The great Cappadocians — Basil of Caesarea, Gregory of Nyssa, Gregory of Nazianzus, and Macrina — taught us that the single most important thing about human beings is that they have been created in the image of God.[3] In the Cappadocian perspective, this image is characterized by reason, freedom, and immortality. Immortality describes the entire career of human being, from its conception in the mind of God before the Fall through its earthly existence and there-

2. See David Rhoads, *The Challenge of Diversity: The Witness of Paul and the Gospels* (Minneapolis: Fortress Press, 1996).

3. Jaroslav Pelikan, *Christianity and Classical Culture: The Metamorphosis of Natural Theology in the Christian Encounter with Hellenism* (New Haven: Yale University Press, 1993), chapters 8, 18.

after. The totality of the human experiment, as it is comprehended by God's will, is defined by the process of retrieving and fulfilling the immortality in which we were conceived by God from the beginning.

This grand doctrine of metamorphosis does not depict a transformation away from the earthiness of our creaturely existence into some other-worldly immortality. Under the images of the First Adam and Christ as the Second Adam and also of the two creations, Adam and Christ, Gregory of Nyssa can write, "The first time, the *Logos* made the flesh; this time the *Logos* was made flesh, so that he might change our flesh to spirit, by being made partaker with us in flesh and blood."[4] Gregory of Nazianzus writes provocatively of this transformation:

> I had a share in the image, but I did not keep it. Christ shares in my flesh that he may both save the image and make the flesh immortal. He communicates a second fellowship with God far more marvellous than the first had been. For then he imparted the better nature to humanity, whereas this time he himself participated in the worse nature of humanity. This is more Godlike than the former action, this is more sublime in the eyes of all who understand.[5]

The Eastern traditions bring all this to expression in their image of *theosis*. For too long, we Westerners have translated this term as deification or divinization and rejected it as an egregious and repulsive elevation of humanity. We know better now, and we recognize that it rightly underscores that human being is not fully what God intends it to be unless and until it is transformed, in the flesh, in its Adamic quality, as God has always intended it, to share fully in God's intended fulfillment of the creation — and this journey of transformation in *theosis* is one that began at our creation.

Transformation and Lutheran Tradition

In our Lutheran understanding of the gospel, transformation is closely related to both justification and sanctification. It is justification by God's grace through faith that enables us to lay claim to the newness that God has

4. Quoted in Pelikan, *Christianity and Classical Culture*, pp. 284-85.
5. Quoted in Pelikan, *Christianity and Classical Culture*, p. 285.

chosen us for, and it is sanctification that refers to the enablement by grace that allows us to bring that newness to concrete expression in our everyday life, even if its forms are fallible. What we call conversion or metanoia is nothing else but transformation. Our Lutheran preoccupation with grace clarifies that this transformation is grounded in God's intention and in God's power for us and within us; it is not a humanly devised project.

Transformation Today

What particular nuances does transformation carry that are essential for our understanding today? I call attention to two: newness and change. *Newness* means that what we look for from God and what forms the content of our hope is something new, something not yet fully known or possessed. Despite much traditional rhetoric to the contrary, Christian faith is not essentially restorationist in its perspective. The hope that burns in our hearts is not only warming, but also so much a part of us that without it we would be torn apart. The grace we experience is likewise a present reality that actually makes our life possible. Strangely, however, the flame of hope and the presence of real grace live within us as much in anticipation as in present reality, as much tomorrow as today, and as much unfinished in us as they are completely a part of us. Like the ancient Habiru who became the Hebrews — the Israelites who came to Palestine — we are have-nots who are in the process of always receiving what can never be fully possessed, we are never haves who can count their riches. Little wonder that when we speak in technical theological terms, we say that God's creation and God's promise for that creation are thoroughly eschatological! When we think of God's good gifts and God's good presence, we think of that which is new, not yet fully known nor yet fully possessed.

If we truly believe that our lives are constituted by God's grace, and that this grace is the gift of God's transforming promise, then we recognize that our lives and their promise are woven on the loom of *change* and process. It is a fundamental mistake to think of our lives and of God's grace as a solid unchanging core that remains untouched as it moves through changing terrain. The Habiru were not constituted by a core of nomadic homelessness that changed incrementally into landownership through the experience of the Exodus and the Conquest of Canaan. It is true that most of the ancient Hebrews, too much of the time, held to the image of themselves as having arrived. They gave Yahweh thanks for having saved them from poverty and for translating them into the condition of possessing and prospering. The prophets reminded them forcefully that in thinking thus, they had missed the point of their own history. Their being was defined by a constant receiving — receiving the new realities that God gives, which can never be possessed fully, and being transformed in the process, only to find that transformation itself is never complete. This is difficult for us to understand, just as it was for the Hebrews. We demand closure, whereas God grants only new visions of open-endedness. We long for a steady-state creation in which our place is clear, certain, and comfortable, but God gives us an evolutionary creation in which clarity is always transforming itself into ambiguity, certainty into vulnerability and riskiness, comfort into challenge. And just as there was never an Eden in which our existence was different from this, so we know of no future Heaven in which transformation will no longer define us.

Transformation is in itself a summary of what Christians believe, the epitome of our faith. It is a transformation that characterizes our actual present existence and that of the world we live in, as well as the future hope to which we hold, our personal hope beyond our own physical death, and also our hope for the future of the cosmos, the entire creation.

The character of God as good and loving is essential for our understanding of transformation, just as it is for interpreting all of God's works. What we say about God's work in creation, judgment, the governance of history, fulfillment — all of these are dependent for their meaning on our conception of the character of the God who is doing the creating, judging, governing, and fulfilling. Our tradition tells us that God is fundamentally good and loving. Even those traditions that give prominence to God's judgment, to law, as well as gospel, give the priority to love and goodness. The work of God is a working out of God's character, from creation to eschatological fulfillment. This understanding is given dogmatic status in our concepts of the economic and immanent Trinity, where we say that what God does in history is utterly consonant with who God is in God's own inner being. And even though we cannot step inside God's mind, we rest our faith on the conviction that that mind is revealed in the love of Jesus Christ. Theologically and dogmatically there are no other options for us as Christians: Whatever we believe God to be willing and doing, finally crystallizes into goodness and love.

The weight of our belief in transformation rests also on this understanding of God's character, because that character defines the motivation for our being transformed, and also both its methodology and its goal.

Transformation as Ecclesiological Focus

We cannot adequately speak about the church and its place in salvation unless we understand also the centrality of God's will and work of transformation. When early Christians called themselves People of the Way, when the church understood itself as a *communio viatorum,* a community of pilgrims, they were giving expression to this central insight — that the church is constituted by the work of God in Christ as transformation. When we speak of ourselves as the church catholic, we remind ourselves that we stand in this broad tradition. When we speak of ourselves as a community grounded in the Protestant principle, *ecclesia semper reformanda est* (the church must always be reformed), we acknowledge that it is a tradition of always receiving what cannot be possessed, never a tradition of having once-and-for-all arrived in the Promised Land. As Joseph Sittler once observed, there is a sense in which the quintessence of being Christian is actualized more in the person of Moses peering into the distance from Mount Nebo than in the crowds who were getting their feet wet as they walked through the Jordan River into Canaan.[6]

The worldview of transformation is not so much the perspective of an essential self being repaired and rendered more desirable as it is a sense of a self in the process of becoming — not a defined self being altered so much as a self whose definition is in the entire process. Intentionality, planning, and control are part of the process, but the sense of undergoing a process that is not in our control, of being shaped as much as we do the shaping, is even more prominent. We are in the process of becoming something whose outcome and aim we cannot fully or even very adequately comprehend. We are not the potters of highly successful persons as much as we are ourselves on the wheel of the potter, whom we call God in Christ.

6. Joseph Sittler, "The View from Mount Nebo," in *The Care of the Earth and Other University Sermons* (Minneapolis: Fortress Press, 1964), pp. 75-87.

Transformation: God's Hopes for the World, the World's Hopes for God

The awareness of possibilities and the transformation that prepares for the realization of possibilities constitute a concrete point of contact between God and the world. This is a point where God's hope for the world becomes actual and accessible for the entire creation, including human persons. Conversely it is also a point where the hopes of the world for God likewise become actual and accessible — even when those hopes are articulated in terms that do not use the name of God. Mission that is centered on possibility recognizes this point of contact between God and the world and also understands that it is of the very essence of the church that it be a community in which there is a forceful expression of God's hopes and the world's hopes.

There is no single insight concerning the church's mission that is more significant than this one: that in our preaching, teaching, worship, pastoral care, personal interactions, and public ministry, we are a community in which these hopes are a prime reality, and we are called to become a community in which their primacy becomes ever more clear. If the church is not such a community, then its existence is trivial; it is just another institution, and it has lost its sense of why God created it in the first place. The church cannot be church apart from its being a community where God's possibilities and hopes are engaged and where the transformative work of God is welcomed and nurtured. If we wish to relate the church to salvation, we will focus on the church as this community of possibility and transformation, where God's hopes and the world's hopes interface. Only in communities such as these does talk of salvation make sense.

Grief, anxiety, joy, and expectation are significant experiential signals of the process of transformation, both among individuals and communities, precisely because transformation involves the passing away of the old and emergence of the new. All of these four characteristics of experience may be authentic and also inauthentic. Grief at the loss of that which has nourished our faith and the cause of God in the world is authentic in Christian terms, while grief attached to the loss of that which nourished our idolatries and which caused pain and starved the faith of others is inauthentic grief. Precisely the converse analysis may be made of that which brings joy and encouragement. The depth and richness of God's transforming work will always call into question our grief, anxiety, joy, and expectation when they are grounded in falsehood and superficiality, just as it will provide strength and energy for that which is grounded in the work of God's spirit.

Why devote so much time to discussing a worldview centered in transformation? Because, I contend, *unless we can identify with the worldview of transformation we cannot enter into mission that conforms to the gospel, nor will we possess an adequate ecclesiology for mission in our time, nor can we relate that ecclesiology to salvation, because only as we share in God's transforming work can we truly be available to the possibilities that God intends to bring forth in the world and through the church. If the church's mission is not oriented toward transformation, it will not be God's mission, as our Christian tradition teaches us to understand God.*

Empirical Foundations of Transformation: Locating Mission in God's World

Empirical studies make it unmistakably clear that the world in which our mission takes place is a world that is not only continually undergoing transformation, but a world that is constituted by transformation. Christians, for whom belief in God as Creator is fundamental, would expect this conclusion from empirical studies. The implication is obvious: The God who calls us to mission intends transformation, and the world in which we carry out mission is by its nature conditioned by transformative processes.

Theoretical interpretations of the empirical world are nearly unanimous in proposing evolutionary ideas as the key to understanding both the world and our placement in it. The comprehensive theory of evolution reinforces the theological interpretation of this essay: evolution is not simply a concept of change, it also describes processes in which novelty emerges within matrices of natural stuff and natural causes. Furthermore, evolutionary theory presupposes a concept of nature that is undergoing continuous transformation, rather than the idea of a static essence whose attributes change. As psychologist David Loye has pointed out, transformation theories are not only grounded in the theoretical studies of biology and chaos science, but are "organic and ecologically grounded . . . embedded within and rising out of nature . . . not imposed" from the outside.[7] Niels

7. David Loye, "Can Science Help Construct a New Global Ethic? The Development

Gregersen's discussion in this volume is an example of this interpretation of emerging novelty in one of its more sophisticated aspects as suggested by the sciences of complexity, namely, nature's own capacity to create novelty under the conditions of autopoiesis.

Loye goes further and argues that *moral* transformation is integral to the processes of the world. He describes these processes of transformation as inclusive of both genders, crossing all boundaries of faith, philosophy, and social placement, trans-evolutionary (attested by biological, cultural, and cosmic evolution), and action-oriented (in contrast to traditional nonactivist and noninterventionist theories of transformation).[8]

Such conclusions from the sciences are of enormous importance for our thinking about our mission as Christians. Even though we bring a particular perspective to bear, we do not bring the concern for transformation to the world — it is already implanted in the world by virtue of its creation. Furthermore, we are not the only ones who are dedicated to transformation — people from every faith and philosophy, from all occupations, are also committed to it.

It is no surprise that theological interpreters of science, such as Teilhard de Chardin,[9] Karl Schmitz-Moormann,[10] and John Haught,[11] have provided significant theories of the processes of transformation that God works within the framework of evolution. Scientific theorists also describe the transformation in evolutionary processes, without, of course, entertaining any notions of God. The evolutionary process is charted in cosmic terms, and also in terms of terrestrial evolution and biocultural evolution.[12] It is helpful to survey briefly each of these phases of evolution, under the guidance of the thinkers just mentioned.

Gregersen's work underscores the transformative character of the

---

and Implications of Moral Transformation Theory," *Zygon: Journal of Religion & Science* 34 (June 1999): 228.

8. Loye, "Can Science Help Construct a New Global Ethic?" pp. 228-30.

9. Pierre Teilhard de Chardin, *The Human Phenomenon*, A New Edition and Translation by Sarah Appleton-Weber (Brighton, U.K.: Sussex Academic Press, 1999).

10. Karl Schmitz-Moormann, *Theology of Creation in an Evolutionary World* (Cleveland: Pilgrim Press, 1997).

11. John F. Haught, *God After Darwin: A Theology of Evolution* (Boulder, Colo.: Westview Press, 2000).

12. Eric Chaisson, *Cosmic Dawn* (New York: Little, Brown, 1981) and *The Life Era* (New York: Atlantic Monthly Press, 1987).

physical world in terms of the processes of what is now called "complexity" (including physics, chemistry, biology, and information sciences). Schmitz-Moormann calls attention to the fact that the creation is not the unfolding of what originated at the beginning, but rather nature's response to a call from the future. He coins the term *creatio appellata,* the "called-forth creation," in which becoming is creation's answer to God's call.[13] He places this notion alongside the doctrines of *creatio ex nihilo* and *creatio continua.*

Biological evolution on planet earth, decisively interpreted by Charles Darwin, is also a realm of transformation. Gregersen's work on complexity and autopoiesis makes this evident in the biological realm as much as in physical processes. John Haught, building on Teilhard and Alfred North Whitehead, speaks of the evolutionary testimony to the *unfinished* character of the creation.[14] This unfinished aspect is correlated with hope within an eschatological perspective on the world and also with an understanding of God's power as an alluring, persuasive force, rather than a coercive force. This perspective on God's power agrees with Schmitz-Moormann's emphasis that God intentionally fosters freedom in the creation. Haught suggests the concept of creation as "letting be," in which God's persuasive power is exercised within the biblical idea of self-emptying *(kenosis).*[15]

The focus of these thinkers on physical and biological aspects of nature is not ordinarily associated with the theological idea of mission. However, as I have already suggested, the testimony of these sciences is significant for our reflection on mission, since it indicates how our theological insights are rooted in the very nature of the world that God has created — even within the nonhuman dimensions of that world. Viggo Mortensen himself has given attention to these sciences.

Historical-cultural studies are thoroughly consistent with these natural scientific researches, as all of the thinkers I have mentioned thus far would agree. These studies provide further empirical interpretation of the world in which mission is located. The phenomenon of globalization, for which Viggo Mortensen has also expressed concern, emerges in this historical-cultural domain. It is one of the major elements, he insists, in the contemporary "dominant culture," about which he writes: "Christianity in the

13. Schmitz-Moormann, *Theology of Creation,* p. 121.

14. Haught, *God After Darwin,* pp. 37ff.

15. Haught, *God After Darwin,* chap. 7.

new millennium will be shaped in the encounter with the dominant culture of this time, which is globalization."[16] He has adopted the terminology of "productive encounter/critical distance" to describe our approach to globalization.[17]

Although Mortensen himself does not give so much attention to this fact, it is important to understand that globalization is a facet of human culture and history undergoing transformation in our time and giving rise to new realities. This transformation is expressed in quintessential ways in the phenomenon of globalization, but it is larger than this phenomenon. Ewert Cousins is one of those thinkers who has spoken of this vast set of transforming events in terms of a First and Second Axial Period.[18] It is helpful to rehearse briefly Cousins' argument.

The Axial Period concepts are said to provide a deeper understanding of our times than the terms "modern" and "postmodern." The Axial Period concepts build upon the work of Karl Jaspers,[19] who suggested that in "the period between 800 and 200 B.C.E., peaking about 500 B.C.E., a striking transformation of consciousness occurred in three geographic regions, apparently without the influence of one on the other."[20] In this period there came into existence the great schools of Chinese philosophy (Confucius and Lao-tze), the Upanishads emerged in Hinduism, as well as the new religious traditions of Buddha and Mahavira, the Jewish prophets (Elijah, Isaiah, and Jeremiah) who called forth a new moral awareness, and the Western philosophy of the Greeks — the pre-Socratics, Socrates, Plato, and Aristotle.

> The First Axial Period ushered in a radically new form of consciousness. Whereas primal consciousness was tribal, Axial consciousness was individual. This sense of individual identity as distinct from the tribe and from nature is the most characteristic mark of Axial consciousness. From this flow other characteristics: consciousness that is self-reflective

16. Viggo Mortensen, "Areopagus Revisited: The Dialogue between Science and Religion and the Dialogue between People of Different Faiths," *Zygon: Journal of Religion & Science* 37 (March 2000): 64.

17. Mortensen, "Areopagus Revisited," p. 78.

18. Ewert Cousins, "The Convergence of Culture and Religions in Light of the Evolution of Consciousness," *Zygon: Journal of Religion & Science* 34 (June 1999): 209-19.

19. Karl Jaspers, *Vom Ursprung und Ziel der Geschichte* (Zurich: Artemis, 1949).

20. Cousins, "The Convergence of Culture and Religions," p. 211.

> and analytic and that can be applied to nature in the form of scientific theories, to society in the form of social critique, to knowledge in the form of philosophy, and to religion in the form of mapping an individual spiritual journey. This self-reflective, analytic, critical consciousness stood in sharp contrast to primal mythic and ritualistic consciousness.[21]

There was also a loss in this Axial consciousness, namely, the alienation from nature and the tribe, and the organic relationships of community. However, the great religions of the world as we know them today grew out of this period, including Christianity and Islam, the two religions that emerged from the roots of Judaism. "The common structures of consciousness found in these religions are characteristic of the general transformation of consciousness effected in the Axial Period."[22]

If we note the monumental significance of the First Axial Period and its restructuring of human consciousness, we can appreciate the depth and breadth of the assertion that we are now in a Second Axial Period. Cousins writes: "Like the first it is happening simultaneously around the earth, and like the first it will shape the horizon of consciousness for future centuries. Not surprisingly, too, it will have great significance for world religions, which were constituted in the First Axial Period. However, the new form of consciousness is different from that of the First Axial Period. Then it was individual consciousness; now it is global consciousness."[23]

The transformation of consciousness that is engendered by the Second Axial Period is defined over against the First Axial Period, but goes in different directions. The forces of divergence were the critical motor of the earlier transformation, whereas convergence drives the current axial movement. This convergence (to draw once again on the thought of Teilhard de Chardin) does not obliterate the identities of the particular persons and groups and identities that inhabit the globe, but in "center-to-center" union, the convergence includes the dynamics of individuation within itself. Teilhard called this double rhythm "complexification," which does not contradict the term as Gregersen discusses it, but is a richer, metaphysical concept.

21. Cousins, "The Convergence of Culture and Religions," p. 213.
22. Cousins, "The Convergence of Culture and Religions," p. 213.
23. Cousins, "The Convergence of Culture and Religions," p. 215.

> Although in the first millennium B.C.E. there was a common transformation of consciousness, it occurred in diverse geographical regions within already differentiated cultures. In each case the religion was shaped by this differentiation in its origin and developed along differentiated lines. This produced a remarkable richness of spiritual wisdom, of spiritual energies, and of religious-cultural forms to express, preserve, and transmit this heritage. Now that the forces of divergence have shifted to convergence, the religions must meet each other in center-to-center unions, discovering what is most authentic in each other, releasing creative energy toward a more complexified form of religious consciousness.[24]

This new form of consciousness will not accept the First Period's alienation from the earth and community, but will seek to re-establish the unity with them, as well as with the primal consciousness that preceded the First Axial Period — not in any sense to undo that first transformation, but rather to take it in new trajectories. Further, the new consciousness will not be content with the spiritual path of the First Axial Period, which tended toward heavenly realms at the neglect of the earthly. Rather, it will direct its attention also to the solution of the earthly problems of environment, poverty, war, and injustice.[25]

I have chosen the work of Ewert Cousins as my guide to this new transformation of consciousness, but the work of Mihaly Csikszentmihalyi, Eric Chaisson, Solomon Katz, David Loye, and Ervin Laszlo, to mention only a few thinkers, could be brought to illuminate the cultural-historical events that Cousins describes.

Beyond Theology and Location: Transformation as Challenge to Mission

To this point, we have given attention to the idea of transformation as theological mandate to which mission must respond and as description of the world in which mission takes place. Now the discussion moves to a

24. Cousins, "The Convergence of Culture and Religions," p. 216.

25. See also Lesher, "The Challenge of Global Ethics: Learning and Organizing," *Zygon: Journal of Religion & Science* 34 (June 1999): 255-63.

brief consideration of transformation as the challenge and object of mission. Our perspective underscores the relationality or ecology of mission: Mission takes its start from the gospel that announces God's will for the world that God has also created. As God's creation, the world in which mission takes place is not fundamentally alien or "other" from the gospel and the church, but rather co-existent with the church in the creation. This accounts for the strange fact that transformation is both subject and object of mission, a characteristic both of the world to which mission extends and of the gospel that informs mission.

We could devote our full attention to elaborating this subject/object character of mission as transformation. It raises a number of questions, such as: If transformation is already the ground of the world's processes, in what sense is our mission "to" the world? Just what does the mission of transformation contribute to a world that is already constituted by transformation? In this context, we can only assert that because of finitude and sin, the world does not fully comprehend its own transformational nature, nor does it see clearly what the goal of transformation is. *Formally stated, the mission of the church aims to comprehend more fully and proclaim clearly what the world's transformation is really about and what God intends for it. This includes the message that God accomplishes transformation under the conditions of sin and finitude, that is, under the conditions of grace that transforms even sin and finitude.*

Here we can only survey some of the configurations in which transformation challenges our mission.

The Empirical Sciences

Today we are dependent upon the sciences for knowledge of the world, and our understanding of transformation is significantly informed by their contribution. At the same time, the sciences also constitute a field for mission. There are two aspects to the challenge that the sciences pose to mission. First, although many scientists are Christians and members of the church, the scientific community as such has been alienated from the church and its life for several centuries — so much so that many superficial and distorted stereotypes of the church's antagonism to science have become widespread, both in the scientific community and in the larger society. These conditions point to the *pastoral* challenge of our mission to science. Our mission will want to reach out to relate the Christian community to the scientific community.

Second, the intellectual and conceptual component of the Christian faith has failed to engage the worldviews of the sciences, with the result that the common view of society is that Christian faith is hostile to science and that it holds to a "primitive" set of concepts that science cannot accept. Christian faith, like most religious faiths, accepts as normative articulations of wisdom about the world that are millennia old. Even though much of this wisdom is profoundly relevant to life today, its form is for the most part archaic. This puts it, prima facie at least, at odds with scientific knowledge, whose articulations are continually articulated in new and current forms. The challenge to communication between archaic forms and current ones is difficult at best, even for those persons who understand that archaic forms are not necessarily to be understood literally. Unfortunately, most religious believers today, as well as most scientists, consider ancient religious formulations to be literally intended. Fundamentalists, of course, in both science and religion hold this literalism to be the norm, and so do other conservative religious adherents. Until both scientists and Christian believers gain more awareness of the uses of language, and the differences between scientific and religious language, there will be little constructive engagement between Christian faith and science. This set of concerns comprise the *intellectual-conceptual* aspect of our mission to science.

Technology

Technology represents the "humanification" of the nonhuman natural systems. Today there is no natural space that has not been conditioned by human culture in the form of technology. Technology has reshaped our understanding and our experience of the world and of ourselves. It engenders experiences that are in themselves new to human life.

From their origins, for example, human beings have been conditioned to be alert to the large and sudden challenges that come their way, producing immediate consequences: the pounce of a tiger in the jungle, the stampede of elephants, lightning and thunder, avalanches, warfare. Our sensory systems are not suited to notice the very small, the microscopic challenges that may have no immediate consequences for us, but may threaten us over the long haul: smoking tobacco and ingesting other slow-acting toxic substances, polluting streams upstream from their irrigation functions, polluting the air, handling radioactive substances, and the like. Technology (coupled with scientific knowledge) enables us to be aware of these microscopic, long-term effects. Awareness of these microscopic events engenders a range of new experiences that must be integrated into our interpretation of life and our assessment of behaviors, even moral behaviors.

Technology allows us to intervene in natural processes in ways that were unimaginable even a generation ago. This is apparent in the practice of medicine, particularly as it pertains to the beginning and ending of life. It is a new experience for us to be obliged to decide when a loved one must die after having been kept alive by medical interventions for weeks or months or even years. It is a new experience for us to become aware that the baby in a mother's womb has lethal genetic defects and therefore might be aborted. It is also new to us that science-based in vitro fertilization technology can give babies to women who are otherwise not able to bear children. Genetic engineering pushes still further into areas of new experience.

Since life, birth, and death are themes of great significance to Christian faith, these new experiences must be understood, interpreted, and morally engaged by religious believers as they attempt to put their worlds together in the world-building activity.

Consequently, technology poses two challenges to our mission that are comparable to those of science. The *ethical* challenge concerns the ways in which we use technology. The *intellectual-symbolic* challenge focuses on the ways in which technology is refashioning our images of what it means to be human, particularly in terms of our capability to shape and reshape human nature itself. Although these challenges are especially vivid in the realms of genetics and medicine, they also arise in the realms of computer technology and artificial intelligence. The concept of *cyborg* will no doubt become a familiar element for theological and ethical reflection, since it images human beings in intimate relation to technology, so intimate that technology is no longer external to human life and nature, but internal to its very constitution.

The Plurality of Cultures and Religions

The convergence that Cousins speaks of, as well as the globalization that Mortensen himself has discussed, brings our mission to the challenge of defining ourselves and the gospel in a pluralistic world and, as Cousins suggests, entering into the interactions that deepen understanding and, even more, allow each particularity to be enriched by the others and to attain the more complex consciousness that can allow the values and experiences of other particularities to converge with our own.[26] This challenge, too, possesses both *pastoral-evangelistic* and *intellectual-theological* dimensions. Presently neither Christian community life nor theology has a clear sense of how to share in the convergence of cultures and religions that is part of the dominant culture in which we live and that will shape our Christian identity. This deficiency is a major item for the agenda of mission.

A Final Word

Transformation as mission means that we are challenged (1) to acknowledge and understand transformation in its broadest terms, (2) to participate in it in ways that conform to and witness to the gospel, (3) to allow it to influence our worldview, (4) to shape our theological understanding in ways that can take the measure of transformation, and (5) to make our distinctive Christian contribution to how we understand and share in transformation. My assumption has been that transformation is the work of God, in the creation and in the providential course of the creation towards its final consummation. If this assumption is true, then every aspect of our mission will be permeated by it — not only in our understanding, but even more in the ways in which we share in the transformation of the world.

26. Cousins, "The Convergence of Culture and Religions," pp. 216-17.

Is There Hope in the Midst of Suffering? Images of Christ in Latin America

WALTER ALTMANN

I. Introduction: Is There Meaning in Suffering?

Suffering has been one of the most difficult issues in theological reflection. It touches not only our understanding of the meaning of life and of God, but also our very experience of God and with God. It has been said that after the horror of Auschwitz it has become impossible to talk of God, at least of a loving God. On the other hand, it has been the experience and the testimony of countless Christians throughout the centuries that they were not left alone in the midst of the most cruel forms of suffering, which would indeed seem to be unbearable. It has been said that the blood of the martyrs constituted the seed of the church.

Leonardo Boff, the well-known liberation theologian from Brazil, has said, supporting Dorothee Sölle, that while there *is* no meaning in suffering, "we can *endow* it with meaning."[1] This seems to me to be correct. Meaningless situations of suffering can be turned into meaningful expressions of Christian faith and love. Ultimately, faith confesses that nothing, no powers whatsoever, not even the power of death — as the Apostle Paul has put it — can separate us from the love of God, which was revealed in

1. Leonardo Boff, *Passion of Christ, Passion of the World: The Facts, Their Interpretation, and Their Meaning Yesterday and Today* (Maryknoll, N.Y.: Orbis Books, 1977), p. 107.

This article is part of a paper presented in Finland, July 6, 2001.

Christ Jesus (Rom. 8:38-39). Death, this last "enemy" of God to be destroyed (1 Cor. 15:26), can be a "gain" when Christ is our life (Phil. 1:21).

However, this can by no means signify that we will accept passively the reality of meaningless suffering. On the contrary, the existence of suffering of this kind is a permanent call to overcome the causes of suffering and, when this is not possible, to express a compassionate solidarity with those who have to bear suffering. Therefore, this other distinction by Leonardo Boff[2] is pertinent as well: we distinguish between a suffering which has been imposed upon people, which is the result of prevailing structures or actions of injustice, and that other form of suffering which is the consequence of voluntary action to prevent or to overcome meaningless or unjust forms of suffering. While you may never accept the first form of suffering as "natural" or as "God's will," and fall into resignation, you may be called to take upon you the second form of suffering, which is part of the cost of discipleship, as Dietrich Bonhoeffer has taught us, and therefore, in this case, as God's will indeed.

If, ultimately, our understanding of suffering has to do with the way we understand and experience Jesus himself, then it will be significant for us to look into the way Jesus Christ is perceived and seen in different contexts. In the following I shall explore a variety of images of Christ in Latin America, especially images of the cross, asking about their meaning for faith, experience, and action in this continent.[3] I shall comment on pictures of Jesus and the cross, from Latin America, in their variety, especially as they appear in catechetical materials in base communities. The aim will be that of drawing attention to how suffering has been perceived in Latin America, but also of leading to those perspectives that raise hope and trust beyond the reality of suffering.

II. How Is Christ's Suffering Perceived?

1. Throughout the history of the colonization of the South American continent, two christological images became crystallized above the others: a

2. Boff, *Passion of Christ,* pp. 117-28.

3. In a different way I have developed — and presuppose it here — the question of Christ's images and their meaning from a Latin American point of view in "A Latin American Perspective on the Cross and Suffering," in *The Scandal of a Crucified World: Perspectives on the Cross and Suffering,* ed. Yacob Tesfai (Maryknoll, N.Y.: Orbis Books, 1994), pp. 75-86.

dead Jesus, and Christ, a celestial monarch.[4] The sculptured images of the dead Christ show him laid out, totally defeated and impotent, bleeding and with an expression of unspeakable suffering. These images of the dead Jesus remain in the crypts of the churches throughout the year, exposed to the devotion of the people. During Holy Week and at Corpus Christi they are carried out in procession, and people repeat the stations of the cross through the *via sacra.* A good example from the colonial art is *The Dead Lord,* a sculpture by friar Domingos da Conceição, from the years 1679 to 1681.[5] Typical is the almost naked and bleeding body of Jesus, not so typical that Jesus' head is somewhat raised, giving almost the impression of being still alive. The pain of Jesus is revealed more impressively, though, in *The Flagellated Christ* of Antonio Francisco Lisboa, O Aleijadinho (known as "The Crippled"), from the latter part of the eighteenth century.[6] Son of a Portuguese man and a black slave woman, O Aleijadinho became probably the greatest artist of Brazil's colonial period, in spite of his physical disability acquired possibly through a leprosy that affected the nerves of his hands, arms, and legs.

2. In relation to the image of Christ as a heavenly monarch, George Casalis[7] gives account of several examples of churches in New Mexico and Colombia, where Christ and the Blessed Virgin are portrayed as Ferdinand of Aragon and Isabella of Castile. It may well be that the tradition was not as strong in Portugal's colonies. Nevertheless, you can find, of course, the identification of the holy with wealth and power, for example in the richly decorated churches from the time of the great gold discoveries in the eighteenth century. Saints too could be portrayed richly dressed and adorned, like the example of Saint Benedict and Saint Escolastica, by Domingos da Conceição, in the main altar of the Saint Benedict Monastery in Rio de Janeiro, one of the richest churches in Brazil.[8]

3. In contrast to those pictures from colonial times, let me come to examples of catechetical materials under the spell of liberation theology.

4. See José Míguez Bonino, ed., *Faces of Jesus: Latin American Christologies* (Maryknoll, N.Y.: Orbis Books, 1983), especially George Casalis, "Jesus — Neither Abject Lord nor Heavenly Monarch," pp. 72-76. See also my article mentioned in the previous note.

5. *Arte no Brasil,* v. 1 (São Paulo: Abril Cultural, without year), pp. 100-101.

6. *Arte no Brasil,* v. 1, p. 388.

7. See note 4 above.

8. *Arte no Brazil,* v. 1, p. 100.

Hermann Brandt[9] has called attention to the enormous influence of the genus of what he calls *Kleinliteratur:* leaflets, pamphlets, and booklets of a very unpretentious makeup, usually of anonymous authorship, but widely used as catechetical and liturgical materials by the base communities throughout Latin America, especially in the 1970s and 1980s. In fact, in those materials you can find in a very direct form the theme of Jesus' identification with the poor and needy, so dear to liberation theology. Quite often the drawings will represent Latin America or a certain region or country of Latin America as in bondage or crucified. The first examples portray South America in chains like Jesus (see p. 201), and the crucified Argentina and its poor people (see p. 202). The significant title of the first picture reads, translated into English, "The history of Christ repeats itself in the history of the people that struggle for liberation." The second one wants to foster a journey in faith and hope, but relates this issue with the suffering of the thousands who were killed and disappeared during the Argentinean military dictatorship.

4. I mentioned the processions of the *via sacra.* Traditionally the *via sacra* has fourteen stations of meditation related to the passion of Jesus. The fourteen stations are the following: "1. Jesus is condemned to death; 2. Jesus receives the cross; 3. Jesus falls for the first time; 4. Jesus meets Mary, his mother; 5. The Cirenese helps Jesus to carry the cross; 6. A woman called Veronica dries Jesus' face; 7. Jesus falls for the second time; 8. Women of Jerusalem weep as they see Jesus pass by; 9. Jesus falls for the third time; 10. Jesus is stripped of his clothes; 11. Jesus is nailed onto the cross; 12. Jesus dies on the cross; 13. The body of Jesus is taken down from the cross and placed in the arms of his mother; 14. Jesus is buried." Under the influence of liberation theology, there was regularly added a fifteenth station: "Jesus, after being dead for almost three days, lived again and is alive among us."[10]

Not only a fifteenth station will be regularly added. The description of the different stations can also be significantly changed, to express that Jesus' story can be found among the fate of the people. For example: "1. The big ones plot against Jesus; 2. Jesus is betrayed; 3. Jesus feels anguish facing death; 4. Peter denies Jesus; 5. The people let themselves be deceived

9. Hermann Brandt, *Gottesgegenwart in Lateinamerika: Inkarnation als Leitmotiv der Befreiungstheologie* (Hamburg: Steinmann & Steinmann, 1992), pp. 94ff.

10. *Via sacra da fraternidade* (without place and year), p. 32.

CEBI/Sul, *A história de Cristo se repete na história do povo que luta pela libertação* (São Leopoldo, 1986), cover.

Juan José Díaz, *Para Caminar con Fe y Esperanza*
(Buenos Aires [?], 1982), cover.

by the chiefs and prefer Barabbas; 6. Jesus suffers torture; 7. The governor washes his hands; 8. Condemned as subversive; 9. Jesus carries the cross; 10. A peasant helps Jesus to carry the cross; 11. The women accompany Jesus to the cross; 12. Jesus dies on the cross; 13. Jesus is buried; 14. He is risen; 15. The way of the people."[11] We notice that in this example, besides describing the stations within the reality of Latin American dictatorships (subversion and torture, peasants and women, but also betrayal and the people's illusion), Christ's resurrection is already the fourteenth station, leaving room for "the way of the people" in the fifteenth station. It is the theme of following Jesus that has taken a central place in Christology in Latin American liberation theology.[12] The title of the booklet reads: "The cross of Jesus in the life of the people" (see p. 204).

The fact that the poor people have to carry the burden of the cross can be placed in different concrete situations, like the following example from Mexico. The settler says: "We have suffered this type of housing for many years" (see p. 205). Or this other: "Jesus' *via sacra*" (see p. 206). As a final example in this section, it should be noted that Christmas and Jesus' birth can also be placed in the midst of various situations, relevant for the people on the fields and in the cities, in leisure or in political participation. The banner that is carried by the people reads: "Political participation is a right of everybody" (see p. 207).

It should be emphasized that these catechetical materials, in spite of the harsh realities, always indicate hope and the perspective of resurrection. Other Latin American artists came to express simply the horror of Jesus' death. The best examples are given by Guido Rocha, a Brazilian sculptor who had to go into exile. His depictions of Christ on the cross simply and vividly express the horrifying agony of those who were tortured by the military dictatorships in Latin America. Asked why he would make so many Christs, he answered: "I am so far away, and I want to make a sculpture of my people. Since being a child, in Minas (Gerais), I learned that no one resembles the people more than Christ."[13]

5. Nevertheless, there are other forms of expressing who Christ was and is, forms that show happiness and freedom. The Sandinista Revolu-

11. Prelazia de São Félix do Araguaia, MT, *A cruz de Jesus na vida do povo* (Petrópolis: Vozes, 1985), summary on p. 5. See the illustration on p. 204, below.

12. Especially in the Christologies of Leonardo Boff and Jon Sobrino.

13. Apud Ulrich Schoenborn, *Fé entre história e experiência:* Migalhas exegéticas (São Leopoldo: Sinodal, 1982), p. 122; pictures of Rocha's sculptures are found on pp. 134-35.

Prelazia de São Félix do Araguaia, MT, *A cruz de Jesus na vida do povo* (Petrópolis: Vozes, 1985), cover.

CRISTO COLONO

HEMOS SUFRIDO ESTAS VIVIENDAS DURANTE MUCHOS AÑOS

Cristo colono (no place or year of publication given), cover.

Arquidiocese de Campinas, *A via sacra de Jesus . . .*
(Campinas, no date of publication given), cover.

CNBB Sub-Regional VI, *Natal em comunidade*
(Senhor do Bonfim/BA, no date of publication given), cover.

tion represented one of those moments. After the Revolution, Ernesto Cardenal, then as Minister of Culture, went back to the Island of Solentiname, where he had worked with peasants and fishermen and women. The experiment had been destroyed by the bombs of the Somoza dictatorship. Now the people expressed their belief through the arts, especially paintings. They are extremely colorful. Jesus on the cross does not seem to suffer. The women bring flowers, and even the bleeding hands and feet look almost like a decoration, a feeble memory of the sufferings of the people, which belong now to the past.[14] Also the cemetery, where Jesus was buried and where he cannot be found anymore, is full of flowers. Behind the man portrayed in the picture (the resurrected Jesus himself or, possibly, a disciple come to the graveyard, anyhow a common person from the people), we see in the open tomb the flag of the Sandinista Front. The accompanying text says: "The news is not only his [Jesus'] resurrection but also ours."[15]

6. Yet, colorful and happy representations of Jesus' crucifixion can be found in other contexts, too, not only in the midst of the experience of the revolutionary liberation. It may simply express a basic hopeful attitude towards life by Latin American peoples, even in the midst of hardships. One example may be the typical colorful wooden crosses from El Salvador, a popular handicraft from that country. They are made in a great variety. Usually Jesus does not seem to be nailed on the cross at all, but rather the cross, with a beautiful scenery of a common people's village, constitutes only the background for Jesus in a sovereign attitude of blessing. His gesture does not reveal the pain of an executed person, but proclaims vividly the victory over death (see p. 209). But there are crosses that portray women on the cross, in Jesus' place, and the women in various tasks in the midst of the community — a beautiful example of expressing the dignity of women, so harshly discriminated against and oppressed under the traditional Latin American *machismo* (see p. 210). Some crosses will even bring simply the abundance and beauty of natural life without any people.

7. Another good example can be found in the best Brazilian painter of naive art, José Antônio da Silva.[16] He painted a full series of pictures of

14. *Los campesinos de Solentiname pintan el evangelio: Texto de Ernesto Cardenal* (Managua: Ediciones Monimbó, 1982), p. 63.

15. *Los campesinos de Solentiname,* pp. 66-67.

16. See Ladi Biezus, "A Paixão segundo Silva," *Icaro* 116: 22-27, and cover (with pictures).

Wooden cross depicting a victorious Christ (El Salvador)

Wooden cross depicting women in various tasks (El Salvador)

Jesus' passion. One of the pictures shows the women under the cross, another Jesus' triumphant entrance into Jerusalem on Palm Sunday, but already foreshadowed by the prospect of death on the cross; black crosses are in the midst of the welcoming multitude. On a third picture, a man of the people — already aged? — is portrayed on the cross. He looks more like someone accepting his fate than suffering under pain. On a fourth one, we see "Joseph of Arimathea lowering Christ from the cross among clouds of hope: a tragic event, but surrounded by transcendent light."[17] In relation to a fifth picture, Ladi Biezus writes:

> To depict the 14th station, the burial, Silva decided to paint a scene that is not described in the Bible: a number of followers pay their last respects to Christ, who lies on flowers, far above the ground. The onlookers, their eyes wide open, appear to hesitate between awe and hope; it seems that they finally see the light. Amid the perplexity of the people, the hills are illuminated by a golden light, which could be the dawn of the definitive day. This may be just a hint of the Resurrection according to Silva.[18]

Again, therefore, as in the catechetical materials we presented, Jesus' death on the cross is not the last word, but is seen in the light of his resurrection.

8. Where do we find ourselves today? The 1990s have brought profound changes in the political, social, economic, cultural, and religious scenery in Latin America and the world. The crudest military dictatorships, but also the Sandinista revolutionary experiment, belong to the past. Yet a globalized economy has deepened the gap between rich and poor, and created a new category of excluded ones, who in many ways long for the past when they still were under the category of exploited ones. In this sense, all the images of Jesus identifying him with the sufferings of the people are obviously still relevant. On the other hand, "liberation" by no means seems to be at hand. On the contrary, while the prevailing ideology tries to convey the message that there is no alternative to the currently given system — history has come to an end! — people perceive that the way to a just social order is still a very long one, but nevertheless a necessity and a possibility. A sense of citizenship and active participation in society and political life has

17. Biezus, "A Paixão segundo Silva," p. 24.
18. Biezus, "A Paixão segundo Silva," p. 29.

to be built. This means, as well, that previously neglected dimensions are being incorporated into theological reflection, like the cultural and ethnic ones. The indigenous crucified Christ, by Gustavo Pavel Egüez, from Ecuador,[19] in the painting called the *Cry of the Excluded,* is a good example. The death of the indigenous Christ is inserted into the reality of the indigenous people and their magic world. Their cry is also hope. The Holy Spirit, in the shape of a dove constituted by human hands, doesn't leave room for doubts about the dignifying perspectives of solidarity.

Is there really reason for hope? Where do we get the strength for the necessary perseverance? Can Jesus' cross illuminate this journey? Can Jesus' resurrection function as a horizon of hope calling us towards the future? The movement of base communities seems to answer with a realistic but nevertheless confident yes. The poster for the tenth interecclesial encounter of the base communities, which took place July 2000, in Ilhéus/ Bahia (Brazil), is perhaps not very artfully designed but has great symbolic strength (see p. 213). The themes of these encounters of base communities — mostly poor lay people who often travel by bus for thousands of kilometers — are more of an ecclesiological nature. But to a certain extent the poster has implications for our christological concern, as well. Latin America (within it, we can depict Brazil) is portrayed as a gigantic foot. It is — and the base communities with it — on its way. It is, of course, a long journey. The various dimensions of this journey form a cross, itself under Jesus' cross. In its center there is the Bible. On the bottom there are the people in their cultural and ethnic plurality, with a *dream* (the word can be found on the lower part of the cross). The arms of the cross present the words *commitment,* on the right, and *journey* ("caminhada"), on the left.[20] In this journey the people need the *memory* — this is written on the upper part of the cross — , memory of the liberating event on Jesus' cross, which however, like a rising sun, brings the dawn of a new future. Thus — perhaps only in this way, but in this way as a concrete experience — we may endow suffering with a meaning: it gives birth to new life.

19. In: *alai* 333, Ano XXV/II Epoca, 29 mayo 2001, cover.

20. It is hardly possible to translate adequately the Portuguese word *caminhada.* In its root there is the word *caminho,* way. *Caminhar* would be "to walk." The term *caminhada* is often used for demonstrations and processions. But it conveys a sense of spontaneity and freedom. God's people are on their way towards an open but beautiful future.

10º ENCONTRO INTERECLESIAL
Ilhéus - Bahia - 11 a 15 de julho 2000

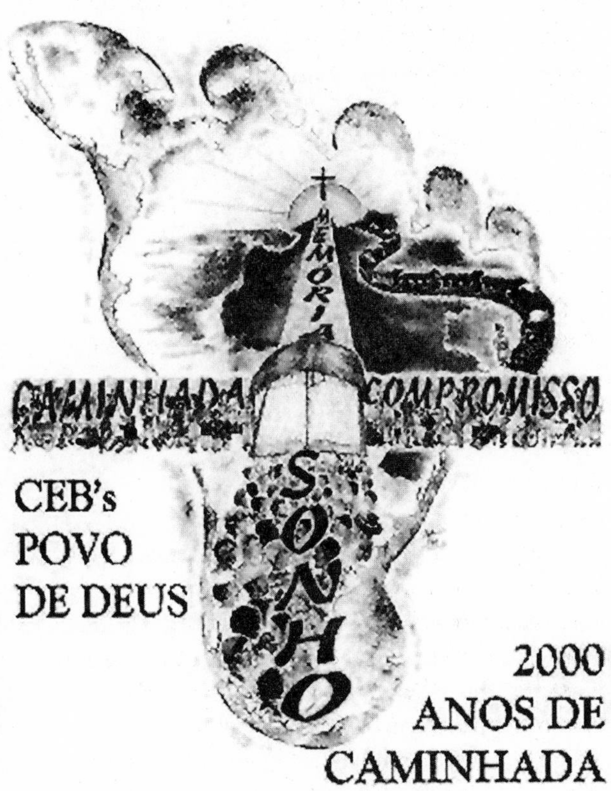

10.° Encontro Intereclesial: Ilhéus — BA —
11 a 15 de julho de 2000, *CEBs:
Povo de Deus, 2000 anos de caminhada:
Texto-base* (Paulo Afonso:
Ed. Fonte Viva, 1999), cover.

Faith in a World of Risks: A Trinitarian Theology of Risk-Taking

NIELS HENRIK GREGERSEN

Do the semantics of risk take the place of earlier societies' calculations with God?

Niklas Luhmann, *Observations on Modernity,* 1999.

The Globalization of Risks

On September 11, 2001, when the two towers of the World Trade Center in New York were attacked by hijacked airplanes and a few hours later crumbled and destroyed the lives and dreams of some 3000 innocent people, the pervasiveness of risk in ordinary life was tragically combined with several elements of globalization. Globalization refers first and foremost to the global world market, which works across the lines of national economies and different lifeworlds. The terrorists no doubt carefully selected the World Trade Center. The al-Qaeda network behind the September 11th terrorism also employed another asset of globalization: modern information technologies. From the faraway mountains of Afghanistan the attacks on New York were prepared, coordinated, and launched. Local actions have global effects, propelled by the globalizing agencies of modernity. As a result, Jerusalem is everywhere.[1]

1. To use the term coined by my colleague in the English Department, Hans Hauge. A

It is here that the idea of a "world risk society" (Ulrich Beck) enters the picture. There are the risks that we each individually take in our lives. But there are also the risks that we run as a consequence of the fact that we live in an interconnected world. Risks, however, are not equally shared. The poor people of this world are far more vulnerable to risks such as natural disasters, diseases, or polluted water. However, second-order risks increase with the complexification of society. The specialized institutions of highly differentiated societies are particularly vulnerable to targeted attacks, even though they also have the resources to absorb the instabilities.

In what follows I aim to relate current sociological thinking on risk to central issues of Christian faith such as trust, hope, and love. I shall argue, however, that major parts of current sociological wisdom occlude the role of religion in coping with risks. What we find in standard sociological literature is a *myth of replacement.* The common assumption of authors such as Anthony Giddens and Ulrich Beck is that religion is basically a premodern phenomenon in which people address external dangers by taking recourse to fate or divine providence; by contrast, modernity is described as the attempt to control risk via science and technology; finally, "reflexive modernity" (the preferred ideology of sociologists) is characterized by the discovery that the calculation of risk is no longer possible. I shall argue that this macro-sociological thesis relies on gross simplifications. Modern notions of risk have not superseded notions of fate and givenness. Any risk calculus, after all, measures a given risk against the background of relatively stable parameters. The risk of getting a genetic disease, for instance, is measured against the background of the general laws of gene recombination. But also, the postmodern discovery that risks are not finally controllable has been part of the wisdom of ordinary Christians since antiquity. The sociological supersessionism is thus ill founded. My counter-thesis is that we simultaneously live with all three elements of uncertainties: (1) the awareness of external dangers that befall us, (2) the attempt to control the ubiquitous threats or risks, and (3) the awareness that we, in the end, live in an uncontrollable world. Christian faith has in fact been able to articulate all three aspects of risks and risk-taking, as is also acknowledged by a third sociologist, Niklas Luhmann. In the final

helpful overview on the discussion of globalization can be found in David Held and Anthony McGrew, "The Great Globalization Debate: An Introduction," in *The Global Transformations Reader* (Cambridge: Polity Press, 2000), pp. 1-45.

part of the essay, I therefore propose a theology of risk and risk-taking, guided by a phenomenological analysis and in critical discussion with current sociological theories. In particular I shall argue that a trinitarian theology can understand God as a risk-taking God. As I hope to show, the seemingly secular topic of risk studies contains untapped resources for articulating what it means to have faith in a loving God while fully acknowledging the pervasiveness of dangers, risks, and the untamable nature of life.

First-Order and Second-Order Risks

Risk awareness came up in the Renaissance. Etymologically, the term "risk" itself is derived from the Italian "risco" or "rischio," which means both the danger that one is succumbing to, and the venture that one is embarking on. Used first about the hazards of sailing among tradesmen in Italy and Spain in the fifteenth century and onwards, the term is probably derived from the Greek term "riza," which means both root and cliff.[2] If this is so, "risicare" means something like sailing around the dangerous cliffs, and "riscum" is what results from such a venture. Even if this etymology is uncertain, the concept of risk did come up in the Renaissance mercantile world, in which sailors had to take risks and owners wanted to insure the lives of the sailors and their goods. From this sphere the word slowly moved into everyday language, first in the sixteenth century in the Latin languages; only later the concept of risk entered the German and English languages, where it was soon settled in the world of gambling and strategic warfare.

Since then the word has been with us in all the main European languages. However, the idea of risk has increasingly dominated the public perception of existence, especially since the 1970s. First motivated by the threat of nuclear wars, it was primarily the environmental concerns that brought the notion of risk into the center of cultural analysis. Today we know also that our eagerness to take precautions and prevent first-order

2. In the literature, one sometimes meets two other etymological proposals, one from the Arabic word *rizq,* meaning "dependency upon God or fate," and the Latin *resecare,* meaning "cutting up," but this etymology "ist lautlich und begrifflich nicht möglich" (O. Rammstedt, "Risiko," in *Historisches Wörterbuch der Philosophie,* ed. Joachim Ritter & Karlfried Gründer [Basel: Schwabe & Co., 1992], vol. 8, pp. 1045-55, with references).

risks may incur second-order risks upon ourselves. We use antibiotics in order to get rid of inflammations that would otherwise go out of control. By this move, however, we are in a process of making the immune systems of bacteria resistant to antibiotics so that future bacteria will get out of our control. We are now about to see ourselves as part of an evolutionary arms race with risks in which we, like frogs, have to make our tongues stickier in order to catch the still more slippery feet of the fruit-flies of risks.

Now if the very prevention of risks creates new risks we should realize that *safety,* the traditional counterpart to risk, does not exist at all. The road back to Paradise seems to be blocked forever. There seems only one way to proceed: forward. In this perspective, the German social philosopher Niklas Luhmann has argued that we should look for another lead difference: in hyper-modern societies the difference between *risk* and *danger* replaces the premodern difference between risk and safety. A danger, then, is a potential damage that we attribute to the environment, whereas a risk is one that we incur upon ourselves as a consequence of our decisions, including the second-order risk involved in our prevention of first-order risks.[3] The fundamental idea of this attribution theory of risk can be represented in the figure on p. 218.

The Debate Between Realists and Constructionists in Risk Theory

In her recent book on risk, Deborah Lupton has proposed a helpful typology of three dominating positions in current risk theory, a realist position, a weak constructionist position, and a strong constructionism.[4] In the table on p. 219, I have adapted and expanded her formulation in order to stress the lead difference between risk and danger. Admittedly any typology already reflects a stance. My own position is here to be found in the middle category, which maintains the distinction between the dangers

3. See Niklas Luhmann, *Soziologie des Risikos* (Berlin: Walter de Gruyter, 1991), pp. 31-38, and his definition in Niklas Luhmann, "Risiko und Gefahr," in *Soziologische Aufklärung 5. Konstruktivistische Perspektiven* (Opladen: Westdeutscher Verlag, 1990), p. 148: "Der Unterscheidung von Risiko und Gefahr liegt ein Attributionsvorgang zugrunde, sie hängt also davon ab, von wem und wie etwaige Schäden zugerecht werden. Im Falle von Selbstzurechnung handelt es sich um Risiken, im Falle von Fremdzurechnung um Gefahren."

4. Deborah Lupton, *Risk* (London: Routledge, 1999), pp. 17-35.

The Attribution Theory of Risk

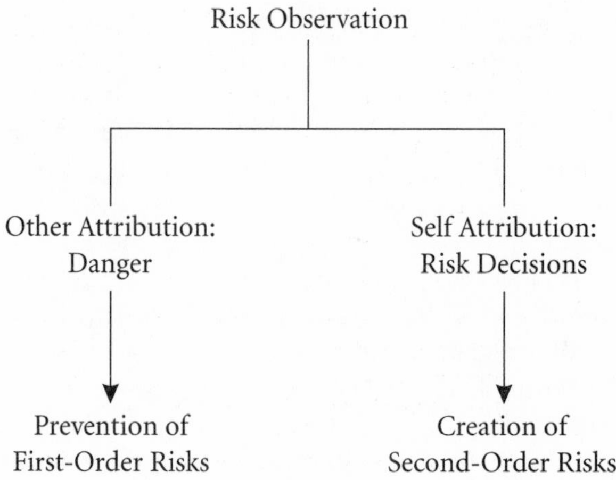

we attribute to the external environment (natural or social) and the risks we attribute to our own novel decisions. The typology is also biased in the way I suggest that both classic realist positions and strong constructionist positions try to occlude the difference between risk and danger.

Realist positions do so by absorbing the existential or relational nature of risk-taking into a notion of putatively objective risks "out there." Risks are mapped directly upon the reality of threats. Most scientific literature on risk falls under this category, driven by our need to know the probable outcomes involved by our technological decisions. *Strong constructionist positions,* by contrast, attempt to absorb the objective character of dangers into a social construction of risk-taking that simply fabricates dangers out of a neutral world in an ongoing process of inner-societal negotiation. *Weak constructionist* positions are legitimately placed in the middle. This category includes the work of sociologists such as Ulrich Beck and Anthony Giddens (even though both are often criticized for being unqualified "realists").[5] It also includes the important work of the anthropologist Mary Douglas on the cultures of risk and blame.[6] Although

5. See Ulrich Beck's response to this type of critique in "Risk Society Revisited: Theory, Politics, and Research Programmes," in *The Risk Society and Beyond: Critical Issues for Social Theory,* ed. Barbara Adam et al. (London: SAGE Publications, 2000), pp. 211-29.

A Typology of Risk Theories

	Epistemology	Type of Theory	Key Questions
1. Realism:	Risk is an objective danger, that can be measured independently of social definitions but may be biased by subjective perceptions in the public realm	Technical sciences Probability theory	What risks exist? How can we calculate and manage risks?
2. Weak constructionism:	Risk builds on objective dangers that are inevitably perceived and mediated through personal, social, cultural, or self-observing processes	Phenomenology "Risk society theory" (Ulrich Beck) "Symbolic Theory" (Mary Douglas) "Attribution Theory" (Niklas Luhmann)	What is our attitude to dangers? How do we understand risk in today's society? How and why do we select risks among the multiple dangers? How do we observe our own risk-decisions?
3. Strong Constructionism:	Nothing is a risk, but everything can be taken as a risk as a product of our decisions or social negotiations	"Governmentalist Theory" (Michel Foucault)	Why do we fabricate particular risks?

she and her co-author Aron Wildavsky have focused on the cultural symbolics of risk, they do not deny that there is a physical substrate of danger behind our cultural codes of risk and dangerousness. According to Douglas such a denial would be irresponsible. Selecting among risks in so-

6. Mary Douglas and Aron Wildavsky, *Risk and Culture: An Essay on the Selection of Technological and Environmental Dangers* (London: Routledge, 1982).

ciety presupposes that there are pre-existing dangers to select from, even though "the real" cannot explain why, for instance, the American population does not care much about environmental pollution, but seems obsessed by sexual dirt, or why European populations, unlike the U.S., are highly concerned about the emergence of multicultural society.

A special note may be appropriate concerning the location of Niklas Luhmann's *Sociology of Risk* in this typology. Luhmann is the social philosopher who more than anyone else has clarified the distinction between risk and danger in his theory of external versus internal attribution (see the figure on p. 218). So far his theory should be located among the weak constructionists, and I am myself appropriating Luhmann's theory from this angle. In his theory of modernity, however, Luhmann often argues that today the idea of dangers (as well as of pre-existing nature) is a leftover baggage from a premodern age that we have (almost) left in reflexive modernity. In late modern semantics, according to Luhmann, we attribute all contingencies to ourselves, that is, we treat them as risks in relation to which danger is only the residual category from which we depart:

> To the extent that society imputes decisions and a corresponding mobility, there are no longer any dangers that are strictly externally attributable. People are affected by natural catastrophes, but they could have moved away from the endangered area or taken out insurance. To be exposed to danger is a risk.[7]

I believe there is a considerable degree of arrogance in a sentence like this, since moving away from, say, the desert areas of North Africa is not an option to all people, and living in an area with occasional volcanoes such as Iceland hardly means that one lives here by virtue of very particular decisions. Admittedly Luhmann sometimes articulates viewpoints that resonate with a strong constructionism. However, he is very well aware of the problem that environmental problems (and problems related to our biological survival) are not easily attributed to any social system.[8] There is, in Luhmann's view, a "limit of risk semantics" that derives from the complex-

7. Niklas Luhmann, *Observations on Modernity* (Stanford, Calif.: Stanford University Press, [1992] 1998), p. 71.

8. Niklas Luhmann, *Ökologische Kommunikation. Kann die moderne Gesellschaft sich auf ökologische Gefährdungen einstellen?* (Opladen: Westdeutscher Verlag, [1988] 1990).

ity of our ecological system.[9] It should be noted that according to Luhmann's general systems theory any systematic operation builds upon the previous history of input-output relations. Therefore, there is always a past of a system that reflects previous interactions between systems and their environments. Thus Luhmann's position could perhaps best be described as an *evolutionary constructionism,* which should be distinguished from a purely social derivation of risks.

II. A Critique of Sociological Supersessionism

In current sociological literature on risk we often find the myth of replacement according to which scientific risk calculation simply supersedes the faith in the future of earlier ages. Anthony Giddens, for instance, sees the modern concept of risk as replacing the ancient notion of fate or *fortuna.*[10] Similarly, Ulrich Beck argues that pre-industrial hazards were "'strokes of fate' raining down on humankind from the 'outside' and attributable to an 'other' — gods, demons, or Nature."[11] By contrast, the risks of the industrial age were perceived within "a logic of control." Finally, today's post-industrial "risk society" is defined as one in which we can no longer control the unintended consequences of our attempts to control the risk that we are taking. "The more we attempt to 'colonize' the future with the aid of the category of the risk, the more it slips out of our control." The dilemma, then, is that the more we know the more we can do (which is risky), but also, that "the less risks are publicly recognized, the more risks are produced."[12]

I do not want here to question that a new awareness of the dangers of risk-taking has been added to the traditional sensitivity to external dangers. What I want to criticize is the scheme of replacement. It seems to me that we today are dealing with the hazards of life in a complex manner that combines strategies towards the future that have been emphasized in premodernity, modernity, and postmodernity. We live *simultaneously* in a premodern world of fate, in a modernizing attempt to control risk, and in

9. Niklas Luhmann, *Observations on Modernity,* p. 73.

10. Anthony Giddens, *The Consequences of Modernity* (Cambridge: Polity Press, 1990), p. 30.

11. Ulrich Beck, *World Risk Society* (Cambridge: Polity Press, 1999), p. 50.

12. Ulrich Beck, "Risk Society Revisited: Theory, Politics, and Research Programmes," in *The Risk Society,* ed. Barbara Adam et al., pp. 215 and 220.

a postmodern awareness of creating risks while trying to prevent them. The very idea of risk leaves us with an intriguing world of paradoxes, since we speak of the risks of future contingents *as if* these uncertain futures were already latently present, as dangers! As acutely seen by Luhmann: Risk "unifies contradictions in the present, lest the paradox [of different co-present possibilities] reappears and solves it another way, namely through risk management."[13]

The Christian Dress Rehearsal of Risk Awareness

In the writings of Niklas Luhmann we find, in my view, a more complex and more appropriate reflection on risk and religion. According to Luhmann, Christianity in particular has offered something like a "dress rehearsal" for the Western modernization process.[14] If there is any basic commitment of Christian faith it is that the world in which we live is not a matter of course, but a contingent order, created by God. The fact that we exist is a kind of miracle in ordinary. Ordinary because contingencies pervade God's whole creation, but a miracle because both the very existence of the world (its *existentia*) and the beautiful way the world has been structured and formed (its quality or *essentia*) are contingent. Christianity departed from the Greek notions of the world's eternity, and of fate. The world is not a given; it is a gift. What I should like to add to this analysis is that there exists also a third form of contingency reflected in Christianity, namely the contingency involved in subjectivity. In this perspective,

> God is not only what we long to see, but what powers the eye which sees. So the light of God is not just "out there," illuminating the order of be-

13. Furthermore, the risk prevention through management carries with it the paradox that it immediately creates unforeseeable second-order risks. See Niklas Luhmann, *Soziologie des Risikos,* p. 39: "Das Erstrisiko der Entscheidung, um die es zunächst geht, wird durch ein zweites Risiko aufgefangen, ergänzt, abgeschwächt, aber, da das zweite Risiko auch ein Risiko ist, unter Umständen auch erhöht." At the same time, Luhmann also knows that we are still confronted with dangers that are not attributable to any specific system of society, namely the problem of ecology. Thus there are "limits of risk semantics. In ecological contexts we find ourselves faced with a complexity that defies an attribution of decisions" (*Observations on Modernity,* p. 73). If this is so, we should avoid perpetuating the myth of a reflexive modernity that leaves behind us the semantics of premodernity and modernity.

14. Niklas Luhmann, *Observations on Modernity,* p. 55.

> ing, as it is for Plato; it is also an "inner light." It is the light "which lighteth every man that cometh into the world" (John 1:9).[15]

Not only the exterior world but also the interior are gifts of faith, hope, and love without which our eyes would be blind to the beauty of the world (and without which we would just perpetuate our selfishness).

According to Luhmann, the particular Christian awareness of contingency can be seen as a kind of "pre-adaptive advance" for the later process of modernization, for Christian faith offers a unified world description that nonetheless is capable of mastering a high degree of fragmentation and inconsistency. "'Diversitas' lies in the intent of God and is a characteristic of perfection."[16] This applies to the ways the world appears as well as to the domain of human decisions. "Contingent" means that which is neither necessary nor impossible, but *is* exactly because the loving God finds pleasure in the existence of such a world.

Inner complexities inhere in the notion of risk. Objective dangers are combined with subjective ventures, the present tense is fused with the future tense, and facts are intrinsically related to values. Nonetheless much sociological literature on risk attempts to temporalize these paradoxes by using the aforementioned scheme of premodern, modern, and postmodern (respectively early modern and late modern).

Another picture emerges, however, if Bruno Latour is right in arguing that "we have never been modern."[17] In a similar way, I would argue that we have never been postmodern. Rather postmodernity is characterized by living in a *simultaneity of times,* in which we may use the insights of many generations in coping with the many faces of reality. While this analysis is at odds with the standard view in textbook sociology, it is supported by comparative anthropology. According to Mary Douglas, the obsession with risk in today's societies can be seen as part of the general human wish to shun the dirt and flee the margins of society that remain sources of social disorder. In this perspective, risks are the splinters in our eyes because they offend our moral worldview of orderliness. However, since most margins of danger are hidden to us, any society has to select among the poten-

15. Charles Taylor, *Sources of the Self: The Making of Modern Identity* (Cambridge: Cambridge University Press, [1989] 1992), pp. 129f.

16. Niklas Luhmann, *Observations on Modernity,* p. 55.

17. Bruno Latour, *We Have Never Been Modern,* trans. Catherine Porter (Cambridge, Mass.: Harvard University Press, [1993] 1997).

tial risks. Public opinion may thus diverge as to which risks we are to face and which we are outselecting. However, according to Douglas, the new situation is that science and technology are no longer seen as a tool for guarding us against risk but as a major cause of risk-acceleration. "Once the source of safety, science and technology have become the source of risk."[18] In modernity, thus, religion was more or less ruled out of risk-perception. In the meantime, however, the downfall of the idea of a technologically perfect risk-calculation has paved the way for a still increasing risk anxiety. The modern hope for a "hygienist utopia"[19] is no longer socially plausible.

Rather than replacing religion, as argued by the supersessionists, this renewed sense of the paradoxes inherent in the notion of risk brings back to mind the religious dimensions of risk. The concept of risks involves a fragile fusion of the facts of the present moment with future contingents, indeed an old topic in the doctrine of divine foresight. However, the idea of risk-taking also brings together an awareness of the fate of the pre-given boundary conditions with the awareness of the human freedom of risk-calculation, while still acknowledging that risks remain in principle incalculable, at least for finite agents. How can these three elements of risks be redescribed theologically?

III. A Trinitarian Theology of Risk and Risk-Taking

A risk-taking attitude is one by which we cope with uncertainty in the acceptance of potential losses but in the expectation of an overall positive outcome. Accordingly, any religion that values contingencies positively has the potential of nurturing a risk-taking attitude. We saw that Niklas Luhmann, against this background, argued that premodern Christianity in fact functioned as a cultural "pre-adaptation" to the self-reflective state of our present-day risk societies. Indeed, Christianity values at least three forms of contingency. The fundamental contingency is the positive gift of existence, to which is related the risk of ultimate perdition. Secondly we

18. Douglas and Wildavsky, *Risk and Culture,* p. 10.

19. R. Castel, "From Dangerousness to Risk," in *The Foucault Effect: Studies in Governmentality,* ed. G. Burchell, C. Gordon, and P. Miller (London: Harvester/Wheatsheaf, 1991), pp. 281-98, 289.

have the gift of the non-trivial qualities of life to which corresponds the risk of trivialization. Finally there is the gift of being enabled to see and appreciate the beauty of the world, to which corresponds the risk of dullness. However, even though contingencies are valued positively, the risks finally come down on the side of that which should be shunned. The idea that something important may be gained by risk-taking, and only by risk-taking, is not within the scope of the traditional dogmatics of premodern Christianity.

Faith and Human Risk-Taking

The seeds for a more radical appreciation of risk are nonetheless present at a deeper, first-order level of Christian awareness, below the threshold of second-order theologies. Thus, the teaching of Jesus suggests a dauntingly positive view of human risk-taking. In the parable of the entrusted talents, a master hands over to his slaves a certain number of talents. Some went out to trade with them and went back with more money. One of the slaves, however, was so terrified by his master that he immediately went off to dig a hole in the ground; there he hid the entrusted talent. As the story runs, however, this strategy of safety was punished by the master, who took the one talent given to the servant and handed it over to the risk-willing servants (Matt. 25:14-30). It is in this context that the general maxim is spoken that "to those who have, more will be given, and they will have an abundance; but from those who have nothing, even what they have will be taken away."

The point is clearly that the strategy of safety fails for certain, whereas risk-taking may pay off, and if it succeeds, it will do so abundantly. A similar positive view of putting at stake can be found in many strands of the Jesus-tradition (the calling stories; the windstorm on the sea, etc.). The followers of Jesus were after all those who had given up the safe ordinaries of work and family life. Similarly, the early church consisted of those who had left the sanctuaries of temple, tradition, and national identity (cf. Mark 7:5). The church understands itself as nomadic church, the wandering people of God, and a person's life history as a pilgrimage of learning. The recurrent idea in these biblical traditions is that only the one who is willing to risk a loss will prevail, and only the one who is willing to face uncertainty on the streets of life will find God. The gift of life demands a risk-taking attitude, even to the point of losing one's life for the benefit of others. Yet the world is made up so as to favor and reward a risk-taking attitude. "Unless a grain of wheat falls into the earth and dies, it remains just a single grain. But if it dies, it produces much grain" (John 12:24).

If the world thus provides a habitable framework for risk-taking, the sociological supersessionism is not only simplistic as a historical analysis; it is also philosophically untenable. For no risk-taking takes place in a vacuum. Risk and fate cannot be pitted against one another since the first always takes place in the framework of the latter. Or, expressed in theological terms, the world is created by the benevolent God in such a manner that it invites a risk-taking attitude, and rewards it in a long-term perspective. In a twofold way, risk-taking is a non-zero game. The gifts of risk-taking are greater overall than the potential damages, and by risking one's life one does not take anything away from others; the risk-taker explores new territories rather than exploits the domains of the neighbor.

Risk Views and No-Risk Views of Divine Providence

One issue here is whether a human risk-taking can be valued positively (with all the necessary *caveat*). Another is whether the particular emphasis on risk in self-reflexive modernity can illuminate the way in which we may speak about God as a risk-taker. In short, does the concept of risk apply only to finite agents, or also to God?

Interestingly, current theologies of providence are almost divided into two camps: those who are proponents of the no-risk view and those who endorse a risk view of divine providence.[20] On the traditional or *no-risk view,* God is governing the world without ever losing control of its creatures, without any limits to divine foreknowledge, and without ever being vulnerable to a form of disappointment. Strong expressions of this view can be found in premodern Calvinism. Hear the *Westminster Confession* of 1647:

> God, the great Creator of all things, doth uphold, direct, dispose, and govern all creatures, actions and things, from the greatest to the least, by his most wise and holy providence, according to his infallible foreknowl-

20. E.g., Paul Helm, *The Providence of God,* Contours of Christian Theology (Downers Grove, Ill.: InterVarsity Press, 1994), ch. 2.

> edge, and the free and immutable counsel of his own will, to the praise of the glory of his wisdom, power, justice, goodness, and mercy. (V.1)

The question is, however, whether this sort of second-order theology is in line with the first-order biblical stories about God's genuine interaction with the world of creatures, and with the recurrent references to divine compassion, and even repentance. The story of Abraham's negotiation with God in his intercession for Sodom (Gen. 18:16-33), or the story of Moses who succeeds in changing God's initial plan to destroy the Israelites (Exod. 32) are often explained away as sheer anthropomorphisms. In the no-risk view, God does not negotiate and cannot regret, for God's plans are unalterable. God cannot even feel compassion for the sinners, for God is presumed to never be affected. Before the foundation of the world, God has decreed the future contingents; divine knowledge is without gaps since it is immediately co-present with all times: past, present, or future. Accordingly, the biblical reference to God's affections, such as the heavenly joy of the conversion of sinners, is taken as a human expression of the fact that a conversion is in accordance with God's eternal plan for humanity.

On the *risk view,* by contrast, God is taking an actual risk by creating a world endowed with freedom. In an interesting way, ideas of divine risk-taking have come up across a wide spectrum of current theological thought. Thus, intimations to a theology of a divine risk-taker can be found both in very liberal strands of Christian theology such as process theology and within evangelical theology, especially in the so-called "openness of God" model.[21]

Process theology, to my knowledge, has not yet developed a theology of risk, but the key elements are certainly in place for such a move. According to Alfred North Whitehead, God is not an imperial ruler in control of

21. Process theology has many faces, but an influential and fairly representative position can be found in John B. Cobb, Jr., and David Ray Griffin, *Process Theology: An Introductory Exposition* (Belfast: Christian Journals, 1976). The manifesto of the openness perspective is Clark H. Pinnock et al., *The Openness of God: A Biblical Challenge to the Traditional Understanding of God* (Downers Grove, Ill.: InterVarsity Press, 1995) followed by Clark H. Pinnock, *Most Moved Mover: A Theology of God's Openness* (Carlisle: Paternoster Press/ Grand Rapids: Baker Academic, 2001). An internal discussion of differences and common ground between the two groups can be found in *Searching for an Adequate God: A Dialogue between Process and Free Will Theists,* ed. John B. Cobb, Jr., and Clark H. Pinnock (Grand Rapids: Eerdmans, 2000).

the world. However, process theology is distinctive in holding that the limitation of divine power is not the result of a self-restraint in God, but arises from a metaphysical necessity. God's power is always and everywhere limited by the world, which is assumed to be a co-eternal principle alongside God. For this reason process theologians refuse to speak of an original creation "out of nothing" as if creation were ever the activity of God alone.[22] Rather, God is conceived as the formative shaper of the world that always existed. Since the uncreated world is itself characterized by inexhaustible creativity, the world's creativity may be said to constitute the "raw material" of risk (in Aristotelian terms: the material cause of risk). Accordingly, God might be interpreted as the formal and final cause of risk. As the "source of novelty" God both creates and accepts what we have termed second-order risks by offering the relevant information for the evolution of higher-order states. The riskiness of creativity is further enhanced by God's wish to form more complex, yet also more vulnerable forms of organization. Thus it seems that process thought does not conceive God as the primary inaugurator of risk, but as the creator of second-order risks. In addition, God eternally absorbs the pains of creaturely risk-taking. In this sense, God is both active love and responsive love — "the fellow sufferer who understands."

With a stronger view of divine creation than allowed for in process theology, Christian thinking has even stronger grounds for affirming God as the prime source of risk. John Saunders has thus argued that the idea of a risk-taking God is consonant with several biblical traditions. Important for his argument is that the anthropomorphic language used about God in the biblical traditions should be taken ontologically seriously. God may not have hands and eyes in the literal sense, but the metaphorical intention of these images is to affirm God's real and reciprocal relations with human agents.[23] Saunders also wants to argue that the idea of a divine risk-taker is conceptually intelligible. The point is that if God establishes a creation with the general strategy of affirming freedom, God cannot but take risks. "Risk taking must be seen as an element in the broader structure of goals and relationships."[24]

22. Lewis Ford, "An Alternative to Creatio Ex Nihilo," *Religious Studies* 19 (1983): 205-13.

23. John Saunders, *The God Who Risks: A Theology of Providence* (Downers Grove, Ill.: InterVarsity Press, 1998), pp. 19-23.

24. Saunders, *The God Who Risks*, p. 172.

On this view, divine omnipotence cannot be treated as an abstract doctrine of a philosophical theology, but should be respecified according to the central commitments of Christian gospel. Not the *size* of God's power (whether it is total or not total) is the relevant question here, but God's *use* of power according to God's own character and will. God "has" an all-determining power in the sense that all that exists, and the way the world is, has its only and sole source in divine creativity. But power is not a commodity that God wants to possess in splendid isolation, but something that God spreads into the network of creation.

Similarly concerning divine omniscience. The interesting question is not whether God knows "all," or less than all. The real issue is what that "all" is, about which God's omniscience is asserted. On the risk-view this "all" must be all-that-can-be-known, given the limitations that God has chosen by creating a world that includes relatively autonomous agents. Both the omnipotence and the omniscience of God should thus be redefined by God's love, materialized in God's will to create and interact with free creatures.

The Divine Risk of Giving Gifts

In what follows I want to develop the concept of a risk-taking God one step further. The focal point will be how a divine risk is involved in the exchange of gifts. In the previous section on human risk-taking we discussed the kinds of risk associated with *receiving oneself as a gift.* We here spoke about the gift of existence, the gift of living in a multifarious world of beauty, and the gift of being able to "see" God's world. By contrast, the fundamental risks of God are connected to the risk involved in *giving gifts.*

In the New Testament God is defined as love. "Whoever does not love does not know God, for God is love" (1 John 4:8). Now if God *is* love (and not only occasionally shows love), love must inform also God's actions in relation to the world. The idea of a creation "out of nothing" may thus be seen as the negative version of the affirmative statement that God's creation comes "out of divine love."[25] This position differs from process thought insofar as the world would not *be* without divine love. The world

25. Paul Fiddes, "Creation Out of Love," in *The Work of Love: Creation as Kenosis*, ed. John Polkinghorne (Grand Rapids: Eerdmans, 2001), pp. 167-91.

is not a metaphysical necessity. The existence of the world depends on the ecstatic love that God eternally *is.*

One could argue that trinitarian theology wants to be nothing than an explication of the sentence that God *is* love.[26] God is the self-related community of Father, Son, and Holy Spirit. In the community of divine love, the principle of creativity is always there, in the form of the Father; the principle of otherness is always there, in the form of the Son; and the principle of ecstasy is always there, in the form of the Spirit. Thus, the "inner" divine life is characterized by a self-relatedness that provides the common matrix for God's "outward" relationality, and the world is created out of God's will to stimulate and enjoy otherness.

However, God does not only give a gift, God also gives Godself as a gift to the world. God's self-communication (or revelation) can be translated as God's self-donating love. The closest analogy to this that we can think of in human life is the situation of proposing; of laying bare one's intentions; of declaring one's love to the beloved other. This move involves a twofold risk: the risk of being misunderstood (a theme to which Søren Kierkegaard recurs in his idea of divine self-giving), and, of course, the risk of being rejected. By revealing oneself to the other, one is exposed both to the risk of *negligence,* and to the risk of *not being accepted.*

Thus the divine dilemma is here that different responses on behalf of the creatures are possible to the divine initiative, and these responses cannot be forced if God is really love. In *The Risk of Love* (1978), the Anglican theologian William Hubert Vanstone has developed a phenomenology of love, in which he points to three marks of authentic love. The first mark is *limitlessness.* True love does not impose very specific limits on the conduct of the other, but "accepts without limit the discipline of circumstances."[27] True love is not conditional, but shows its *largesse* by wanting to enlarge its sphere of influence while at the same time accepting the restraints of the other. Second, authentic love knows about the *precariousness* of love. Love avoids the distortion of possessive control, which would be nothing but extended selfishness. Accordingly, the lover is often depicted as a "waiting figure,"[28] which patiently awaits the free response of the other. Third, love

26. Regin Prenter, "Der Gott der Liebe ist. Das Verhältnis der Gotteslehre zur Christologie," *Theologische Litteraturzeitung* 96 (1971): 401-13.

27. W. H. Vanstone, *The Risk of Love* (New York: Oxford University Press, 1978), p. 44.

28. Vanstone, *The Risk of Love,* p. 49.

is *vulnerable.* The genuine lover is not a detached person, but by laying oneself bare, one's giving is endangered. "Where love is authentic, the lover gives to the object of his love a certain power over himself — a power which would not otherwise be there."[29] Vanstone is here keenly aware of the weak and unguarded position of self-giving love. Giving oneself means being part of a transaction, an exchange that must go back and forth until the gift is received and finds its place in the recipient.

Against this background Vanstone develops an image of the loving creator that is mapped upon the character of the redeemer Jesus Christ, who according to Philippians 2 emptied himself of power in an act of *kenosis* (the Greek term for self-emptying). Vanstone suggests that "the Kenosis of the Redeemer points to, and is the manifestation of, the Kenosis of the Creator: and we may describe as 'The Kenosis of God' that activity of authentic love which is the activity of God in creation."[30]

According to Vanstone, "nothing remains in God unexpended." God is not acting as one who proceeds by an assured program (a "design"), but as one who proceeds stepwise into the unknown future. The divine matrix surpasses the idea of a fixed design. So far the picture expounded by Vanstone has influenced a major part of modern reflection on the divine creation as founded in the kenotic work of Love.[31]

The Threefold Risk of Divine Love

The question is now whether Vanstone's phenomenology of love and risk can be further elaborated.

Allow me first to caution against a reification of risk. Risks are not something given "out there," but risks always exist for somebody in a given situation. Moreover, risks are taken in an environment that exists prior to the risk. Therefore risks, as we saw, cannot simply replace fates and dangers. In a similar way, the risks of God occur in the ambiance of divine Love. When God takes risks, these are always subordinate to the framework of love and gifting in which the risks occur.

29. Vanstone, *The Risk of Love,* p. 51.

30. Vanstone, *The Risk of Love,* p. 59.

31. See the aforementioned collection of essays dedicated to Vanstone: *The Work of Love: Creation as Kenosis* (Grand Rapids: Eerdmans, 2001).

Second, the legitimacy of risk-taking is conditioned by the demand that the size of the risks should be under the catastrophe threshold. Accordingly, divine risks too would be morally tainted, if God imposed risks on the creatures that were in principle unbearable. Thus, by applying the catastrophe limit to God's risk-taking, we might infer the following rule: The more risks God is willing to take within the order of creation, the more God must be able to absorb the risks and restore the loss incurred on the creatures in the order of salvation. If not, divine risk-taking falls out of the logic of love.

Having made these caveats, it is possible to draw on trinitarian theology for the idea of divine risk-taking. Thus the creativity of God, traditionally appropriated to the Father, correlates to the divine acceptance of *taking the risk* by creating otherness. If God created human beings in God's own image (Gen. 1:27f.), God must have provided a space for fresh initiatives among human beings. The so-called "free-will defense" even argues that God could not, *in principle,* have created rational creatures endowed with the capacities for goodness without also risking that these creatures turn themselves against the will of God in the exercise of evil. In the science-theology discussion, this free-will defense has been generalized into a "free-process view" that assigns freedom also to natural processes. The argument is that if God wants to create a genuine otherness in nature, God will also have to grant real autonomy to natural processes.

The point is clear: if God had a definite plan or design for the world, God would infringe the respect for others demanded by love. Instead God seems to be nurturing the creatures, in accordance with their self-development. Thus, even though moral freedom might be exercised by human beings alone, an exploratory freedom is exercised also by biological life forms who are able to learn from and adapt to their environments. God both supports and stimulates complex adaptive systems, some of which are "autopoietic systems" that are able to produce new elements in the process of their development. The pathways are laid down in the process of walking.[32] However, even here the development of freedom goes hand in hand with the interaction with the environment, and in this sense also autopoietic processes take place in a world that is always structured.

32. Niels Henrik Gregersen, "The Idea of Creation and the Theory of Autopoietic Processes," in *Zygon: Journal of Religion & Science* 33, no. 3 (1998): 333-67.

Design and self-organization should not be pitted against one another, since the latter presupposes the former.[33]

At this juncture, another element of divine risk-taking comes to the fore. God is not only taking a risk by giving autonomy to creatures. God is also *enduring the risks* that are incurred by the fact that the world of creation is yet unfinished. The Divine Spirit is seen as the person in God who insists on the fulfillment of creation, while patiently offering the time needed and thus enduring the risks of creation. God is here not only active, but also responsive to the sighs, pains, and laments of creation (Rom. 8:26f.). The Spirit bears the mark of the resourcefulness and proficiency of God in dealing with the adversities as they come up during the process of creation.

But God is not only taking a risk in creating a world of freedom, and not only enduring and overcoming the risks of creation. According to Christian tradition God is also *assuming the victim's role* in the incarnation of the eternal Son. The story of the cross and resurrection of Christ is the story about how God the creator, who has exposed others to risks, also bears the risks and succumbs under the burden of risk. On the cross God is depicted as self-giving, even to the point of death. Since he had no offspring, Jesus is the icon of a loser in the evolutionary arms race. Since he was not able to make use of the protection of social networks, Jesus is the icon of an outsider, who refuses to play the game of success in social competition. Jesus faithfully assumed the risks of life, and crumbled under them.

When Christians believe that God was in Christ, God is thereby proclaimed to be the co-carrier of the costs of creation. In an interconnected world, risks are shared risk, and the creator did not withdraw from the ethics of sharing risks, even to the bitter end. God assumed and adopted a person who tragically failed in his willingness to put himself at stake. However, the cross of Christ is never to be seen in isolation from the event of resurrection. So deeply has Christ united himself with the role of the victims of risk that God does not only passively endure risks, but is also actively transforming those who lose in the game of risk-taking.[34] For, as it is proclaimed, only the one who is willing to lose life, shall gain it.

33. Niels Henrik Gregersen, "From Anthropic Design to Self-Organized Complexity," in *From Complexity to Life: On the Emergence of Life and Meaning,* ed. Niels Henrik Gregersen (New York: Oxford University Press, 2002).

34. See further my essay, "The Cross of Christ in an Evolutionary World," *Dialog: A Journal of Theology* 40, no. 3 (2001): 192-207, esp. 203-5.

Contributors

ANNA MARIE AAGAARD was a member of the Faculty of Theology, Institute of Systematic Theology, University of Aarhus (retired). Her recent publications on ecumenics include "What Does This Look Like? On an Ecumenical Agenda for the Twenty-First Century," Nime Papers 2000, in *Swedish Missiological Themes* 88, no. 4 (2000): 561-76; "Ecclesiology and Ethics," *Studia Theologica* 55, no. 2 (2001): 157-74; and *Beyond the East-West Divide: The World Council of Churches and "the Orthodox Problem"* (WCC Publications, 2001).

WALTER ALTMANN is Professor of Systematic Theology at the Escola Superior de Teologia, São Leopoldo/RS, Brazil and Vice-President of the Evangelical Church of the Lutheran Confession in Brazil (IECLB). He has written a number of articles on ecumenical, Lutheran, and Latin American theology. His main publication is *Lutero e Libertaçao: Releitura de Lutero em perspectiva Latino-americana* (São Paulo, São Leopoldo: Ática, Sinodal, 1994), a shorter version of which was published as *Luther and Liberation: A Latin American Perspective* (Minneapolis: Fortress, 1992).

FRIEDRICH WILHELM GRAF holds the Chair in Systematic Theology and Ethics at the University of Munich. He is the President and executive editor of the *Kritische Gesamtausgabe* of Ernst Troeltsch's Collected Works. His publications embrace numerous articles and books in systematic theology, the history of science and religion, cultural history, and ethics.

NIELS HENRIK GREGERSEN is Research Professor in Theology and Science at the University of Aarhus, Denmark, and President of the Learned Society in Denmark. His recent publications include *The Human Person in Science and Theology* (T. & T. Clark and Eerdmans, 2000), *Design and Disorder* (T. & T. Clark, 2002), and *From Complexity to Life* (Oxford University Press, 2002).

JOHN W. DE GRUCHY is Professor of Christian Studies and Director of the Graduate School in Humanities at the University of Cape Town, South Africa. He has published widely on the theology of Dietrich Bonhoeffer, and on the church and theology in South Africa. His most recent books are *Christianity and Democracy* and *Christianity, Art and Transformation,* both published by Cambridge University Press.

PHILIP HEFNER is Professor of Systematic Theology emeritus, Lutheran School of Theology at Chicago; Editor of *Zygon: Journal of Religion & Science;* and Director of the Zygon Center for Religion and Science. He has published books and articles in historical and systematic theology and in religion-and-science. His major and recent works include *The Human Factor: Evolution, Culture, Religion* (Minneapolis: Fortress Press, 1993); *Natur-Weltbild-Religion* (Munich: Institut Technik-Theologie-Naturwissenschaften and Verlag Evangelischer Presseverband für Bayern e.V., 1995); "The Church as a Community of God's Possibility: The 1996 Hein-Fry Lectures," in *Currents in Theology and Mission* 25 (August 1998): 245-319; and *Technology and Human Becoming* (Fortress Press, 2002), in press.

MUSIMBI KANYORO is General Secretary of the World YWCA and former Programme Secretary for Women in Church and Society in the Lutheran World Federation. She has written a number of articles and books on Bible studies, gender issues, and church.

PETER LODBERG is General Secretary of DanChurchaid and former Associate Professor at the Department of Systematic Theology, University of Aarhus, Denmark. His most recent book is *Dansker først og kristen så — overvejelser om nationalitet og kristendom*/First a Dane then Christian — Thoughts about Nationality and Christianity (Aros Books, 2001).

JOHANNES NISSEN is Associate Professor of New Testament Exegesis at the Department of Biblical Studies at the University of Aarhus, Denmark. He has published a number of books and articles on Bible and ethics. His recent publications in English include *New Testament and Mission: Historical and Hermeneutical Perspectives* (Peter Lang, 1999) and *New Readings in John: Literary and Theological Perspectives* (Sheffield Academic Press, 1999).

ELSE MARIE WIBERG PEDERSEN is Associate Professor of Systematic Theology at the University of Aarhus. She has published a number of articles on eschatology, and on feminist and medieval theology. Her recent publications include *Se min kjole. De første kvindelige præsters historie*/See My Dress: The History of the First Women Pastors in Denmark (Copenhagen: Samleren, 1998) and *Gudsfolket i Danmark*/The People of God in Denmark (Copenhagen: Anis, 1999).

JENS HOLGER SCHJØRRING is Professor of Church History at the University of Aarhus, Denmark. He has published a number of books and articles on modern and contemporary Scandinavian and German church history. His recent publications include *From Federation to Communion: History of the Lutheran World Federation* (Fortress Press, 1997) and *Nordiske Folkekirker i opbrud. National identitet og international nyorientering efter 1945*/The Break-Up of Nordic Folkchurches: National Identity and International Reorientation after 1945 (Aarhus University Press, 2001).

ROBERT J. SCHREITER is Vatican II Professor of Theology at Catholic Theological Union in Chicago, and Professor of Theology and Culture at the University of Nijmegen in the Netherlands. His most recent book is *Mission in the Third Millennium* (Orbis Books, 2001).

VÍTOR WESTHELLE is Professor of Systematic Theology at the Lutheran School of Theology at Chicago. He has published a number of articles on eschatology, theology of the cross, postmodernity, and Latin American theology. His most recent publications include *Voces de Protesta en América Latina* (Mexico: CETPJDR/LSTC, 2000) and *Created Co-Creator: Currents in Theology and Mission* 23, nos. 3-4 (2001).

Index

Index